American Horror Show

TRANSGRESSIONS: CULTURAL STUDIES AND EDUCATION

Cultural studies provides an analytical toolbox for both making sense of educational practice and extending the insights of educational professionals into their labors. In this context *Transgressions: Cultural Studies and Education* provides a collection of books in the domain that specify this assertion. Crafted for an audience of teachers, teacher educators, scholars and students of cultural studies and others interested in cultural studies and pedagogy, the series documents both the possibilities of and the controversies surrounding the intersection of cultural studies and education. The editors and the authors of this series do not assume that the interaction of cultural studies and education devalues other types of knowledge and analytical forms. Rather the intersection of these knowledge disciplines offers a rejuvenating, optimistic, and positive perspective on education and educational institutions. Some might describe its contribution as democratic, emancipatory, and transformative. The editors and authors maintain that cultural studies helps free educators from sterile, monolithic analyses that have for too long undermined efforts to think of educational practices by providing other words, new languages, and fresh metaphors. Operating in an interdisciplinary cosmos, *Transgressions: Cultural Studies and Education* is dedicated to exploring the ways cultural studies enhances the study and practice of education. With this in mind the series focuses in a non-exclusive way on popular culture as well as other dimensions of cultural studies including social theory, social justice and positionality, cultural dimensions of technological innovation, new media and media literacy, new forms of oppression emerging in an electronic hyperreality, and postcolonial global concerns. With these concerns in mind cultural studies scholars often argue that the realm of popular culture is the most powerful educational force in contemporary culture. Indeed, in the twenty-first century this pedagogical dynamic is sweeping through the entire world. Educators, they believe, must understand these emerging realities in order to gain an important voice in the pedagogical conversation.

Without an understanding of cultural pedagogy's (education that takes place outside of formal schooling) role in the shaping of individual identity – youth identity in particular – the role educators play in the lives of their students will continue to fade. Why do so many of our students feel that life is incomprehensible and devoid of meaning? What does it mean, teachers wonder, when young people are unable to describe their moods, their affective affiliation to the society around them. Meanings provided young people by mainstream institutions often do little to help them deal with their affective complexity, their difficulty negotiating the rift between meaning and affect. School knowledge and educational expectations seem as anachronistic as a ditto machine, not that learning ways of rational thought and making sense of the world are unimportant.

But school knowledge and educational expectations often have little to offer students about making sense of the way they feel, the way their affective lives are shaped. In no way do we argue that analysis of the production of youth in an electronic mediated world demands some "touchy-feely" educational superficiality. What is needed in this context is a rigorous analysis of the interrelationship between pedagogy, popular culture, meaning making, and youth subjectivity. In an era marked by youth depression, violence, and suicide such insights become extremely important, even life saving. Pessimism about the future is the common sense of many contemporary youth with its concomitant feeling that no one can make a difference.

If affective production can be shaped to reflect these perspectives, then it can be reshaped to lay the groundwork for optimism, passionate commitment, and transformative educational and political activity. In these ways cultural studies adds a dimension to the work of education unfilled by any other sub-discipline. This is what *Transgressions: Cultural Studies and Education* seeks to produce – literature on these issues that makes a difference. It seeks to publish studies that help those who work with young people, those individuals involved in the disciplines that study children and youth, and young people themselves improve their lives in these bizarre times.

American Horror Show

Election 2016 and the Ascent of Donald J. Trump

Douglas Kellner
*UCLA Graduate School of Education and Information Studies,
Los Angeles, USA*

SENSE PUBLISHERS
ROTTERDAM/BOSTON/TAIPEI

A C.I.P. record for this book is available from the Library of Congress.

ISBN: 978-94-6300-972-0 (paperback)
ISBN: 978-94-6300-973-7 (hardback)
ISBN: 978-94-6300-974-4 (e-book)

Published by: Sense Publishers,
P.O. Box 21858,
3001 AW Rotterdam,
The Netherlands
https://www.sensepublishers.com/

Printed on acid-free paper

TABLE OF CONTENTS

INTRODUCTION TO DONALD TRUMP AND THE AMERICAN HORROR SHOW

The election of Donald J. Trump was an American Nightmare and stunning shock to the political system and body politic unparalleled in recent history. The Trump administration promised to be an American Horror Show unleashing an era of American Carnage that would be difficult to overcome. Yet Trump's war on the media, judiciary system, and other institutions of U.S. democracy have been resisted and countered in the early weeks of his administration, as I document throughout this book. Hence, although U.S. democracy is in a severe crisis with a highly authoritarian president and administration, the forces of democracy are alive and well and a period of protracted struggle and resistance is likely.

My previous book *American Nightmare: Donald Trump, Media Spectacle, and Authoritarian Populism* began with Trump emerging from the gaudy chambers of Trump tower to announce his candidacy for the presidency on June 16, 2015.[1] The text followed his battles during the Republican primaries in 2015–2016, in which Trump emerged as master of media spectacle and the inspiration for an authoritarian populist movement that enabled him to win the Republican presidential nomination, and to square off against Hillary Clinton in the 2016 general election.

American Horror Show: Election 2016 and the Ascent of Donald J. Trump, by contrast, deals with the astonishing last weeks of the 2016 U.S. presidential election, culminating with Trump's stunning electoral victory on November 6, 2017, a day of infamy. The following chapters follow Trump's antics through the transition period, when he assembled his cabinet and top administration officials, to his inauguration as president and first 30 days in office.

In the last weeks of the 2016 presidential campaign, Trump promised to "drain the swamp" of Washington, eliminating corrupt economic, political, and other figures and interests who had long been appointed to key U.S. government positions. Trump ran as an anti-establishment candidate, attacking Wall Street and a political system that represented dominant political and economic interests and carried out policies that largely benefited establishment elites. Trump's followers took up the slogan and enthusiastically chanted "Drain the Swamp! Drain the Swamp!" during the dramatic final days of Trump's campaign. Yet when Trump assembled his cabinet and administration, he brought in Swamp Creatures from the slimy depths of the far right, Republican establishment, billionaire class, military-industrial complex, and extremists who had previously called for the elimination of the cabinet posts to which they were appointed, pandering to a variety of extremist and establishment wings of the Republican party.

American Horror Show will thus show the emergence to the presidency of Donald J. Trump, King of the Swamps, anointing Mike Pence, a politician of the far right and raging homophobe as Vice President,[2] while choosing White Nationalist and extreme rightwing ideologue Steve Bannon as his "Chief Strategist" and consigliere, and picking Republican National Committee Chairman Reince Priebus to be his Chief of Staff. Trump and his associates then assembled a cabinet and administration consisting of a combination of Republican establishment figures and Trump cronies and rightwing extremists, who have already been caught up in controversies, leading, for instance, Trump's National Security Advisor, General Michael Flynn, to resign in February 2017 as I note below.

In this book, I trace the conflict of interests involved in the Trump family's failure to divest themselves of their motley array of economic interests, and show how from the beginning it was clear that one of Trump's key motivations in capturing the presidency was to promote his Trump Organization economic interests and those of his political and economic allies. Not surprisingly, the Trump administration was burdened by scandals from the beginning and provoked unparalleled resistance with the largest anti-administration demonstrations in history in Washington and throughout the world the day after Trump's inauguration, inspiring a Resistance movement active to this day.

Trump's ascendency as 45th president of the United States will likely be seen as the most disruptive opening of a presidential regime in modern U.S. history. Trump and his administration have already waged battles against the media, the courts, the Congress, and the majority of the people of the U.S. who strongly opposed him and found Trump thrust upon them as president because of an outdated and thoroughly dysfunctional Electoral College system, that I will critically analyze and suggest some alternatives to in the following pages.

I attempt to explain how the Trump campaign managed to win the 2016 election and closely follow the scandal of Russian interference in the election which has generated by March 2017, growing calls for a Special Prosecutor to investigate the ties between the Trump presidential campaign and the Russians, a potential scandal which could well bring down the Trump presidency. Indeed, as Trump entered into the second month of his presidency, his Achilles Heel was clearly his connection and those of his highest officials, and a cadre of lower ones, to Russia and its murderous dictator Vladimir Putin.[3] Trump and Putin were both authoritarians who shared a contempt for democratic institutions and freedoms, although it was bizarre and not yet explained why Trump had chosen so many rabidly pro-Russian members for his administration, and why Trump had throughout the election and into his presidency spoken so highly of Vladimir Putin. Trump had never released his tax returns, and there was still a mystery concerning the financial ties between his campaign and Russia, as well as concerning connections between the Trump organization and Russia. The Russian hack into the 2016 election, described in detail in the following pages, was perhaps one of the most scandalous foreign interferences in a U.S. presidential election in history, constituting events that could destroy Trump's presidency as calls multiply for investigations of Trump campaign and organization connections to Russia and Putin.

The fact that Russia, the U.S.'s Cold War adversary, had hacked into the Democrats emails and released emails embarrassing to Hillary Clinton, the Democratic National Committee, and Clinton's campaign manager John Podesta, was an outrageous scandal that honorable members of Congress and wide sectors of the American people are demanding that the government and media investigate. As this text indicates, Trump's National Security Advisor, General Michael Flynn, was forced to resign in February 2017, because of a phone call just before the election with the Russian ambassador, and years of shady connections to the Russians. Shortly thereafter, Jeff Sessions, Trump's Attorney General, lied to Congress about his contacts with the Russians, and was then forced to admit that he had connections and conversations with the Russian ambassador during a period when Sessions was serving as a key advisor to the Trump campaign as they battled to overcome Clinton's lead in the polls while the Russians allegedly leaked information embarrassing to her and her campaign.

Trump's well-received first address to Congress on February 28, 2017, was soon followed by more revelations concerning relations between top officials of his administrations and the Russians, which led to increased calls by March 2017 for congressional investigations and a special prosecutor. Trump, who had resisted sending out his daily controversial and to some crazed tweets for the previous week, went on a Twitter rampage, first posting a photo of Democratic Senator Chuck Schumer and Putin smiling and snacking together with the message: "We should start an immediate investigation into @SenSchumer and his ties to Russia and Putin. A total hypocrite!" Schumer quickly retorted: "Happily talk re: my contact w Mr. Putin& his associates, took place in '03 in full view of press & public under oath. Would you &your team?"[4]

After a similar Twitter blast against Democratic Congresswoman Nancy Pelosi and picture of her with Putin, the now crazed Trump went after former President Obama, and culminated a blast of five successive tweets with the astonishing claim:

> How low has President Obama gone to tapp my phones during the very sacred election process. This is Nixon/ Watergate. Bad (or sick) guy! 4 March 2017[5]

After launching a Twitter attack on the former president, Trump's twitchy Twitter finger returned to more mundane matters, attacking Arnold Schwarzenegger, the former host of his reality TV show *The Apprentice* and protagonist in a recent Twitter war with Trump. The Arnold had just announced his decision to quit *The Apprentice* because "there was too much baggage" (i.e. Trump's continued role in the show as Executive Producer and his propensity to launch Twitter attacks on the Arnold). Trump exploded in fury: "Arnold Schwarzenegger isn't voluntarily leaving the Apprentice. He was fired by his bad (pathetic) ratings, not by me. Sad end to great show."[6]

There was debate over whether Trump was unhinged and totally out of control, or whether his Twitter antics were a clever strategy to distract attention from his campaign's connections with Russia during the election and the burning question of whether the Trump team had conspired with the Russians to defeat Hillary Clinton in the election. There were increasing calls to appoint a Special Prosecutor to investigate the Trump team/Russia links. This story was coming to dominate the news until Trump's Twitter attack on Obama and his outrageous claim, without a shred of evidence, that Obama had bugged his campaign and Trump Tower, which created a new round of outrage as members of the Obama administration and top U.S. intelligence officials flatly denied Trump's claim that Obama had wire-tapped Trump Tower.

Appearing on *NBC News* the Sunday morning that the story broke on March 5, former director of national intelligence James R. Clapper Jr., who had just resigned, flatly denied that a wiretap was authorized against Trump or his campaign during the elections, asserting: "There was no such wiretap activity mounted against the president-elect at the time as a candidate or against his campaign," Clapper said on *Meet the Press.*" Clapper added that he would have "absolutely" been informed if the FBI had sought or received a warrant to wiretap Trump or his campaign, and confidently claimed: "I can deny it."

No major Republican appearing on the weekend talk shows seemed inclined to support Trump's outrageous claims against President Obama, and pundits speculated that Trump had launched the Twitter assault on Obama to deflect attention from investigations of the Trump/Russian connections. So explosive was Trump's unsubstantiated wiretap accusation that FBI Director James B. Comey asked the Justice Department to take the extraordinary step of issuing a statement rebutting it.[7]

Trump's astonishing Twitter attack had offered no evidence or any credible news report to back up his accusation that Obama had wire-tapped Trump Tower, but media analysts concluded that Trump may have been referring to "commentary on Breitbart and conservative talk radio suggesting that Obama and his administration used 'police state' tactics last fall to monitor the Trump team. The Breitbart story, published Friday, has been circulating among Trump's senior staff, according to a White House official who described it as a useful catalogue of the Obama administration's activities. Trump's response also has deepened doubts about his own judgment, not just in the face of the first crisis to confront his young presidency but in dealing with the challenges that lie ahead for the chief executive of the world's most powerful nation."[8]

Trump continued to make the unsubstantiated claim that the Obama administration had wire-tapped Trump Towers, making the milder claim that it was simply under surveillance, but then made the completely outrageous claim that British intelligence had helped the Obama administration do surveillance of Trump Towers, a claim that Her Majesty's Government and the U.S. closest traditional ally, quickly shot down, using words like "ridiculous" to rubbish the Trump allegations, which he claimed he had heard on *Fox News*, along with rightwing websites, his preferred source of information. In a March 20 Congressional House Intelligence Committee Hearing, FBI Director James Comey denied that the U.S. government had done surveillance of Trump Tower and confirmed that the Trump administration was under FBI investigation for alleged contacts with the Russians during the election, ensuring that the Trump/Russian story would be a major issue for months to come, perhaps the defining story of his administration.[9]

Indeed, Trump's call to repeal and replace Obamacare went down in ignominious defeat on March 24 when the Republican Congressional delegation and Trump could not agree on a health care plan that the majority of Republicans would support and so pulled the bill in an incredible confirmation of Trump's incompetency and inability to master the complexities of legislation.[10] The stunning defeat raised questions concerning Trump's competency to make a deal, to fulfill key campaign promises, and to lead the Republican Party which although it controlled the House and Senate was deeply divided and did not trust Trump.

Upon concluding almost two years of sustained research on Trump and his successful win in Election 2016 and ascension to presidency, Donald Trump emerges as the American Id providing an American Nightmare and American Horror show to the shocked citizens of the U.S. and to many billions of people throughout the world. Trump represents the Worst of the Worst of American culture, incarnating in one orange-haired monster from the dankest and vilest swamps of American history, society, economy, polity, culture and psyche, the Worst of the Worst. Yes, Trump is a monster that not the most deranged Hollywood scriptwriter could imagine, and that would require a Dostoevsky, Dreiser, and Sinclair Lewis rolled into one Master of the Deranged, the Corrupted, and the Absurdly Ridiculous, to adequately describe and evoke.

What we know of Trump's business career is a morass of corruption, cons, and criminality of which only surface facts are known,[11] enough of which qualifies him for the Hall of Capitalist Shameful Shame. Further, we do not even know all of those who bailed him out of his many bankruptcies and failed enterprises since he has refused to release his tax and business records. Although more and more information is dripping out weekly on his business and other strange connections with the Russians (watch the *Rachel Maddow Show* nightly on MCNBC for all the scandalous details), we are still waiting for the results of investigations into connections between the Russians and the Trump organization by the FBI, and the House and Senate Intelligence Committees, with growing calls for a Watergate or 9/11 Commission panels of distinguished experts and investigators.

The more we know of Trump's personality, his family, his closest White House Associates, his cabinet members, and major and minor villains in his administration, we see a daily parade of the worst imaginable actions by the worst administration and presidency in memory and is perhaps The Worst President Ever. As for Trump himself, he embodies the worst of American narcissism, stupidity, boorishness, sexual predation, phoniness, mendacity, villainy, kleptocracy, nepotism, and words not even yet invented. Trump is uncultured with no ability to digest books or information larger than a Tweet (not surprisingly, his favored mode of communication); he is asocial and apparently devoid of empathy, unable to grasp or articulate much beyond a sound-bite or Twitter blast, with attacks and invective his distinctive mode of social interaction. Trump is amazingly unpolitical, without an idea, policy notion, ideology, or grasp of how Washington and the presidency works. The result is that he makes pronouncements, signs Executive Orders, and is set to advance legislation that embodies the worst of Republican anti-government "ideas," although, fortunately, his first foray into actual legislation went down to defeat, as Trump, his team, and Republican allies were not able to cobble together an alternative to Obamacare and so Trump-Ryan (un)Care went down to ignominious defeat on March 24, in a stunning demonstration of Trump/Republican incompetency, stupidity, and dysfunctionality, indicative of the whole Big and Smelly MESS of Trumpdom.

Since Trump embodies in spades and to the max HUGE dimensions of the Worst of Everything, it is hard to pin down in a concise manner the very worst features of Trump and Trumpworld. I've tried in this book to delineate some of the worst visible features and actions of Trump and his fellow Swamp Creatures. Yet so much is buried, secret, and as yet unknown, that I am perfectly aware that I have only scratched the surface, and that Trump Studies will continue for decades to disclose one outrageous scandal after another as Trumpdom devolves into what Jean Baudrillard described as The Spiral of the Worst.

Yes, Trump is the Worst who brings U.S. and the world defeat after defeat, as the U.S. devolves from a City on the Hill, the Best Hopes of Mankind, and a Shining Beacon of Freedom and Democracy to a ridiculous and surreal Horror Show, highly entertaining to Putin and the Russian kleptocracy, to the Chinese Leader Xi, and to tin-horn dictators and wanna be Authoritarians everywhere. To be sure, Trump's popularity continues to spiral down with his approval at a shockingly low 34% of the public who approve of Trump's job performance, according to the April IBD/TIPP poll while 56% disapprove of the job he's doing marking the lowest rating during the first 100 Days into his term.[12]

Trump has a gloomy pessimistic view of the world encapsulated in the philosophical vision that: "Man is the most vicious of all animals, and life is a series of battles ending in victory or defeat. You just can't let people make a sucker out of you."[13] Winning is all for one-dimensional Trump, the only purpose of life, the only thing worth pursuing, and the organizing principle of the Donald's existence. To win, Trump will do anything, raising the spectre of what would a losing Trump do with nuclear weapons under his control, and what destruction might his unrestrained Ego and uncontrollable Id unleash if Trump is threatened in any sort of way. Trump has a Hobbesian view of the world where there are enemies everywhere and where the U.S. must use force to pursue its interests and destroy its enemies. It is also worrisome to contemplate that Trump has developed a large following through his demagoguery, and that Donald Trump and authoritarian populism constitutes an American Horror Show, and a clear and present danger to U.S. democracy and global peace and stability.

Los Angeles, California
April 3, 2017

NOTES

[1] See Douglas Kellner, *American Nightmare: Donald Trump, Media Spectacle, and Authoritarian Populism*. Rotterdam, The Netherlands: Sense Publishers, 2016.

[2] Amanda Holpuch, "Before he was Trump's running mate, Mike Pence led the anti-LGBT backlash," *The Guardian* October 4, 2016, at https://www.theguardian.com/us-news/2016/oct/04/mike-pence-led-anti-lgbt-backlash-trump (accessed on March 6, 2017).

[3] For a critical look at Putin that predates his still mysterious connections with Trump, see Martha Gesson, *The Man Without a Face. The Unlikely Rise of Vladimir Putin*. New York: Riverhead Books, 2012.

[4] Trump's Twitter outbursts during the first week in March can be found at https://twitter.com/realDonaldTrump?ref_src=twsrc%5Egoogle%7Ctwcamp%5Eserp%7Ctwgr%5Eauthor (accessed March 6, 2017).

[5] Ibid.

[6] Ibid.

[7] Michael S. Schmidt and Michael D. Shear, "Comey Asks Justice Dept. to Reject Trump's Wiretapping Claim," *The New York Times,* March 5, 2017 at https://mobile.nytimes.com/2017/03/05/us/politics/trump-seeks-inquiry-into-allegations-that-obama-tapped-his-phones.html (accessed March 6, 2017).

[8] Philip Rucker, Ellen Nakashima and Robert Costa. "Trump, citing no evidence, accuses Obama of 'Nixon/Watergate' plot to wiretap Trump Tower." *The Washington Post,* March 4, 2017, at https://www.washingtonpost.com/news/post-politics/wp/2017/03/04/trump-accuses-obama-of-nixonwatergate-plot-to-wire-tap-trump-tower/?utm_term=.ed559ca48b25 (accessed March 6, 2017).

9   Matthew Rosenberg, Emmarie Huetteman and Michael S. Schmidt, "Comey Confirms F.B.I. Inquiry on Russia; Sees No Evidence of Wiretapping," *The New York Times,* March 20, 2017 at https://www.nytimes.com/2017/03/20/us/politics/intelligence-committee-russia-donald-trump.html?_r=0 (accessed March 6, 2017).

10 See Glenn Thrush and Maggie Haberman, "Trump Becomes Ensnared in Fiery G.O.P. Civil War. First Legislative Failure Shows There Is No Escaping Staid Rules of Capitol Hill," *The New York Times,* March 26, 2017: A1, 16.

11 The best studies of Trump's business career and life include Michael D'Antonio, *Never Enough. Donald Trump and the Pursuit of Success* (New York: Thomas Dunne Books, 2015); Gwenda Blair, *The Trumps* (New York: Simon and Schuster, 2000); and Michael Kranish and Marc Fisher, *Trump Revealed. An American Journey of Ambition, Ego, Money and Power.* New York: Scribner, 2016. The best study of Trump, the media, and his long cultivation and exploitation of celebrity is found in Timothy L. O'Brien, *Trump Nation: The Art of Being the Donald.* New York: Grand Central Publishing, 2016 [2005].

12 John Merlane, "Trump Approval Plunges Amid Russia Inquiry, Obama Care Repeal Failure IBD/TIPP Poll" http://www.investors.com/politics/trump-approval-plunges-amid-russia-inquiry-obamacare-repeal-failure-ibdtipp-poll/ (accessed April 3, 2017).

13 Donald J. Trump, cited in Marc Fisher, "We already know what Donald Trump does when he loses: He acts like it never happened. How he responded to business setbacks could predict what he'll do if he isn't the next president." *The Washington Post,* November 3, 2016 at https://www.washingtonpost.com/posteverything/wp/2016/11/03/what-does-donald-trump-do-when-he-loses-he-acts-like-it-never-happened/?utm_term=.1433f1e2c944 (accessed March 6, 2017).

PRESIDENTIAL DEBATES, THE *ACCESS HOLLYWOOD* TAPES, AND DONALD THE DEPLORABLE

Guy Debord described a "society of the spectacle" in which the economy, politics, social life, and culture were increasingly dominated by forms of spectacle. Donald Trump lived the spectacle from the time in New York as a young entrepreneur and man about town he performed his business and personal life in gossip columns, tabloids, and rumor mills. He used PR advisors to promote his businesses and himself to eventually become a maestro of the spectacle when his popular TV-show *The Apprentice* made Trump into a national celebrity. Trump ran his 2016 presidential campaign as a media spectacle with daily tweets that became fodder for TV news, and rallies where he would make outrageous comments that would be replayed endlessly on cable and network news. Trump thus dominated news cycles by making shocking assertions, insulting and negatively defining opponents, and helping construct daily media events through which he was able to define the news agenda.

Yet the Donald Trump Presidential TV-Reality Show also stumbled, choked, and went into crisis mode with the onset of the annual presidential debates in which the two finalists get to duke it out to see who will convince the audience that they deserve the ultimate prize, the presidency of the United States.

U.S. presidential debates have been in the Age of Television, and now New Media, a gladiator spectacle in which the opponents try to destroy each other, while the media personalities who moderate each debate try to positively define themselves and avoid gaffes that could negatively impact their image forever. The first presidential debate on September 27, 2016, was a compelling political media spectacle in which the two candidates showed how they were able to make their case for the presidency under conditions of intense pressure and media focus. From the outset, Trump played to the hilt the authoritarian macho, shouting, insulting Clinton, and trying to dominate the procedure.

Clinton, however, ignored Trump's bullying and blustering, made her arguments against him, and presented her positions on the issues.

As the debate progressed, Trump exhibited a loss of stamina, rambled, became incoherent, and was unable to cogently respond to Clinton's sharp attacks on his business record, his failure to pay taxes, his atrocious attacks on women, and his lack of qualifications to be president. Trump's unraveling during the first debate presented the media spectacle of the Outsider and Macho Man, not ready for prime time, and losing the debate to the cool professional and qualified politician, who was able to provide coherent answers to questions, and look presidential while Trump faltered and appeared increasingly flustered as the debate went on, by the end, he looked like he lacked stamina and was a choker, accusations that he had made against his Republican rivals in the primaries.

The next morning after what commentators on all sides labeled a disappointing, and even disastrous, debate, Trump went on the offensive, lashing out at the debate moderator, complaining about his microphone and threatening to make Bill Clinton's marital infidelity a campaign issue in a spectacle of desperation. There were estimates that 85 million people had watched the debate live on television, and millions more were re-watching it and discussing it at home, work, and online, making it one of the major debate spectacles in US political history. Clinton was exuberant, campaigning with Bernie Sanders the next day, and presenting a united Democratic Party on the offensive.

Presidential debates are the ultimate shared media spectacle and it would be interesting to see if Trump could recover and gain the offensive in the coming political debates and in last weeks of the campaign. At different stages, Clinton and Trump had dominated the presidential spectacle, and anything could happen as the spectacle moved toward its conclusion.

Over the weekend of October 8–9, 2016, media coverage of the campaign was overwhelmed by a videotape of Trump's bragging of his sexual prowess with women that revealed the full extent of his vulgarity, crudeness, and contempt for women. The front page of *The New York Times* featured a full account of Trump's sexual bragging in an October 8, 2016 story: "Tape Reveals Trump Boast About Groping

Women," and television networks and social networking cites played the footage over and over.

A three-minute videotape was found and endlessly replayed of a conversation of trash talk between Trump and Billy Bush, a minor TV celebrity on *Access Hollywood* and member of the Bush clan. Trump boasted that his "star" status allowed him to do what he wanted with women, including married women, telling how, in one case, he "moved on her like a bitch, but I couldn't get there." On the whole, sex philosopher Trump asserted that a "star" like him gets special treatment, and "You can do anything," including "grab them by the pussy." Displaying his vengeful retaliation, he noted that the married woman who managed to resist his cave man charms wasn't really up to The Donald's high standards, as he explained: "I did try and fuck her. She was married. She's now got the big phony tits and everything."

The video clips of Dirty Donald went viral and a nervous Republican establishment went hysterical with Paul Ryan disinviting Trump to a Republican Unity campaign rally, John McCain withdrew his support, and Trump's wife Melania, to whom he was married when the *Access Hollywood* interview took place, said the comments were "unacceptable," but none the less the Donald she knew was a great "leader" (although not much of a husband as he was married to Melania when he bragged about bagging all the women he wanted). There was speculation whether this spectacle of lechery would end Trump's run, but the Shameless One was seen waving at crowds in front of Trump Tower, showing that he was still in the game, and his surrogates claimed that in the coming days the Trumpsters would provide evidence that Bill Clinton's sexual indiscretions were worse.

And so the media spectacle of the 2016 campaign had devolved into gutter sniping trash talk, and Donald Trump demonstrated that yes, he was an outsider and outside the bounds of decorum, decency, and shame. In a campaign of outrageous sexism, racism, xenophobia, insults, and trash talk would this assault on women and decency finally be the viral outrage that went over the top and took Donald Trump into the sewer of filth where even his rabid followers would be loath to follow? Or is this just the way good old boys talk in the locker room, as Trump's surrogates, like thrice-married and serial adulterers

Rudi Giuliani and Newt Gingrich insisted? Would the Authoritarian Populist Leader continue to drive his campaign and Trumpite followers forward, or was the spectacle that had created Trump about to devour him?

Trump and his male defenders revealed a backlash against the more progressive and woman-friendly concept of masculinity that had been evolving since the 1960s and the rise of the women's movement back to the sort of caveman masculinity that had ruled the U.S. and to some extent globally for centuries. Trump and his surrogate good old boys were especially crude, and no politician or public figure in recent history was as blatantly sexist and patriarchal as Donald J. Trump. Trump blurted out that he "respected" women, but his behavior belied this claim and speculation mushroomed about whether suburban Republican women were going to vote for such a Neanderthal.

The last weeks of the campaign would resolve how much of Trump the country could take as Hillary Clinton regained the momentum and scored a double digit lead after she was able to dominate the Second Presidential Debate and make Trump's character and attitude toward women a key issue of the campaign. A series of women then came forward with claims about how Trump had groped them inappropriately, attempted to kiss them, and, in fact, had done exactly what Trump bragged to Billy Bush he was able to do with any woman he liked.

From October 10 and for days to follow, a new woman or two would appear on television with harrowing stories of how Trump had sexually assaulted them, refuting Trump's assertion during the second presidential debate that he had never acted on the claims he made to Billy Bush. In a mid-October summary, the list of new allegations against Trump included:

- Two Miss USA contestants who claimed Trump deliberately walked in on them when they were naked in a dressing room.
- Two women who allege Trump groped or kissed them without consent – one in the first-class seat of an aircraft.
- A claim by a woman that she was groped at a Trump event at his Mar-A-Lago estate in Florida.
- A *People* magazine reporter who says Trump forced himself on her shortly before she was due to interview him and his wife in 2005.

- An incident in which Trump appears to sexualize a young girl. The encounter with the young girl surfaced in a video of a 1992 *Entertainment Tonight* Christmas special in which Trump appeared, according to CBS News. Trump was 46 at the time.[1]

Never before had the networks or cable channels presented such graphic descriptions of sexual assault, and never had a politician been accused of such a vast array of sexual battery. The day after Trump faced the barrage of accusations of groping and sexual assault from scores of women, the Republican nominee went on the offensive attacking the accusers. At a rally in West Palm Beach, Florida, he suggested that he would never have sexually assaulted the woman who claimed that Trump was all over her like "octopus" during an airline flight, claiming: "Believe me. She would not be my first choice. That I can tell you... Just look at her!" In regard to Natasha Stoynoff, the writer from *People* magazine who alleged that Trump pinned her to a wall and stuck his tongue down her throat while she was at his Florida estate Mar-a-Lago to write a first anniversary story about Trump and his then pregnant wife Melania, the mogul told the West Palm Beach crowd: "Take a look. You take a look. Look at her. Look at her words. You tell me what you think. I don't think so."

At the same rally, Trump also crudely disparaged Hillary Clinton, referring to their bodily encounter in the presidential debate stating: "I'm standing at my podium and she walks in front of me, right. She walks in front of me, and when she walked in front of me, believe me, I wasn't impressed." In the following days, Trump continued to attack his accusers in vicious terms describing them as "horrible people, they're horrible horrible liars". Trump insisted that the press was "false and slanderous in every respect," and said "the depths of their immorality is absolutely unlimited."

Playing the card of anti-political correctness, Trump also insisted that: "The Clinton machine is at the center of this power structure. Anyone who challenges their control is deemed a sexist, a racist, a xenophobe and morally deformed. They will attack you, they will slander you, they will seek to destroy your career and your family. ... They will lie, lie, lie." Trump's rant came just minutes after first lady Michelle Obama had stated in a powerful speech condemning Trump:

"I can't believe that I'm saying that a candidate for president of the United States has bragged about sexually assaulting women." She added: "And I can't stop thinking about this. It has shaken me to my core in a way that I couldn't have predicted." While Michelle Obama took a serious tone, in the key battleground state of Ohio, Barack Obama mocked the idea of Donald Trump doing anything for working people and trying to fob himself off as a champion of the workers, when all his life he'd been trying to brand himself as a rich member of the elite, and brag about and celebrate his wealth.

As the days went by, Trump widened the alleged spectrum of the conspiracy of lies and slander directed against him to include not only the media and the Clinton campaign, but "international banks" with whom Clinton allegedly met in secrecy "to plot the destruction of US sovereignty in order to enrich these global financial powers." This screed lead Jonathan Greenblatt, the head of the Anti-Defamation League, to accuse the statement of resembling anti-Semitic tropes used by the Nazis.

Republican leaders were once again challenged as to whether they could support such a vile person, although Trump's core supporters bought his defense that every one of the women were liars and that the barrage of revelations was part of a conspiracy against him by the media, the Clinton campaign, international bankers, global corporations, and shadowy forces who were united in denying Trump the presidency and stealing the White House for the Clintons. As the week went on, Trump added components to the conspiracy against him which emerged as a major campaign motif of the last weeks of the election, as Trump blared over and over that the election was rigged, a claim which cynics saw as a strategy to prepare Trump and his followers for a loss.

The New York Times had published the first story of women who claimed Trump had sexually assaulted them,[2] and in a speech where he was detailing those who were conspiring to steal the presidency from him and his supporters, he included the *Times* and a major Mexican investor Carlos Slim who he claimed was a supporter of the Clintons, bringing a Mexican into the web of conspiracy that Trump was trying to weave, returning to a motif of his opening election rant that Mexicans were pouring across the border and threatening our country.

Going off the rails, Trump intensified his rant against the Clintons, insisting every rally that they were criminals, while his storm troopers chanted "lock her up, lock her up!" Upping his journey into Crazyland, the weekend of October 15–16, Trump insisted Hillary Clinton was on drugs during the previous debate and demanded they he and her take a drug test before the next debate, coming up on Wednesday.

The weekend talk shows continued to dissect the spectacle of the multiple accusations of sexual assault against Trump and whether this would destroy his campaign, while his hapless surrogates tried to defend the indefensible, and explain Trump's claim that the accusations against him by nine women of sexual assault were all lies. Equally difficult, was the task of Trump's surrogates to provide evidence that the election was rigged, as election officials and media pundits kept insisting that it was impossible to rig an election that had so many variables and voting sites.

Both Clinton and Trump disappeared for debate preparation, so drama mounted as the third and final presidential debate took place in Las Vegas on October 19, 2016, which might be remembered as one of the more bizarre and perhaps consequential presidential debates in recent history. The debate opened innocently enough with a question by moderator Chris Wallace of *Fox News* concerning what kind of justices the candidates would appoint to the U.S. Supreme Court, an issue which obsessed conservatives and gave Trump a chance to secure this base. Trump assured his conservative followers that he'd appoint an anti-abortion majority on the court to overturn Roe v. Wade, while Clinton argued that she would appoint justices who would uphold reproductive and abortion rights, as well as LGBT rights, and would support campaign finance reform as well, making a strong appeal to millennials and liberals.

The debate spectacle continued with Trump emphasizing immigration, one of the favorite themes of his campaign, repeating the idea that launched his election bid, as he promised again that he would build a wall on the Mexican border. Yet Trump now backed away from his pledge to deport 11 million undocumented migrants and their 4 million citizen children. Clinton stated that she favored comprehensive immigration reform, like former Republican presidents Ronald Reagan and George H.W. Bush, and argued that Trump's "deportation force" would require a police state that raided homes, schools and businesses.

When the questions inevitably engaged Russia and the WikiLeaks release of stolen e-mail from Clinton's campaign, Clinton argued that the theft showed that Russia's intelligence agencies and its dictator, Vladimir Putin, were siding with Trump "because he'd rather have a puppet as president of the United States." That prompted Trump to lose his composure and start yelling that she was "the puppet," without explaining whose puppet she was and who was pulling the strings. Clinton countered that: "It's pretty clear you won't admit that... Russians have engaged in cyberattacks against the United States of America, that you encouraged espionage against our people, that you are willing to spout the Putin line, sign up for his wish list, break up NATO, do whatever he wants to do, and that you continue to get help from him, because he has a very clear favorite in this race."

Trump interrupted her, sputtering, "You have no idea" who hacked her campaign, and Clinton retorted that 17 military and civilian intelligence agencies have reached the same conclusion that the hacks were attributable to Russian agents, to which Trump repeated again, "Our country has no idea." She replied, "you doubt 17 military and civilian... [agencies]" Trump replied, "Yeah, I doubt it, I doubt it." Clinton pressed on, "Well, he'd rather believe Vladimir Putin than the military and civilian intelligence professionals who are sworn to protect us. I find that just absolutely..." Trump cut Clinton off, speaking over her about how Putin had bested Clinton every time, repeating his strange allegation that Putin was a political strongman who was superior to Obama and Clinton.

The rest of the night continued in the same vein, with Trump accusing Clinton and Obama of causing virtually everything wrong in the country and world, while Clinton tried to argue that all her proposals would be paid for by increasing taxes on the wealthiest Americans, whereas Trump's proposed policies would create trillions in debt. The highlight of the debate, and point that dominated discussion the next day and into the final days of the election, was Trump's truculent message that the country would have to wait and see if he would recognize the results of the presidential election. When pressed by the debate moderator, Chris Wallace of *Fox News*, if he would accept a peaceful transition of power if Hillary Clinton were declared the winner, Trump responded: "I will look at it at the time," and then repeated one of the Republican Party's Big Lies on voter fraud: "If you look at your voter rolls, you will find millions of people there that are registered that shouldn't be registered to vote."

Going off the rails again, Trump suddenly blurted out that Hillary Clinton "shouldn't be allowed to run—she is guilty of a serious crime… in that respect, it is rigged." When Wallace again asked Trump if there would be a peaceful transition of power, he answered: "I will tell you at the time," he replied. "I will keep you in suspense." As if he was playing a role in a reality TV-show, Trump broke a fundamental rule of the political game which mandated that the candidate who gets the least votes in the Electoral College conceded to the candidate that got the most votes. Immediately, the Democrats took Trump's arrogance as evidence he was a demagogue not fit to be president, while some establishment Republicans denounced Trump and insisted that the loser must accept the mandate of the voters.

In addition, Clinton provoked Trump to interrupt her and assert, "nasty woman, nasty woman," a meme which shot through the Internet,[3] convincing many that Trump was too rude for the prime time political game. While clenching his jaw tightly, Trump had started the evening standing erect behind the lectern and not stalking Clinton as he had done the previous debate. He had attempted with difficulty to present serious answers to the questions, but as the night unfolded he could not keep his malignant aggressive instincts under control and began interrupting Clinton, insulting her, repeatedly called her a liar, and rambled and blustered, throwing out wild accusations, and jumping from topic to topic, mixing confused recitations of his main ideas with insults and rambling attacks on Clinton.

The next day the headlines of almost every newspaper in the country highlighted that Trump was refusing to accept election results and that he continued to insinuate that the system was rigged against him. A beleaguered Republican establishment finally got Trump to modify his stand on accepting election results. In a speech in Ohio the day after the debate, Trump dramatically stated that he would accept the results of the election, [pause]—"if I win!" Commentators noted that throughout the campaign season, if Trump did not get his way, he accused the process of being rigged against him and had even claimed past elections were rigged, documenting him as a thorough-going conspiracy theorist who many thought provided a clear and present danger to U.S. democracy with pundits worrying about what Trump and his supporters would do after the election. Gary Legum noted:

> Once again, Trump was not so much a presidential candidate as he was the angry Republican id that has been howling in rage about Hillary Clinton for two and a half decades. He was the avatar of years of conservative frustration, the vessel through which the right could channel every sputtering protest against Hillarycare, every lurid conspiracy about Benghazi and emails, every cruel and cutting scream ever heard in a Usenet chat room or a Breitbart comments thread. He was the final shout into the abyss for the conservative movement, its last impotent sputter before Clinton beats them all by taking the presidential oath of office.
>
> At which point they will start demanding her impeachment, but let's not get ahead of ourselves.[4]

The evening after the debate during the 71st annual Alfred E. Smith Memorial Foundation Dinner at the Waldorf Astoria hotel in New York, the two candidates once again faced off in a televised spectacle in which politicians generally used depreciatory humor to roast themselves while attempting to make humorous but pointed political arguments about their opponents. The event is sponsored by the Catholic archdiocese and assembles New York's elite to raise money for poor children. During presidential election years, the candidates are expected to show up and make witty, self-deprecatory speeches in which each can also take gentle gibes at the other. Breaking with this gentile tradition, Trump began with a self-pitying comment about how the New York political world, who used to love him, had turned against him since he became a Republican. Then in a tasteless attempt at failed Catholic humor, Trump compared himself to Jesus, presenting himself as "a guy who started out as a carpenter working for his father."

After some other weak jokes, Trump turned to nasty, telling the crowd that "Hillary is so corrupt, she got kicked off the Watergate commission," a claim that fact checkers quickly found to be false and that caused the crowd to groan and jeer. As Trump continued his attack on Hillary with email jokes, WikiLeaks jokes, and assorted insults, the crowd began loudly booing the Donald, and network camera shots of the live, televised event showed the crowd erupting in disbelief and horror when Trump remarked that Hillary was there, "pretending not to hate Catholics." Commentators remarked that this was the first time that there were political insults and attacks at the usually good-humored bi-partisan event, and the first time that a crowd loudly booed a candidate for president at the dinner.

In his lackluster campaign during the third week in October, with the election three weeks away, reporters were beginning to speculate that for the first time, Trump was realizing he might lose the election. Speculation became to emerge that Trump was planning to build a new rightwing media empire to mobilize his followers and capitalize on his campaign.

Yet in a campaign event at the hallowed civil war site of Gettysburg, a stone's throw from the place of the bloodiest battle in American history, Trump delivered what his campaign announced as a major policy speech in which he would outline the first 100 days after his election. Deplorable Donald could not resist beginning his talk with attacks on the women who had recently accused him of groping and sexual assault. Trump insisted that: "Every woman lied when they came forward to hurt my campaign, total fabrication." Threatening the women, Trump then blurted out that: "The events never happened," adding: "All of these liars will be sued after the election is over." Continuing his unsubstantiated conspiracy motif, Trump claimed: "It was probably the DNC [Democratic National Committee] and the Clinton campaign that put forward these liars with these fabricated stories."

Later that day, on a rare impromptu discussion with reporters on her campaign plane, with running mate Tim Kaine at her side,

Clinton noted: "I saw where our opponent Donald Trump went to Gettysburg, one of the most extraordinary places in American history, and basically said if he's president he'll spend his time suing women who have made charges against him based on his behavior." By contrast: "Tim and I are going to keep talking about what we want to do if we're given the great honor of serving as president and vice-president."

Trump's "Gettysburg Address" began with a lengthy attack on the women who had leveled sexual assault charges against him and he threatened to sue them after the election. This UnLincolneque grievance tirade was followed by a rather listless list of previous campaign promises to build a wall along the Mexican border, round up illegal immigrants, cancel NAFTA and other trade treaties, cancel Obamacare, and the like. Reading from a teleprompter, Trump seemed low energy and just going through the motions of reading his text. Minutes after he concluded, cable news reported that there was an 11th accusation of sexual assault by a porn star, Jessica Drake, who at a press conference in Los Angeles gave graphic details of how Trump had aggressively come on to her, lured her to his Los Angeles hotel suite for a business dinner, and then assaulted her with unwanted sexual advances. Drake claimed that Trump had also come on to her and kissed her and other women on the lips at a hotel reception and that the other women would confirm Trump's inappropriate behavior.

Although over the weekend, Donald Trump's campaign manager Kellyanne Conway admitted "we are behind" on Sunday talk shows, the candidate himself continued to claim over the weekend and into the next week that he is winning and denounced "phony polls." Speaking in a rally in St Augustine, Florida, Trump falsely claimed that pollsters were "oversampling Democrats," using a "voter suppression technique" to discourage Trump supporters from voting. He tweeted: "Major story that the Dems are making up phony polls in order to suppress the the Trump [sic]. We are going to WIN!" Yet almost every poll has shown a steady lead for Clinton since late July and pundits were starting to call the election for Clinton – polls and predictions that we now know were far off the mark.

Trump also continued his fierce attacks on "rigged media," while previewing his own Trump TV on Facebook, featuring Trump campaign operatives minutely dissecting the latest Hillary Clinton conspiracy scandal. Trump denounced the press as being composed of "thieves and crooks", and claimed that it may be even more corrupt than his rival "Crooked Hillary". It was overlooked, however, that Facebook and other social media sites were constantly publishing fake news stories, circulating outright falsehoods like the Pope, or Denzel Washington, had endorsed Trump for President, or that the Clinton Foundation was accused of gun-running.[5]

Trump's rants were seen by pundits as defensive gestures preparing him for a big loss as polls were predicting a 93% chance of a Clinton victory. Trump's activities on October 25 and 26 seemed to indicate that he was thinking more about business and the future of his organization than his campaign. There were announcements that Trump would engage in no more fundraisers for the Republican Party during the reminder of the campaign on a day when Tim Kaine allegedly attended five Democratic Party fundraisers, according to an interview with him on *The Rachel Maddow Show*.

On Tuesday, Trump held an event with employees of Trump National Doral resort in Miami, and his opening gambit was to assemble his apparently mostly Latino employees and get them to cheer him on. He opened with an attack on Obamacare and claimed that his employees were having "lots of problems with it" (there were media reports that monthly premiums were going up more than 20 per cent next year). Unfortunately for Trump, the manager of the resort had to confess that Trump's employees were covered by private insurance from the organization and did not use Obamacare.

The next day, instead of spending the morning in one of the battleground states where polls show him trailing Clinton, Trump attended a ribbon-cutting ceremony at his newly renovated and opened hotel at the Old Post Office on Pennsylvania Avenue in Washington where he had held a press conference declaring that Obama was born in the U.S. and blaming Hillary Clinton for the entire birther movement. Privileging business promotion over campaigning in the last two weeks of a hard fought campaign inevitably raised questions about whether Trump was really more interested in business than politics, or recognized he was losing and was planning for his return to business after the presidential race.

Trump's talking point in his ceremony opening the hotel was that it had come in "under budget and ahead of schedule." Yet he couldn't resist saying: "Congratulations, Newt, on last night. That was an amazing interview. We don't play games, Newt, right? We don't play games." That interview was a clash between former Speaker of the House and thrice married adulterer Newt Gingrich and Trump nemesis Megan Kelly on *Fox News*. When Ms. Kelly brought up whether the sexual assault accusations against Mr. Trump were taking a toll on his poll numbers, Gingrich asked why Bill Clinton's accusers weren't getting covered, and when Kelly answered by saying that on her show they had been covered, Gingrich lost it, accusing Kelly of being "fascinated with sex." She retorted that she was "fascinated by the protection of women." Gingrich continued to bluster and Kelly signed off by telling him: "You can take your anger issues and spend some time working on them."

The story became the highlight of the day, dominated the news cycle, and once again sent the message that Trump and his surrogates were clueless in dealing with women and unaware how angry women were becoming with the Trump campaign as their poll numbers with women continued to plummet.[6] There was also widespread recognition that Trump's brand had taken a beating during the course of a vicious campaign in which the businessman repeatedly made incendiary remarks about Mexicans, women, Muslims, immigrants, African-Americans, and whatever other group offended him. There were reports of efforts afoot to remove Trump's name from some of the New York residential towers he had built when people began selling their apartments, saying that they were ashamed to be living in a building with TRUMP on it.[7] And in Hollywood, activist James Otis attacked the Trump star on the Walk of Fame and badly defaced it.

Meanwhile, the Clinton campaign deployed the star power of Michelle Obama in North Carolina on Thursday, with the first joint appearance of the two first ladies. Both warned sharply against voter apathy, and Obama called Hillary "sister" and noted that "Hillary doesn't play," after ticking off Clinton's professional accomplishments and highlighting her qualifications to be president to the jubilant cheers from the 11,000 who came to see the joint appearance at Lawrence Joel Veterans Memorial Coliseum. Closing her argument, Ms. Obama stated: "She (i.e. Hillary) has more experience and exposure to the presidency than any candidate in our lifetime – yes, more than Barack, more than Bill – so she is absolutely ready to be commander in chief on Day 1. And yes," Obama paused for dramatic effect, "she happens to be a woman."

The Clinton campaign was given a final gift by Donald the Deplorable before the biggest shock and setback for Clintonland which appeared to be headed for an easy win, maybe a landslide. On Friday, October 18, 2016, there were announcements that a former Miss Finland had become the 12th woman to openly accuse Trump of sexual assault. Ninni Laaksonen alleged in an interview with the Finnish newspaper *Ilta-Sanomat* that Trump had groped her before an appearance on *The Late Show with David Letterman* in 2006. Ms. Laaksonen claimed: "Before the show we were photographed outside the building. Trump stood right next to me and suddenly he squeezed my butt. He really grabbed my butt." Donald's butt-grabbing would be completely overshadowed by an October Surprise that would have momentous consequences for the election and the U.S. political future.

THE OCTOBER FBI BOMBSHELL AND COMEY'S INTERVENTION

On Friday, October 29, 2016, FBI Director James Comey dropped a bombshell that is perhaps the most stunning and, for many, outrageous, intervention in a presidential election by a top official of the judicial branch of the government in U.S. presidential history. Director Comey released a letter to 12 Congressmen saying that the FBI had received a collection of emails that the FBI would review to determine if they improperly contained classified information, and that the emails "appeared to pertain" to Hillary Clinton's email investigation.

Over the past year, the FBI had investigated Clinton's email, and over the summer determined that she was not guilty of any crime concerning her private email server. Many in the FBI and Justice Department were outraged with Comey's rekindling of the Clinton email crisis 11 days before the election. There were immediate leaks to the media that the Justice Department had opposed Comey sending out a letter on an FBI investigation in progress, which was supposed to be secret, and in particular releasing a political bombshell so close to an election when such intervention was specifically prohibited. Further, senior law enforcement officials informed the media that it was unclear if any of the emails were from Mrs. Clinton's private server, and indicated that although Comey said in his letter that the emails "appear to be pertinent," the FBI had not yet examined them. Jane Mayer reported in *The New Yorker* that Comey's letter had been opposed by Attorney General Loretta Lynch who had argued Justice Department tradition mandated secrecy and not releasing information that could affect an election.[8] Mayer reported:

> Comey's decision is a striking break with the policies of the Department of Justice, according to current and former federal legal officials. Comey, who is a Republican appointee of President Obama, has a reputation for integrity and independence, but his latest action is stirring an extraordinary level of concern among legal authorities, who

see it as potentially affecting the outcome of the Presidential and congressional elections.

"You don't do this," one former senior Justice Department official exclaimed. "It's aberrational. It violates decades of practice." The reason, according to the former official, who asked not to be identified because of ongoing cases involving the department, "is because it impugns the integrity and reputation of the candidate, even though there's no finding by a court, or in this instance even an indictment."[9]

Within hours, other government officials leaked that the email trove in question came from a device shared by Anthony Weiner, a former Democratic congressman from New York, and his then wife Huma Abedin, a top aide of Hillary Clinton. Further, the "unrelated case," in which Comey had claimed brought the emails to light, involved an F.B.I. investigation into illicit "sexting" from Weiner to a 15-year-old girl in North Carolina.[10] Trump and his camp were overjoyed by the new bombshell, leading the candidate, who had been complaining that the election was rigged, to concede at a campaign rally in New Hampshire that: "Maybe, it's less rigged than I thought... Perhaps, finally, justice will be done." To the cheers of "lock her up" from his supporters, Trump claimed: "Hillary Clinton's corruption is on a scale we have never seen before. We must not let her take her criminal scheme into the Oval Office."

In a brief press conference, Clinton told reporters in Iowa that she learned of the newly discovered emails only after the letter to Congress was made public, and that: "I'm confident whatever [the emails] are will not change the conclusion reached in July," she said, referring to Director Comey's announcement that no violation of law had turned up in a probe of Secretary Clinton's private e-mail server, and that the FBI was dropping the investigation. Pressing the FBI to release more information about Comey's letter, Clinton insisted that: "Therefore, it's imperative that the bureau explain this issue in question, whatever it is, without any delay." Asked about the connection to Weiner, Clinton replied: "We've heard these rumors. We don't know what to believe."

An angry John D. Podesta, chairman of Clinton's election campaign, sent out a memo proclaiming: "Director Comey's letter refers to emails that have come to light in an unrelated case, but we have no idea what those emails are and the director himself notes they may not even be significant." California Senator Dianne Feinstein stated: "The F.B.I. has a history of extreme caution near Election Day so as not to influence the results. Today's break from that tradition is appalling."

The rest of the day and into the weekend stinging criticism of FBI Chief Comey from both Democrats and Republicans erupted, as well as from government officials speaking on and off the record. Comey appeared on the defensive, saying in an internal email to FBI employees that he had felt obligated to inform Congress, and conceding: "we don't know the significance of this newly discovered collection of emails." Government officials were said to be deeply upset about Mr. Comey's decision to go to Congress with the new information before it had been adequately investigated, and "several officials who spoke on the condition of anonymity," said that Comey's intervention "appeared to contradict longstanding Justice Department guidelines discouraging any actions close to an election that could influence the outcome. One official complained that no one at the F.B.I. or the Justice Department is even certain yet whether any of the emails included national security material or was relevant to the investigation into whether Mrs. Clinton had mishandled classified material in her use of a private email server."[11]

The press was even fiercer in its criticisms of Director Comey with a barrage of articles attacking the director in the *Washington Post*.[12] Matthew Miller, director of the Justice Department's public affairs office from 2009 to 2011, appeared throughout the day on cable news shows and his Twitter feed criticizing Comey's intervention, and wrote in a *Washington Post* Op Ed:

> FBI Director James B. Comey's stunning announcement that he has directed investigators to begin reviewing new evidence in the Clinton email investigation was yet another troubling violation of long-standing Justice Department rules or precedent, conduct that raises serious questions

about his judgment and ability to serve as the nation's chief investigative official....

This case in particular has exposed how Comey's self-regard can veer into self-righteousness, a belief that only he can fairly adjudicate the appropriateness of others' conduct, and that the rules that apply to every other Justice Department employee are too quaint to restrict a man of his unquestionable ethics.

That is a dangerous trait. The director of the FBI has great power at his disposal. Congress has seen to fit to provide FBI directors with nearly unfettered independence, including a 10-year term designed to stretch beyond any one president's tenure.

With that independence comes a responsibility to adhere to the rules that protect the rights of those whom the FBI investigates. Comey has failed that standard repeatedly in his handling of the Clinton investigation.[13]

I quote this at length as I cannot recall another instance of a former government official criticizing so fiercely the head of the FBI, and calling into question his fitness to govern. The controversy over Comey's bombshell raged throughout the weekend and the election had entered new uncharted waters. Earlier, in the week, there were reports that Trump supporters would take up arms and mobilize to assault what they might see as a stolen election if Trump lost. Certain of his followers interviewed on TV and in the press indicated that they had threatened to take up arms and carry out a "revolution," in response to Trump's charges that the election was rigged and that they should take action if Clinton was declared the winner.[14] Now if Trump won, Clinton's supporters would rage against problematic FBI interference in the election which was surely among the most contested and bizarre in U.S. history.

The weekend political news and commentary shows were dominated by Comey's letter and the bipartisan response with Democrats fiercely attacking his unprecedented intervention in a presidential election, while Trump and his inner circle, but not all Republicans, praised Comey. Clips were played throughout the day juxtaposing Trump's attack on FBI Director Comey when he announced he was not pressing charges against Clinton over her email issue in July, contrasted with his praise of Comey after he had inserted the issue into the presidential campaign, stopping Trump's precipitous fall toward apparent defeat and giving him a chance to pull it out; one amusing clip showed Trump attacking Comey and the FBI on a talk show on Friday morning and praising him Friday afternoon following the release of his letter, giving the phrase "flip flop" new life.

Further, speaking in Las Vegas on Sunday afternoon, Trump accused Clinton of bribing Attorney General Beverly Lynch with the promise of reappointment, a rather shocking and outrageous comment made with no evidence whatsoever. Taking the high road of extreme hyperbole, Trump thundered that Clinton had "set up an illegal server for the obvious purpose of shielding her criminal conduct from public disclosure and exposure," leading his followers to explode into ecstatic paroxysms of their collective desire for political purges of their enemies: "Lock her up! Lock her up!" Trump also joked: "We never thought we were going to say thank you to Anthony Weiner," recognizing that he would have had little chance of winning if Comey hadn't decided to muck around in Weiner's email and then insert his investigation – before there were *any* findings! – into the election, thus giving Trump a chance to come from behind and eventually surge ahead.

Senate Majority Leader Harry Reid released a letter with a scathing attack on Comey, warning that the FBI Director may have broken the law: "Your actions in recent months have demonstrated a disturbing double standard for the treatment of sensitive information, with what appears to be a clear intent to aid one political party over another. My office has determined that these actions may violate the Hatch Act, which bars FBI officials from using their official authority to influence an election. Through your partisan action, you may have broken the law." Reid concluded his letter with a personal rebuke of the FBI director, writing: "Please keep in mind that I have been a supporter of yours in the past," noting that he had fought to secure

Comey's confirmation through Republican filibusters, "because I believed you to be a principled public servant. With the deepest regret, I now see that I was wrong."

Reid was referring back to Comey's earlier press conference and Congressional hearing where he explained why he was not pressing criminal charges against Hillary Clinton for her private email server issue, and to the 1939 Hatch Act that mandated that Federal Officials should not use their office to influence elections. In the course of his earlier testimony exonerating Clinton, Comey had nevertheless called her actions "reckless," and made other critical comments about her that were deemed by experts unseemly and partisan, breaking with FBI protocol and tradition. Now Reid and others were claiming that Comey had actually violated the Hatch Act and illegally intervened in a political election, leading one wit to post a comment on *The Daily Koz* demanding to "lock him up!"[15]

Democratic congressman Steve Cohen on Sunday night called for Comey to resign, and argued that Comey's letter "was plainly premature, careless and unprecedented in its potential impact upon a presidential election without a speck of information regarding the emails in question, their validity, substance or relevance". Former attorney general Eric Holder and dozens of former federal prosecutors signed and released a letter critical of Comey,[16] claiming that Comey broke from Justice Department policy when he sent the letter to Congress about the Clinton email investigation. The former prosecutors pointed out that Comey's disclosure had "invited considerable, uninformed public speculation" about Clinton's emails, which was indeed the case.

There were also reports that the FBI had been investigating connections between Trump's previous campaign managers and top officials in his campaign and the Russians, leading Harry Reid to accuse Comey of withholding information about the FBI's investigation into computer hacks into Democratic Party officials and organizations, which were allegedly carried out by Russian intelligence with possible links with various former advisers to Donald Trump. Indeed, there was an obvious double standard at play in the FBI's release about their investigation into Clinton's email and silence on their investigation into Trump's Russian connections, with Comey making an explosive and unprecented public intervention into publicizing the former and remaining quiet about Trumpster Russian connections and the computer attacks against the Democrats. Indeed, Comey had never mentioned the hacks into Democratic party severs or indicated the FBI was doing anything to investigate them.

Other senior Democratic Party Senators, including Dianne Feinstein, Patrick Leahy, Ben Cardin and Thomas Carper, released a letter written to Comey, demanding a full briefing on the new emails by Monday. Anonymous officials had leaked to the *Associated Press* that FBI investigators had known for weeks that they might find pertinent emails on Weiner's device, but claimed that Comey had not been briefed until Thursday, and then on Friday rushed to publicize what was supposed to be a secret FBI investigation, thus acting with unseemly and seemingly partisan haste.

On Monday, October 31, 2016, MediaWorld was buzzing with reports that the FBI had received a warrant to search Weiner and Huma Abedin's laptop for Clinton emails, and that FBI director James Comey had been told that his unprecedented disclosure into an ongoing investigation may have broken the law. Speculation raged over the possible impact of the FBI's email investigation would have on Clinton's election chances, and whether the FBI would determine the results of the 2016 election, just as the Supreme Court had determined the results of the 2000 election, in both cases subverting the U.S. constitution and presidential election traditions, and undermining the will of the people and U.S. democracy.[17]

Throughout the day, attacks continued on Comey's questionable insertion into the election with former Attorney Generals and top Justice Department officials and legal experts fiercely attacking Comey. Bush administration attorney general Alberto Gonzales noted: "To throw out this kind of letter without more information, without really knowing what the facts are with respect to these additional emails, I think was a mistake." Richard Painter, George W. Bush's top ethics lawyer from 2005 to 2007, claimed that Comey's letter had "very likely" violated the Hatch Act and federal law barring public officials from using their position to influence the outcome of an election. Moreover, Painter claimed that he had filed a complaint with the Office of Special

Counsel to investigate Mr. Comey's action.[18] In addition, 100 former federal prosecutors signed a statement attacking Comey for inviting "considerable, uninformed public speculation" about the Clinton email case before establishing, by the FBI director's own admission, investigative relevance of the material and had compromised the "non-partisan traditions" of the Justice Department and the FBI.[19]

CNBC reported on November 1, 2016, that in early October, Comey had fought successfully to keep the FBI's name off a government report regarding evidence that Russia was attempting to interfere in the presidential election. CNBC claimed that while Comey believed the report was accurate, he did not want to sign on to it so close to the election – raising again the double standard question of why Comey was hesitant to release information or associate the FBI with investigations into potential crimes by members of the Trump campaign team while eagerly releasing a letter that could harm Hillary Clinton and the Democrats. Indeed, Comey's letter had dominated the news cycle for days and raised intense speculation as to whether Comey's intervention could bring down Clinton and many Democratic Party candidates locked in close elections that would determine the fate of the Senate and House, and thus American politics for years to come.

Further, Comey was being compared to two of the worst villains in recent American history: former FBI Director, J. Edgar Hoover and disgraced Communist witch-hunter Joseph McCarthy, who used smear and innuendo to attack his opponents, two words being frequently applied to Comey's intervention into the presidential campaign.[20] Douglas Brinkley, a presidential historian and professor at Rice University, said, perhaps more acutely, that "Comey has become the Ken Starr of the 21st century," citing the federal prosecutor who attempted to destroy the Clinton's in the 1990s and who just resigned in disgrace as president of Baylor University. Reports had circulated concerning a number of rapes on the Baylor campus by athletes which the Baylor Administration, under Starr's "leadership," had, in effect, covered over, leading the sanctimonious Starr to resign.

There were also damning reports about Donald Trump that were being published and received some discussion in the mainstream media. David A. Fahrenthold published an article in *The Washington*

Post titled "Trump boasts about his philanthropy. But his giving falls short of his words."[21] The story opens with an account that in October 1996, Trump crashed a charity gala for the Association to Benefit Children which was celebrating the opening for a new nursery school serving children with AIDS. Trump reportedly barged in and "sat down in a seat saved for Steven Fisher, a developer who had given generously to build the nursery." Trump reportedly plopped himself down in a row reserved for major benefactors beside then-Mayor and later Trump nastyman Rudy Giuliani, former mayor David Dinkins, TV stars Frank and Kathie Lee Gifford, and other celebrities and major donors. Fahrenhold reports:

> "Nobody knew he was coming," said Abigail Disney, another donor sitting on the dais. "There's this kind of ruckus at the door, and I don't know what was going on, and in comes Donald Trump. [He] just gets up on the podium and sits down."

> Trump was not a major donor. He was not a donor, period. He'd never given a dollar to the nursery or the Association to Benefit Children, according to Gretchen Buchenholz, the charity's executive director then and now.

> Afterward, Disney and Buchenholz recalled, Trump left without offering an explanation. Or a donation. Fisher was stuck in the audience. The charity spent months trying to repair its relationship with him.

> "I mean, what's wrong with you, man?" Disney recalled thinking of Trump, when it was over.

Fahrenthold reported how for the last months, he had been calling every major charity and philanthropist in the New York and Florida area where Trump frequented, and could discover almost no donations from Trump, thus putting in question Trump's boasts about his philanthropy. The *Post* investigation uncovered, among other things, that the charity to which Trump has given the most money "appears to be his own: the Donald J. Trump Foundation." Further, as had already been reported, the Trump Foundation has been funded largely by other people, and that records indicate that it has received nothing from Trump himself since 2008. Further:

> One of the foundation's most consistent causes was Trump himself.

> New findings, for instance, show that the Trump Foundation's largest-ever gift – $264,631 – was used to renovate a fountain outside the windows of Trump's Plaza Hotel.

> Its smallest-ever gift, for $7, was paid to the Boy Scouts in 1989, at a time when it cost $7 to register a new Scout. Trump's oldest son was 11 at the time. Trump did not respond to a question about whether the money was paid to register him.

For years, Trump had repeatedly bragged what a great philanthropist he was, but that appeared to be another con. There was also an investigation into Donald Trump's taxes by *The New York Times* which reported that Trump had for years used loopholes of questionable legality that were later outlawed to avoid paying any taxes.[22] The article notes: "Donald J. Trump proudly acknowledges he did not pay a dime in federal income taxes for years on end. He insists he merely exploited tax loopholes legally available to any billionaire – loopholes he says Hillary Clinton failed to close during her years in the United States Senate."[23]

The article recounts how in the 1990s Trump almost went bankrupt because of bad overinvestments in the Atlantic City casino industry and noted, an already reported and documented story, that Trump's loss of $946 million one year allowed him to avoid paying any taxes for twenty years thereafter because of tax loopholes for real estate developers. The Trump stories brought back the narrative that Trump, trumpeting himself as an outsider, was a big-league insider who had gamed the system for his own benefit, was only out for himself and his bottom-line, had suffered many disastrous business failures that had cost his investors, banks, and contractors who he claimed he couldn't pay hundreds of millions, and that rather than being a great businessman as he and his deluded supporters claimed, he was really one of the great con men of all time.

THE FINAL WEEK, THE NOVEMBER SURPRISE, AND BANANA REPUBLICANISM

It is safe to say that after the pyrotechnics of the past week, anything could happen in the final seven days of the campaign. The race was tightening, there was a media frenzy, and the electorate was suffering perhaps unparalleled anxiety over the election. Lesly Alderman published an article in *The New York Times* which revealed that: "A study released by the American Psychological Association revealed that 52% of American adults are coping with highly levels of stress brought on by the 2016 election, according to a national Harris Poll."[24] The poll indicated that 59% of Republicans and 55% of Democrats acknowledge that the election has become a major source of stress. "Both sides apparently were generating fears of what would happen after the election and worried on both sides about secrecy leading to increased levels of mistrust of government."

Astonishingly, the FBI muddled into another partisan election scandal by publishing on its website 129 pages of internal documents related to a years-old investigation into former President Bill Clinton's pardon of a fugitive Democratic donor Marc Rich in the 1990s.[25] Although FBI officials claimed that the timing of the release was purely coincidental and that they were published after Freedom of Information Act requests, and were posted "automatically and electronically to the FBI's public reading room in accordance with the law and established procedures," it looked bad for the FBI that they were attacking Bill Clinton when there was an uproar about their assault on Hillary's campaign.[26] The FBI documents were released from an FBI Twitter account called @FBIRecordsVault, which had been dormant for more than a year, until it happened to release materials pertaining to a 1990s Clinton scandal. In response, Senate Minority Leader Harry Reid pointed out that Comey possessed "explosive information about close ties and coordination between Donald Trump, his top advisers, and the Russian government," but had stayed quiet about this scandal, allegedly because he deemed it too close to the election! Reid reminded Comey that the FBI director may have violated a federal statute, the Hatch Act, that prohibits government officials from engaging in activities that can influence an election, and concluded that: "Through your partisan actions, you may have broken the law."[27]

Barack Obama weighed in on the Comey scandal on November 2, 2016, delivering a stinging critique of the FBI, and insisting in his first interview after Comey's controversial decision with the online outlet *NowThisNews*: "I do think that there is a norm that when there are investigations, we don't operate on innuendo. We don't operate on incomplete information. We don't operate on leaks. We operate based on concrete decisions that are made. When this was investigated thoroughly the last time, the conclusion of the FBI, the conclusion of the justice department, the conclusion of repeated congressional investigations was that she had made some mistakes but that there wasn't anything there that was prosecutable." Obama said Clinton made an "honest mistake" by using a private email server as his secretary of state, something that was now "being blown up into just some crazy thing". New voters hear "all that noise" and wonder whether they should be worried about Clinton's conduct, he added, but said he had absolute confidence in her.[28]

Meanwhile, the 16-year-old North Carolina teen who reportedly received the lewd "sexts" from Anthony Weiner, accused FBI director Comey of putting politics ahead of her own well-being and subjecting her to a rash of unwanted media attention, writing in a letter to *Buzzfeed*: "The FBI asked for me to speak to the media as little as possible. I have tried to stay quiet, but Comey has upset me…The last thing that I wanted was to have this become political propaganda. I told my story originally to protect other young girls that might be a victim of online predators. I thought your job as FBI Director was to protect me. I thought if I cooperated … my identity as a minor would be kept secret. That is no longer the case. I have been even been blamed for … costing Hillary the election. Why couldn't your letter have waited until after the election, so I would not have to be the center of attention the last week of the election cycle? *I now add you to the list of people who have victimized me.*"[29]

Obama and other Democratic Party surrogates campaigned in swing states on Wednesday with less than a week until election day, with early voting results reportedly far in excess of the same stage in 2012. Speaking in Florida, Trump repeated familiar attacks on the media, singling out reporter Katy Tur of NBC, naming her four times and pointing her out in the crowd, while his audience booed. Trump thundered: "These people are among the most dishonest people I've ever met, spoken to, done business with. There has never been anywhere near the media dishonesty like we've seen in this election." Pointing to Tur, Trump went on: "They're not reporting it. Katy, you're not reporting it, Katy, but there's something happening, Katy. There's something happening, Katy."

While Trump attacked Katy Tur for not celebrating the awesomeness of his campaign, Tur's sister network MSNBC devoted 48 minutes of a 60 minute show to covering Trump, almost ignoring Clinton, and indeed, throughout the campaign, Trump had received by far the most TV coverage, so one of the Big Lies of the Trump campaign was that the mainstream media was an instrument of the Clinton campaign. Trump has gotten more media coverage than any other candidate in the primaries and general election, and although there was justified media criticism of Trump and his campaign, there had long been and continued to be strong media critique of Hillary Clinton.

On Thursday, with five days to go before the election, the Trump campaign brought out his wife, Melania, to make her first solo appearance of the election since the Republican national convention in July. It was revealed shortly after Melania's convention speech that it was plagiarized in part from a Michelle Obama speech, and Melania withdrew from the campaign trail. Yet scandal trailed her and the Trumpsters had to deal with a story that modelling pictures of Melania appeared in publications one year before she had officially filled out her immigration and work permits, raising questions whether she had broken immigration laws.[30]

There was high anticipation for Melania's speech scheduled before a small audience in the Philadelphia suburbs where the Trump campaign was trying to shore up Republican voters. In a short address televised live by the cable networks, Melania Trump called for a gentler and kinder America, where children can spend time on social media without fear of bullying and harassment. Melania intoned: "Our culture has gotten too mean and too rough, especially to children and teenagers. It is never OK when a 12-year-old girl or boy is mocked, bullied or attacked. It is terrible when that happens on the playground and it is absolutely unacceptable when it's done by someone with no name hiding on the internet."

Ms. Trump promised as a first lady, she would work to combat online bullying, which was described by commentators as ironic, or even hypocritical, since her husband was the most notorious cyberbully in history, using his Twitter feed to mock and degrade his opponents and attack women who have criticized or offended him. Deplorable Donald also has a pattern of retweeting posts from sites and individuals who regularly spread racist, anti-Semitic and Islamophobic hate speech, as well as white supremacism. Indeed, it had recently been revealed that the Ku Klux Klan national newspaper had endorsed Trump and his slogan to "make America great again" (for conservative white people).[31]

More reporting and heated discussion of the FBI attack on the Clinton campaign continued to develop. Spencer Ackerman wrote in *The Guardian* that "The FBI is Trumpland," and that an anti-Clinton atmosphere in the FBI spurred leaking, according to FBI sources.[32] Ackerman wrote that a "highly unfavorable view of Hillary Clinton intensified after James Comey's decision not to recommend an indictment over her use of a private email server" in July. This allegedly spurred "a rapid series of leaks damaging to her campaign just days before the election," and pressured FBI Director Comey to speak out indicating the new material that the FBI was investigating. *Fox News* reported that an indictment against Clinton was forthcoming, and Trump and his surrogates quickly spread this false information on the campaign trail and via surrogates, forcing the FBI to deny the report.

A curious *Fox News* montage was played of an interview with Trump surrogate and former New York mayor Rudy Giuliani who laughed when on October 26, Martha MacCallum, a *Fox News* host, asked Giuliani about Trump presidential campaign activity during its last two weeks, answering: "We got a couple of surprises left," Giuliani answered with a big smile. When pressed if these were "October Surprises," he responded: "I call them early surprises in the way we're going to campaign to get our message out, maybe in a little bit of a different way. You'll see. And I think it'll be enormously effective. And I do think that all of these revelations about Hillary Clinton finally are beginning to have an impact."

Three days later, Comey dropped his bombshell that new emails which may pertain to Clinton's use of a personal email server while Secretary of State, raising questions whether Giuliani, who constantly brags of his inside FBI connections, knew in advance about Comey's letter. Yet on November 2, 2016, continuing his TV and campaign appearences on behalf of Trump, Guiliani admitted to Megyn Kelly on *Fox News*: "You have outraged F.B.I. agents that talk to me. They are outraged at the injustice. They are outraged at being turned down by the Justice Department to open a grand jury. They are convinced that Loretta Lynch has corrupted the Justice Department."

In this astonishing intervention, Giuliani accused the Justice Department and the Attorney General Loretta Lynch of corruption, a highly inflammable charge for a former mayor and prosecutor to make. Giuliani's outrageous comments fit right into the Trump campaign's twofold "argument" that the system is rigged and Hillary Clinton is criminally corrupt. Indeed, for weeks Trump had been droning on about Clinton's "criminal scheme" and "criminal conduct," which was given substance by Comey's letter, a barrage of rumors by Giuliani and the Trump campaign that criminal indictments were going to be levelled against Clinton, and a new line of attack which apparently would be Trump's closing line of attack in his election campaign.

Meanwhile, another major Trump surrogate was disgraced. New Jersey Governor Chris Christie's political career sustained a serious blow after two of his former allies were found guilty of conspiring to shut down the nation's busiest bridge to punish a local mayor who had refused to support the governor's reelection bid. Although Christie wasn't charged in the "Bridgegate" trial, the case produced a steady stream of new allegations against the governor that probably will haunt him whether Trump wins or loses. There was testimony in the trial that Christie had been informed about the shutting of the bridge and resultant traffic jam and laughed, although the rest of his life, this would stain his reputation, as would his involvement in Trumpworld, portending a dim future for the one-time superstar of the Republican party.

As the campaigns went into the last weekend November 5–6, 2016, both opponents crisscrossed the country in search of votes. The Clinton campaign had a concert with Hillary and J-Lo and Jay-Z in Florida, and Katy Perry and other stars held concerts for Clinton, as she attempted to get millennial votes. Clinton campaigned with Bernie Sanders and her surrogates Barack Obama, Joe Biden, and other Dem superstars stumped the nation to bank votes for Hillary. Trump seemed to have only his family to campaign for him, and there was a scare in Nevada when a false report about a man with a gun in the crowd forced secret service agents to hustle him to safety when someone yelled "gun!" and a mob of Trump supporters started beating on the demonstrator. The brave young man had entered a Reno rally for Trump alone with a sign denouncing Trump and had been beaten by Trump supporters and hauled away by police and secret service. Donald Trump Jr. tweeted how his brave father had escaped an assassination and went right back on stage while Clinton stopped her rally during a rainstorm. In fact, the protestor did not have a gun and the spectacle portrayed another out of control violent mob at a Trump rally.

The same day, there was a report that the *National Enquirer*, a weekly tabloid that had viciously attacked the Clintons and Obamas for years, had suppressed a story about a long-time affair Trump had with a beauty queen during the early years of his marriage to Melania.[33] The pre-election edition of the *National Enquirer* headlined "3 Election Eve Bombshells" (which were, in fact, recycling of old anti-Clinton stories), and contained on the cover an unflattering picture of a red-eye and unsmiling Hillary Clinton with capitalized bullet-points

• CORRUPT!
• RACIST!
• CRIMINAL!

These inflammatory charges were followed with balloons announcing:

EXCLUSIVE 1	EXCLUSIVE 2	EXCLUSIVE 3
FBI EMAIL INDICTMENT	CLINTON FAMILY	WHITEWATER
SHE'LL BE PARDONED –	CHEF TELLS ALL!	PROSECUTORS
BEFORE	'HILLARY	BREAK THEIR
OBAMA	USED "N"	SILENCE
LEAVES	WORD &	'HILLARY
OFFICE!	HATES	BLACKMAILED &
	BLACK PEOPLE!'	INTIMIDATED US!'

The *National Enquirer* smears provided precisely the Trump propaganda that Trump was spewing out every day on the campaign trail. The goal was to create negative images in the working class readers of the *Enquirer* that conveyed their worst image of Clinton and provided fodder for Trump's daily attacks on "Crooked Hillary," flaming the call of Trump's followers to "lock her up!" Interestingly, there was also an appeal to African Americans conveying the ludicrous and slanderous allegation that Hillary "used the 'N' word & hates black people," when the truth is that Donald Trump uses regularly more documented racist language than any U.S. presidential candidate in recent history.

As Election Day neared, pundits obsessed over polls, tightening races, and predictions flew fast and furious. The Sunday talk shows buzzed with speculation on the latest polls, campaign strategies, and the key events of the campaign so far. The candidates continued to cross the country in search of votes with frenzy mounting concerning how many people had engaged in early voting, and the breakdown into party votes of black, Latino, young, female, and college educated voters which would be Clinton's coalition as Trumps core constituency were white men and voters with low education levels. The Trump camp had apparently sent out flyers and on-line messages telling citizens how to vote for Hillary on-line, a fraud that would suppress their votes as this was not allowed. Trump also told voters who had voted early for Clinton to contact their voting sites to change their votes, a tactic that could cause delay and confusion, and thus suppress votes. Courts ruled in North Carolina against Republican voter suppressing tactics, and there was worry that voters would follow Trump's demand that his voters show up to monitor polling places so that there would not be stolen votes, calling on his faithful to in effect violate voter suppression and intimidation laws and cause havoc on voting day.

There were also worries that voting sites would be hacked and even that the entire Internet would be taken down, causing chaos on election day. The previous week had seen some servers hacked and major sites like Amazon, Netflix, and various business sites taken down for hours. There had been rumors for weeks that Russia wanted to disrupt the U.S. election to show the fragility of American democracy, so panic pervaded many sectors of the electorate, the parties and campaigns, and electoral officials as Election Day loomed on Tuesday.

Trump's closing argument appeared to be that Clinton was a criminal who would shortly be indicted and cause a constitutional crisis if she were elected. On Thursday, *Fox News* had reported that the FBI had an indictment ready for Clinton and that soon she would be officially indicted. Trump immediately conveyed on the campaign trail the news of the criminal indictment that would soon arrive. Quickly afterward, however, *Fox News* anchor Bret Baier apologized for falsely reporting that investigators had determined Clinton's private email server was hacked "by five foreign intelligence agencies" – and that an investigation would lead to an indictment after the election. Baier acknowledged that "there is no evidence" for either statement, and thus neither of his reports about Clinton were accurate, raising the question whether Giuliani with his FBI connections, or someone in the Trump campaign was responsible for the disinformation and Big Lie that would possibly allow Trump to take the election.

Trump's line of argumentation was disrupted as a shock came out of nowhere that FBI Director James Comey had released another letter informing told Congress on Sunday that the F.B.I. had seen no evidence in a recently discovered trove of emails to change his conclusion in July that Hillary Clinton should face no charges over her handling of classified information. Later in the day, it was revealed that the emails were duplicates of what the FBI had already seen or were not pertinent to Mrs. Clinton's email case, making the whole issue a Big Nothing about Nothing, raising the question why the FBI Director had caused so much drama and controversy by writing the letter in the first place before he had examined that materials in question.

The Democrats were relieved with Brian Fallon, a representative for the Clinton campaign, saying in a post on Twitter that: "We were always confident nothing would cause the July decision to be revisited… Now Director Comey has confirmed it." Many Democrats were outraged though that the past nine days had been dominated by the FBI uproar, about 40 million citizens had voted early, and the initial FBI letter may have irrevocably harmed Clinton and some Democratic Party candidates.

The Republicans, by contrast, were in a state of panic and frenzy with Kellyanne Conway, Trump's campaign manager, appearing on Sunday days shows right after the Comey announcement, melted down on camera, as she poured out a torment of abuse against all the crimes of Hillary Clinton, a motif that was now the fraying DNA of the Trump campaign. Conway lamented the fact that Comey had inserted himself into the election again, while a tightly wound Trump was muttering again on the campaign trail how the system was rigged and Clinton was "protected," as if the government were an extension of the mafia with certain agencies providing hitmen, assassins, and protectors.

While Trump did not comment on the FBI November Surprise in detail, in a Reno campaign stop, Deplorable Donald continued to call Clinton the most corrupt person to ever seek the presidency and predicted: "Hillary Clinton will be under investigation for a long, long time … likely concluding in a criminal trial," while his supporters chanted "lock her up." "You have to understand, it's a rigged system, and she's protected," Trump said.

Never before in recent presidential history, had a candidate so assiduously criminalized his opponent, with the support of the tabloid media and the FBI. Trump and his surrogates carried out an indictment, trial, and jury verdict against Hillary Clinton without her opportunity to respond in a court of law and to defend her rights to have a fair trial, impartial judge, jury of peers, and the legal rights afforded every citizen. Trump and his surrogates were operating outside of the legal system by condemning Clinton out of hand as guilty, thus undermining fundamental rights of all defendants and citizens to have their day in court. The FBI participation in this procedure would seriously put in question its legitimacy and reputation.

From the intense discussion of the FBI's intervention in the campaign, violating the Hatch Act, there were establishment worries that the FBI would suffer a legitimation crisis for its flip-flopping and the dramatic insertion of the FBI Director twice in the last ten days of the campaign. There was intense speculation concerning what impact Comey's conclusion that Clinton was innocent after all would have on the outcome of the election, or whether his earlier intervention doomed the Clinton campaign. For Trump had gained ground against Clinton over the past ten days and key battleground Senate seats were drawing closer and the Democrats hopes to take control of the Senate was now in question as polls rose for Trump and many Republican Senate candidates.

Media reports had claimed before the first Comey letter that the Trump camp was in disarray, divided, and could not explain to Trump how it was losing,[34] but now his campaign appeared resurrected. Trump team officials had been able to wrest his Twitter account from him, so for the last ten days Trump had stayed on teleprompter script as he tried to indict Clinton and did not become the story of the day himself from crazed late night Tweets. The media never really had perceived the extent to which Trump and his minions had become the Judge, Jury, and would-be Executor of Hillary Clinton who was indicted daily by the Trump campaign which claimed that she was guilty of great crimes and promised that she would be punished in a paroxysm of vengeful malice never before visible in a modern political presidential campaign.

This Banana Republicanism was reminiscent of the worst kind of dictatorships and authoritarian movements in the modern era with a demagogic leader who would cleanse society of its evils and solve single-handedly its problems. "I am the ONE who can fix it," Demagogic Don had intoned at the Republican National Convention and Trump had consistently presented himself as a rogue leader who would operate outside the boundaries of the rules of the political game and would play by his own rules.

While the Trump camp was in disarray and confusion, during the last 48 hours of the campaign, the Clinton camp displayed a powerhouse lineup of superstars from the worlds of entertainment, sports, and politics, to campaign for Hillary. During the last days of the election contest, Hillary had campaigned with Beyoncé and Jay Z, Katy Perry, and an all-star line-up of Democratic Party superstars, led by the Obamas and Clintons, and Bernie Sanders. On Sunday, just after the latest Comey bombshell, Clinton appeared in Ohio, alongside LeBron James, the Cleveland Cavaliers star and a revered figure in the battleground state. In New Hampshire, Sunday evening Clinton was joined by Khizr Khan, the Gold Star father whose family Trump attacked in an August clash after the conventions which had proved disastrous for the Republican nominee who began dropping in the polls. The Clinton campaign has used Mr. Khan in television ads as a spokesperson for inclusion and religious tolerance, and he had also proved capable of throwing Trump off-message.

On Monday, the day before the election, both Trump and Clinton crisscrossed the country, hitting key swing states. Trump went to five campaign stops, greeted by uproarious crowds at each stop. The Clinton campaign carried out a monster rally in Philadelphia, before Fennell Hall, the birthplace of American democracy. Crowds of more than fifty thousand rapturously listened to Bruce Springsteen sing some of his most memorable songs and praise Hillary Clinton. Both Michelle and Barack Obama appeared making strong closing statements for Hillary Clinton who appeared with her family and the Obamas in a triumphant spectacle of Democratic Party unity.

On the eve of the election, *New York Times* columnist Charles M. Blow tried to make sense how people who profess traditional Republican, moral, or Christian values could possibly support Donald Trump and concluded that it was impossible to explain why "values people" could vote for Trump because:

Donald Trump is a bigot.

Donald Trump is a demagogue.

Donald Trump is a sexist, misogynist, chauvinist pig.

Donald Trump is a bully.

Donald Trump is a cheat.

Donald Trump is a pathological liar.

Donald Trump is a nativist.

Donald Trump's campaign has proved too attractive to anti-Semites, Nazis and white nationalists, and on some level the campaign seems to be tacitly courting that constituency.

Donald Trump – judging by his own words on that disgusting tape and if you believe the dozen-plus women who have come forward to accuse him of some form of sexual assault or unwanted sexual advance – is an unrepentant predator.

To put it more succinctly, Donald Trump is a lowlife degenerate with the temperament of a 10-year-old and the moral compass of a severely wayward teen.

There is no way to make a vote for him feel like an act of principle or responsibility. You can't make it right. You can't say yes to Trump and yes to common decency. Those two things do not together abide.[35]

SPECTACLE OF HORROR: BREXIT PLUS, ANGRY WHITE PEOPLE, AND THE NATIONAL NIGHTMARE

19th century German philosopher Friedrich Nietzsche believed that all political ideologies are rooted in the herd psychology of resentment which is directed against superior individuals and classes and the state. In particular, Nietzsche developed a vitriolic attack on the modern state, finding it to be a "new idol" that is "the coldest of all cold monsters," run by annihilators" who continuously lie and re-lie. "Everything about it is false," Nietzsche claims (1954 [1883]: 160–163). Nietzsche consistently attacked as well German nationalism, writing: "If one spends oneself on power, grand politics, economic affairs, world commerce, parliamentary institutions, military interests – if one expends oneself in *this* direction the quantum of reason, seriousness, will self-overcoming that one is, then, there will be a shortage in the other direction" (1968b [1889]: 62) i.e. culture, art, religion, and the development of personality. Trump's followers appear to be a variant of Nietzsche's mass men seething with resentment, while Donald Trump himself is a cauldron of resentment, who has deeply internalized a life-time of deep resentments, and thus is able to tap into, articulate, and mobilize the resentments of his followers, in a way that Democrats and other professional politicians just have not been able to do. Part of Trump's followers resentments are resentment of politicians, and Trump's ability to tout himself as outside of the political system has been a major theme of his campaign and an apparently successful way to mobilize voters.

The sources of the deep resentment of Trump's followers are manifold. In terms of economics, many people feel that they are screwed over by the system, not recognized, and are angry at those who they see as beneficiaries which Trump has been able to scapegoat as immigrants, people of color, and the elites. His followers are resentful of paying taxes to the state and not having any political power which they believe Trump is giving them as part of his movement. The working class segment of Trump's followers is also resentful of not getting adequate recognition and recompense which they believe they are entitled to as workers, supporters of families, and patriots. Trump's people believe that he alone will be oriented toward their interests and solve all their problems – all dubious hopes but all grounded in deep resentments and adulation of their leader. We shall see, however, that the choosing of Trump's cabinet and key administration posts shows an individual oriented toward his own billionaire class, the military, and Republican bureaucrats.

Election Day, November 8, 2016 looked like it was going to be a good day. The weather was bright and sunny throughout the country, there had been record early votes, and although voting lines were long in many parts of the country there were no major accounts of voting machines not working, there were only sporadic accounts of some machine irregularities, and no major reports of voter suppression, or charges of fraud, or of fights between the "observers" that Trump had sent to polling places to "monitor" voting procedures. There were many accounts of record voting, initial reports that Latinos had turned out in large numbers, and that the Clinton election machine was out in force making sure its' supporters got to the polls. Pundits were relatively calm, though like everyone else, tired of the longest, most contested, dirtiest, and nastiest election in memory with two of the most unpopular candidates who had ever won their party's candidacy meeting in a titanic battle that would determine the fate of the world.

As the first results started to pour in with the polls closing at 7:00 p.m. EST, the cable news patrols were calmly gearing up for a long evening. Final polls showed Hillary Clinton 3–6 points ahead in the national polls, and predictions appeared across the board indicating victory. Her campaign camp was cheerful and optimistic, gathered in a ballroom of the Jacob K. Javits Convention Center where her supporters were packed in and ready for a victory celebration. The building had a glass ceiling over its atrium which the Clintonites hoped to symbolically break that night with the first woman President. The Trump camp, by contrast, appeared glum and depressed, as its followers gathered in the New York Hilton about a mile and a half from the Clinton event and did not appear particularly cheerful.

Then the results of the election tabulation started pouring in and it was clear from the start that a stunning upset was in the making. While pundits had proclaimed that Hillary Clinton had many state electoral paths to victory, it was said that Trump had few, all of which involved a "steep" and to many near impossible climb. Soon, however, it was clear that Trump had the momentum and Clinton's path to victory appeared more uncertain, and then unlikely with every hourly tabulation of voting results. For several hours, the "too close to call" states remained frozen, although Trump only had to win one of the six or so states that had not yet been decided.

Around midnight, Clinton campaign manager John Podesta appeared at the Convention Center to tell the dispirited Clintonites waiting for Hillary to speak at the Javits Convention Center that since the election had not been called, they should go home and that Hillary would speak tomorrow. Shortly afterwards, there were reports that Clinton had called Trump and that he was arriving at the hotel ballroom to address his followers. Republican Vice President-designate Mike Pence and his family assembled on stage to greet the happy Trumpsters and to introduce Trump and his family.

Trump announced that Clinton had called him to concede and that he was ready to assume the presidency and called for unity, as he evoked the country's great potential which he would help realize promising great things, without specifics or alluding to what he had actually campaigned on. Reading from a teleprompter, Trump intoned: "Now it's time for America to bind the wounds of division. It is time for us to come together as one united people. It's time." That, he added, "is so important to me." Offering an olive branch to Hillary Clinton, who he had called a criminal and threatened to throw in jail if he became president, Trump softened and said the country owed Hillary "a major debt of gratitude for her service to our country."

Donald Trump President?! How the hell had this happened?! For hours, pundits tried to make sense of the stunning upset, and figure out how Trump had won, confounding the pollsters, pundits, and party officials of all major organizations. It was clear that the pollsters were wildly wrong, as in the Brexit election in the UK when polls and politicians thought that the vote for Britain to exit the European Union (hence Brexit) would be defeated. In fact, a nationalist surge and revolt against the British establishment (all major parties supported staying in the European Union) voted to leave the European Union and go it alone. The day after, stock markets tumbled, the British establishment was in shock, and many people who had voted for Brexit weren't sure what they had voted for, and there were many reports of buyer's remorse.

Trump had promised a "Brexit plus, plus, plus," and even "Brexit Times 5" and had delivered.[36] He had played the ultranationalist and anti-immigration card from the beginning, creating an "America First" movement. It had been clear for some time that his supporters were obviously angry at and alienated from the political establishment, enabling Trump to win the Republican primaries against scores of establishment candidates, including Jeb Bush who was broadly believed to win before the primaries began, and who was one of the first to fall victim to Trump's ability to define "losers" and destroy his opponents. Trump brought into his campaign some of the most extreme components of the alt-right and had a tenuous and often hostile relation to the Republican Party establishment. Many top members of the Republican Party national security establishment signed petitions to vote for Clinton and denounced Trump. Previous Republican presidential candidates like Mitt Romney and John McCain denounced and distanced themselves from Trump, and the Bush family side-lined themselves during the campaign and were reported to have not voted for Trump.

Hence, Trump had mobilized an authoritarian populist movement with himself as leader that somehow never was understood by the media, political, and academic establishment (with some exceptions who I have drawn on in this book). Trump himself constantly bragged about what a wonderful movement he had created, praised the large and boisterous crowds at every rally (often held 3–5 times per day), selected which media could attend his rallies (bound up in pens), which he ritualistically summoned his followers to boo and insult. He daily chided the media for not "telling what's going on" (i.e. seeing that he had unleashed an angry populist movement that was alienated from the establishment and bound to Trump as the one person who can help the country and "Make America Great" again).

Trump's main pitch was that he was the candidate of "change" while Clinton represented the status quo and the establishment. Clinton and the Democrats argued that change could be good or bad, and that Trump's proposed changes were reckless and dangerous. Yet Trump's slogan of "change" worked as polls showed that "change" was an important issue for the electorate, and that 83% of those to whom change was an important issue had voted for Trump.

Trump's victory was in part a "whitelash," a rebellion of angry white people who were totally alienated from the established political system and responded to an attack on it. Although there were parallels with Bernie Sander's anti-establishment campaign and supporters, Sanders, by contrast to Trump, offered a positive vision of the future and specific policies concerned with health care for all, free higher education, the protection of the environment, and other progressive issues. Trump played the race card, the gender card, and spewed extreme alt-right invective against people of color, Muslims, women, and other groups who attracted his bile and ire.

Those who claimed that racism was dead in mainstream American politics found out this was just not true, and, sadly, the 2016 election showed that sexism is alive, well, and virulent in the land of the free and the home of the not-so-brave dupes who fell for Deplorable Donald's con. Because of Trump's alienation of Latinos, African Americans, Jews, Muslims, and many ethnic groups; his appalling attitudes and treatment of women revealed on the *Access Hollywood* tape and accounts of women who claimed he had sexually abused them; and because the Trump campaign did not have a conventional organization, strategy, message, or any plans for the country outside of building a Wall, banning Muslims, and assembling deportation forces to round up undocumented immigrants – all of which were said to be impossible – it was widely believed that Trump had no chance of winning. There were, however, armies of angry and alienated voters who turned out on election day, often in record numbers in rural parts of the country, small towns, and neighborhoods that often had low voting turn outs. Initial demographic reports indicated that Trump's core constituencies were angry white men, and white men and women and others without college degrees. After winning the Nevada Republican caucuses,

Trump affirmed that he "loved the poorly educated," tipping his hat to a demographic that had never, to my recollection, appeared in discussions of the electorate or was seen as a core base of a presidential candidate.

In fact, one could argue that Trump's followers were mis-educated and that the election demonstrated a frightening crisis of education in the country. Trump's victory was prepared by decades of rightwing books and websites, *Fox News* and Talk Radio, and social networking that attacked the government, the welfare state, climate change, and political and intellectual elites, while promoting racism, sexism, xenophobia, homophobia, and any number of biases and misconceptions. The miseducated section of the country was full of misperceptions and prejudices that were easily manipulated by Trump and his surrogates, first, against the Republican establishment, and then against Hillary Clinton and the establishment writ large.

Election 2016 is thus in part a "whitelash" against "P.C. culture" (i.e. political correctness which criticizes racism, sexism, homophobia, and other forms of bias while advocating a more open, inclusive, and tolerant culture). Trump's anti-P.C. brigades saw their white male privileges under assault during the Obama years, where whites were no longer necessarily seen as superior to blacks and people of color, men were challenged by uppity women, gay and lesbian marriage and rights were allowed, and immigrants were allegedly permitted to pour into the country and take over "American" jobs.

Adding to the mixture of prejudice and anti-establishment animus in Trump's followers, and fueled by often legitimate anger in the sectors of the industrial parts of the country which saw a loss of jobs without adequate retraining or creation of other ways to make a living, and you have a perfect storm for a Trump election win. The high-tech and global economy had left behind industrial workers, as well as those lacking the education and the skills for the emerging high-tech economy. They were angry and seeking a radical alternative and found their vehicle and champion in Donald J. Trump.

As in classic authoritarian movements, the followers accepted the pronouncements of the leader as gospel truth, and although Trump lied more outrageously than any candidate in recent U.S. history, his followers turned out in droves throughout the country shouting hateful slogans and repeating Trump's lies and deception. Like classical authoritarian demagogues, Trump produced scapegoats and others who were seen as threats against whom Trump could mobilize his followers. The scapegoats Trump projected were not only Muslims and immigrants, but "the establishment" and a shadowy cabal of global capital with which Trump identified Hillary Clinton, successfully making her part of the enemy against which Trump railed. Trump played the "forgotten men and women" card effectively, and presented himself as the people's savior, although it was not clear what he would actually deliver to his followers.

The lack of critical thinking and disregard for facts and truth in Trump's followers demonstrates failures of the education system in the U.S. and the need for a democratic reconstruction of education if U.S. democracy is to survive. Democratic elections require an informed electorate, capable of distinguishing truth from falsity, right from wrong, and to see through lies and deception. Donald Trump had been a celebrity and con man for decades and his skills in seducing and bamboozling the public helped him enormously in the election. He is positioning himself as the first aggressively post-factual president and citizens and the media must hold him accountable.[37]

An informed electorate means an educated electorate, and good jobs in the current economy require higher education, or specialized skills, to level the playing field. This, in turn, requires federal, state, and local government to expand the sector of higher education, and to provide access, training, and financial support to those sectors of the society, which included Trump's base, to help them better their own lives.

Obviously, the pundits and politicians did not understand the dynamics of Trump's authoritarian populist movement, how he articulated their anger and alienation in his tirades against trade deals, immigration, and shadowy forces like international bankers and global elites, a discourse and strategy reminiscent of European fascist movements. Trump himself had no party apparatus, political ideology, or disciplined message and cadres. Yet he and his campaign were able to use social media effectively to mobilize groups and they had organized data collection with their followers' email and social networking sites which they apparently effectively used to turn out voters.[38]

In retrospect, the Democrats were out of touch with major forms of communication and the electorate. While they spent millions on television ads, mailings, and conventional political communication, the Republicans were mobilizing social media, including fake news sites that were claiming that Hillary Clinton was selling arms to terrorists, involved in sex rings with children, and other outrageous crimes, while fake stories claimed that Trump was endorsed by the Pope, Denzel Washington, and others who would never support the Trumpster.[39] The mainstream media and most political insiders overlooked this subterranean network of fake news stories which was circulating daily spurious stories that were sent to hundreds of thousands of people and which surveys after the election claimed that the majority of recipients believed these fake news stories.

Hence, whereas the Obama campaign in 2008 used the relatively new media of Facebook, YouTube, and other emergent forms of social media very effectively to mobilize the young and multicultural Obama base, the Clinton campaign relied on old media and a conventional get-out-the-vote ground game, while the Trump camp was perniciously using new forms of (a)social media in a fashion that subverted all norms of political decency and truth, and perhaps did lasting epistemological and moral damage to political communication and the norms of a democratic election and truthfully informed electorate.

It was clear that the country was much more divided than had been perceived and one of the major divisions was between the sectors of U.S. society that represented what German social theorist Ferdinand Tönnies distinguished as sectors and sociological types of *Gemeinschaft* vs. *Gesellschaft,* generally translated as "community and society."[40] The latter represents urban, secular, and liberal "society" versus more rural, religious, and traditional "community." The more liberal sectors who voted for Clinton and the Democrats were better educated and were inclusive of multicultural forces that constituted the so-called Obama coalition, while the more traditional rural, small town, and conservative forces were less tolerant and inclusive, and inclined to want walls built around their communities and borders rather than to imagine a more open, multicultural, and inclusive society with bridges to a democratic future.

Interestingly, both the Trump campaign, and earlier the Bernie Sanders campaign, had made globalization a hot-button issue, and it turned out that the Trump coalition was strongly anti-globalization, as many of the rust-belt workers, or those in depressed industrial areas, had lost their jobs to globalization, as corporations moved factories to developing world countries where wages were lower and there was less regulation. While Sanders had correctly indicated the problem for workers as an issue of out-of-control corporations moving factories to developing countries to get lower wages, less regulation, and higher profits, Trump translated the issue into bad trade deals and rule by a corrupt global elite that the Clintons were part and parcel of (for some of Trump's alt-right supporters this was a Jewish elite and as noted, the Trump campaign used anti-Semitic images and discourses in its propaganda).

For academic critical theorists like myself, globalization is theorized as a complex matrix of the contemporary era that contains economic, political, and cultural dimensions, including a neo-liberal corporate global economy, global promotion of democracy and human rights, and inclusive and hybrid global cultures.[41] Trump and his followers flattened globalization to an economy run by global elites that had given workers a rotten deal. Indeed, part of globalization was an unregulated global economic order that included trade deals like NAFTA and the TPP, which the Clintons supported, along with mainstream Republicans and Democrats alike. Yet in fact Trump was himself part of this global elite with businesses and investments all around the world. Trump had himself benefitted his entire life from globalization and had never, to my knowledge, shown any reservations toward globalization, or trade, until the election when his campaign discovered that there was anger at the global elite and the globalized economy that shut down U.S. factories and moved jobs to developing countries.

On election eve and no doubt for days, months, and perhaps years to come, there would be analysis of what happened and how a confluence of forces had made possible what was being touted as the biggest upset in American presidential history, and perhaps the biggest shock and blow to the system that had ever occurred in an election in the U.S., perhaps with catastrophic consequences. The word of the day was "stun" with a "stunning upset," "stunned voters," a headline that the "Trump win stuns many D.C. residents," and predictions how the "Trump victory may stun the markets."[42] In fact, the initial reaction to the Trump election was a frightening drop in global markets including a record 800 plus drop in Dow Futures during election night. Yet the next day after a conciliatory Trump speech and gracious concession transition speeches by Clinton and Obama, the Dow Jones hit a record high as fat cat investors anticipated the joys of an unregulated market and lower taxes, and in the days after the election the market continued to rise to record levels into December and beyond, although it also exhibited instability with swings up and down from day to day.

The reasons for the electoral stunning of America and the world are many, and one major factor was perhaps Clinton fatigue and the unpopularity of Hillary Clinton, who was only surpassed by Donald Trump in terms of political negatives. Indeed, the ubiquitous polls, and poll-obsessed media pundits, always mentioned Clinton's negatives that obviously helped define her and suppress her votes. Never before had the spouse of a previous president run for office and never before had a woman come so close to winning the presidency who had been more maligned.

For decades, there has been an anti-Clinton industry which since the 1990s had published countless books, articles, blogs, and made documentaries and other artifacts denouncing the Clintons and the many scandals that they had been involved in since the days when Bill Clinton was Governor of Arkansas and then two-time President of the United States.[43] There were countless congressional hearings, reports, investigations, slander, innuendo, and lies that had tarred the Clintons, producing in many quarters a demonization of them which intensified in the era of the Internet and Social Media, with *Fox News* and rightwing websites like Drudge and Breibart winning pride of place, or place of national disgrace, along with Rush Limbaugh and the screeching voices of rightwing Talk/Hate Radio.[44]

Throughout the long campaign season, the media had devoted countless hours of news time dissecting Clinton's role as Secretary of State and particularly her role in the Benghazi tragedy where American diplomats were killed in a chaotic period of the Libyan civil war in 2011. There were Congressional hearings and endless media discussion of Clinton's role with the Republican Party inviting the mother of a young man who had died at Benghazi to the Republican National Convention where the distraught mother accused Hillary Clinton personally of murder of her son, which shamelessly exploited the bereaved mother and smeared Clinton. While informed political analysts said that Clinton had ably defended herself in the all-day grilling she underwent at the Congressional Benghazi Hearings, Trump and his team continued to manipulate the tragedy and maliciously insinuate that she was personally responsible for the deaths in the tragedy.

Further, there was probably more media coverage of controversy over Hillary Clinton's personal email server than any issue in the campaign. Her violation of relatively new State Department rules concerning using office servers for classified information was taken as representing all of her negative traits. In her defense, it could be argued that previous Secretaries of State and other government officials had used private servers, but the Clinton personal server was the first time the relatively new requirement had been pursued or been made an issue. As a consequence, Clinton was villainized in the media for months over her email server, including the James Comey FBI intervention into the election that undercut her momentum and may have helped cost her the election.

In any case, negative Hillary Clinton memes had been produced to villainize her for decades, and Donald Trump and his surrogates relentlessly deployed these negative memes and created new ones. Trump had successfully labelled his Republican Party primary opponents with derisory names starting with "Low Energy Jeb," "Lyin' Ted," "Little Marco," and his other Republican opponents, and early on came up with "Crooked Hillary." This negative branding of Clinton became a mantra at his rallies with ritualistic chants of "lock her up," displaying posters and web-images of Secretary Clinton with a bullseye target on her face and an assortment of extremely negative visual images, as well as a torrent of sexist and obscene insults to negatively define her.

As noted, Trump's closing argument was demonization of the Clintons as a "criminal enterprise," and Hillary as a "criminal" who he would make sure went to jail. Trump was aided in his criminalizing of Hillary Clinton by FBI Director James Comey whose stunning announcement on October 21 that the investigation of Clinton's email was reopened because of discovery of communications devices shared by Anthony Weiner and Clinton's close associate Huma Abedin. Previous to Comey's intervention, Clinton had ten point leads nationally and in many key states, and looked like she was coasting to an easy victory. Her camp was shocked by Comey's unprecedented FBI intervention into pivoting her political campaign from presenting a positive vision of the future to attacking Trump to offset her own growing negatives. Although Comey announced two days before the election that nothing compromising had been found on the latest computer search, the damage was done and once again there were wide-spread doubts about Clinton's trustworthiness.

Trump, of course, capitalized on Clinton's problems droning on and on about her "corruption" and "criminality," and adding a slogan that he was going to "drain the swamp" of corruption. Indeed, never before had a candidate been so villainized by a campaign and sectors of the media and culture industry as Hillary Clinton. The fact that Clinton was the first woman candidate to engage in a serious run for the presidency also had to factor in as part of the explanation for Trump's shocking victory. Trump and his surrogates, like the vile sexist Rudy Giuliani, had constantly raised questions of Clinton's health, stamina, and capacity to serve which were sexist dog-whistles that women should not be considered for the presidency.

The WikiLeaks scandal and FBI Director James Comey's two letters also were important factors that contributed to Clinton's defeat and Trump's victory by highlighting Clinton's email problems that had been a major campaign theme for Trump and his supporters. If indeed Russian intelligence had hacked the DNC severer, as well as the email of Clinton's campaign head John Podesta, as U.S. intelligence sources claimed, this would be an unparalleled foreign intervention in a U.S. election. Just as scandalous, as far as is known, a U.S. intelligence service like the FBI had never intervened in a U.S. presidential election before. The Clinton team blamed the two Comey letters for Clinton's defeat in a conference call to donors and major supporters days after the election, claiming the first letter stopped her momentum, a claim that could be confirmed by the drop in her poll numbers after the Comey bombshell. Further, the Clintonites claim that the second letter, which indicated there was nothing of relevance on the Weiner/Abeden computer, allegedly mobilized Trump's voters, as the Trump campaign argued that the FBI turn-around was part of a rigged system that was trying to deny Trump his rightful election victory, and helped the Trump campaign mobilize anti-establishment voters.

There would be a cottage industry of insider books on the Clinton campaign that would allege strategic mistakes and criticize a campaign that had no compelling major themes and a weak candidate. Yet it should also be pointed out that Trump ran a campaign that connected with broad sectors of the disenfranchised and miseducated public, and had created an authoritarian populist movement that was devoted to its leader. Indeed, the Trump campaign had drawn on the swamp of the vilest tendencies toward racism, sexism, Islamophobia, xenophobia, and fear and hatred of the Other which for miseducated white men and women was Barack Obama, Hillary Clinton, and their multicultural coalitions. Clinton and Obama were also positioned as the "Establishment" against which Donald Trump alone stood. In fact, Clinton grew up in a modest middle-class family, and worked her way through Wellesley, Yale Law School, and many public service jobs, before serving as First Lady of Arkansas and the United States, and then U.S. Senator from New York and Secretary of State. Her latter accomplishments indeed identified her as part of the U.S. establishment, and she was successfully positioned by the Trump campaign as an exemplar of the elite and the establishment who represented the status quo while Trump represented change and the people. Of course, Donald Trump himself was establishment to the core, and had struggled mightily his whole life to be seen as part of the elite, with mixed success. Yet Trump's supporters saw him as one of them and the voice of their FUCK YOU! and middle finger shot to the establishment.

Michael Moore engaged this situation in his film *Michael Moore in Trumpland*, released shortly before the election, where he addressed a group of ordinary voters, including Trump and Clinton supporters, as well as those undecided, who supported third party tickets, or who simply did not want to vote. Moore spent most of the film delivering a lecture in an old movie theater in Wilmington, Ohio where the audience listened intently as Moore mixed jokes and humor with an impassioned plea to vote for Hillary Clinton, who he said he deeply admired, although he had voted for Obama in the 2008 primaries and Sanders in the 2016 Democratic Party primary. He explained that living in Michigan he understood why working people were alienated, hurting, and angry, but tried to make the argument that Clinton would be better than Trump to address the problems confronting the country.

Yet Trump won and he won by winning swing states in the rust belt, which usually went Democratic in presidential elections. In addition, he won higher numbers of white men and women than any previous candidate and a higher than expected number of Latinos. Ironically, although Trump and his hard-core supporters vilified the media and ritualistically chanted "Fuck CNN!" during his rallies, it was CNN and other media, especially cable television, which had empowered Trump and proved to be a major factor in his victory. Trump received billions of dollars of free television time, and received by far the most TV coverage of any candidate. During the Republican primaries, the cable news channels would announce Trump's next campaign speech in crawlers and would discuss his latest campaign events and speculate about his coming speech, which they would broadcast live, often uncut, and then spend hours discussing. No other Republican candidate received a fraction of the coverage that Trump received, and Clinton and Sanders also barely received any coverage during the primaries, with Sanders often cut off for days, even though he was, like Trump, drawing large and enthusiastic crowds.

While there were mainstream media critiques of Trump, on the whole he got perhaps more publicity than any previous candidate, in part, because, as CBS News President Les Moonves confessed,

Trump brought in high ratings and thus made money for the broadcast networks.[45] Further, Trump often set the news agenda for the day with early morning tweets that were discussed into the day, followed by his rallies and often outrageous statements that set the agenda for the rest of the day. Hence, although Trump attacked the "lying media" in every stump speech, he was enabled and empowered by the mainstream broadcast media from the beginning of his campaign, which made it a popular reality TV show, while also cultivating the swampland of social media with daily virulent Twitters attacking all and sundry, fake news, and the peddling of hate on the campaign trail.

The initial Establishment reaction was shock as stock markets crashed globally on election night, and there was panic throughout global financial and political circles.[46] The Establishment was indeed suffering a stunning and unanticipated shock with unforeseeable consequences. While on one hand, Trump was a hardcore establishment business and media figure, he was unknown as a political figure, and his campaign did not inspire confidence in his ability to govern or his fitness for office.

In *American Nightmare*, I described the similarities between a Trump rally and a Nazi spectacle and noted resemblances between Trump's authoritarian populism and German National Socialism. Like Germany and Italy in the 1930s, it had appeared that the two-party system in the U.S. collapsed in the 2016 U.S. presidential election with the Republican party taken over by a vulgar outsider who was contemptuous of their party apparatus, traditions, conservative ideology, and traditionalist attitudes and habitus. Trump associated himself at the highest level of his campaign with alt-right figures like his campaign CEO Steve Bannon who were dedicated to the destruction of the Republican party, and although the Republicans held on to their majority in the House and Senate, it was unclear whether the Republicans could resume their previous identity or were overtaken by Trumpism with unforeseeable results.

There was, of course, also the possibility that the Republicans could control Trump and use him to put through a rightwing wet dream agenda, and that a Trump/Republican alliance could wipe out all the progressive gains of the Obama and Clinton eras. Bolstered by the wave of Trump's followers coming to the polls to vote for him, the Republicans retained control of the Senate and the House. Whereas the Republican-establishment feared that revulsion to Trump would destroy the Republicans and give control of the political system to the Democrats, perhaps for the foreseeable future, it was the Democrats who were in existential crisis after the election, while Republican fat cats plotted to increase their wealth, pursue their corporate agenda, and control the Supreme Court for the foreseeable future.

The Democrats were in obvious disarray with the stunning upset that no doubt ends Hillary Clinton's political career, puts in question and puts on the line for destruction, the political legacy of Barack Obama, and raises the question of who will lead the Democratic Party and what will be its future. A barrage of WikiLeaks, said to be engineered by Russian intelligence with the complicity of Julian Assange, had embarrassed the Democratic Party leading to the resignation during the primaries of Debbie Wasserman-Schulz who Wiki-Leak email showed to be unfairly favorable to Hillary Clinton and showed her associates discussing in email how Bernie Sanders could be attacked (which led to their being fired). The highly respected Democratic Party operative Donna Brazile, who became leader of the Democratic National Committee during the election, was fired from her CNN position when a WikiLeaks email revealed that she had leaked a question in an upcoming CNN debate to Hillary Clinton, an act that effectively puts in question her career in U.S. politics.[47]

Clinton campaign leader John Podesta also had his emails hacked, causing threats to his future career, and other Democratic party operatives, whose embarrassing comments were revealed in leaked emails, found their career imperiled (some were fired). The hack of the Democrats put in question emails as an instrument of political communication and raised questions of how the U.S. should deal with hacker organizations like WikiLeaks and protect its national communication infrastructure which had revealed itself vulnerable to foreign intervention and mischief.

Indeed, in retrospect the WikiLeaks were even more consequential than was first believed and might have played a significant role in

Clinton's and the Democratic Party's defeat. This is especially distressing if it is true that Putin and Russian intelligence were involved in the WikiLeaks hack and publication, as apparently U.S. intelligence services, but not Donald Trump, concluded. Never before had a foreign power interfered in a U.S. election and when the power is Russia, long the U.S.'s Super Adversary, the consequences of a foreign power able to steer a U.S. election are alarming and unforeseeable.

Rachel Maddow pointed out on MSNBC during the long unfolding of the American Nightmare on election night that Third Parties too were partly responsible for the stunner, as the 2% or 3% of the votes that the Libertarian Party and Green Party had siphoned off could have been decisive in some closely contested states. I have myself voted for Libertarian and Green Party candidates over the years, so do not want to villainize third parties. Yet I suspect there will be finger-pointing at the third parties and their leaders and sharing in blame for Trump's stunner, just as Ralph Nader was demonized after the 2000 presidential election when Green Party votes in Florida and New Hampshire deprived Al Gore of the election and ushered in eight years of the horror show of the Bush-Cheney Gang.[48]

Trump, of course, could be much worse than the Bush-Cheney Gang whose tax cuts for the rich and wars in Afghanistan and Iraq shot up the federal deficit trillions of dollars and helped trigger a global financial crisis in 2007–2008 which it took eight years of the Obama administration to crawl out of. Trump had never served in public office before, he had antagonized the two political parties and more broadly the political class, he had savagely attacked the mainstream media on a daily basis, had banned media outlets who criticized him from his events, and threatened as President to put restrictions on freedom of speech and liberalize libel laws making it easier to sue the hell out of his critics.

Moreover, Trump had criticized generals and the military and claimed he knew more than they did about ISIS and fighting terrorism. He had attacked NATO and the system of alliances and treaties that had protected the U.S., Europe, and other parts for the world for decades since the end of World War II. The foreign policy establishment, U.S. allies, and foreign governments everywhere were in fear of the consequences of a Trump presidency. And although he claimed to be a successful businessman, there were major questions about his business failures and the extent of his wealth. Trump had never released his tax forms, so it still was not clear what his actual businesses involved, who he owed money to, and who he had been involved with. Trump was not putting his economic interests into a blind trust as all Presidents had done before him, and he had made it clear that his family would continue to run his businesses, creating gigantic conflict of interest issues.

Most alarmingly, it was not at all clear what economic policies he would pursue, who would be his economic advisors, and if he would start trade and tariff wars with the U.S. major trading partners. Would Trump continue to believe that climate change was a hoax and would he try to pull the U.S. out of global climate change agreements? Scandalously, climate change was not discussed in the presidential debates and hardly became an issue in the campaign. Scientists agree that climate change is one of the most significant issues of the day and a clear and present danger to the survival of the earth and human and other species. Would a President Trump acknowledge climate change, would he do anything about it, and would he continue to surround himself with climate change deniers and bring on the apocalypse? There were indeed many dangers and unforeseen consequences of a Trump presidency, and an American nightmare could become much worse.

UNFORESEEN CONSEQUENCES OF A TRUMP PRESIDENCY

When one political party loses an election to the winning party, there is always a ritual transition of power and the notion of a peaceful transition to power is one of the defining features of the political ideal of U.S. democracy. One of the most shocking events of the last days of the election was when Donald Trump would not promise that he would concede to Hillary Clinton if the vote count indicated that she won, as complaints about a "rigged election" and a system that "protected" the Clintons was one of Trump's closing lines.

By contrast, Clinton had called Trump to concede when it was clear she had no path to victory, and she gave a gracious concession speech the next morning making a call for national unity, working together, but fighting for what you believe in. The audience was in tears with many openly sobbing and others registering shock that they had not yet come to terms with. After her remarks, Clinton mingled with the crowd, thanking her campaign workers for their efforts and trying to smile and carry on amidst the heartbreak and national and indeed global tragedy.

Shortly thereafter, a surprisingly chipper Barack Obama accompanied by Vice President Joe Biden walked to the White House Rose Garden to address the nation. Obama announced that he had invited Donald Trump to the White House the next day to discuss the transition and praised the George W. Bush administration for a gracious and helpful transition to the Obama administration when he had just won the presidency eight years before.

The next morning a somber and slightly stunned Donald Trump arrived with his wife and some of his entourage for a meeting at the White House between President Obama and President-Elect Trump, and the previous and next First Ladies. These encounters were followed by meetings between Trump and the Republican leaders who gave the Trumps an inside look at the hallowed insider halls of establishment power which Trump had never viewed upfront and close, and that would now be the site of his coming battles.

The normalization of Trump was crowned by the press which broadcast live a friendly exchange between a commanding Obama and a subdued Trump with both men exchanging compliments, after months of bitter insults, and with Trump proclaiming how he was honored to be in the White House and looked forward to Obama's advice. The normalization spectacle continued with an excited House Majority Leader Paul Ryan showing the great view from his Congress office site of Washington, and the two one-time rivals appeared to be good old boy buddies, leading the punditry to gush about unity, peaceful transition of power, and the majesty of the office, all of which Trump had mocked and attacked in recent months with his divisive rhetoric, refusal to say that he would accept results of the election, and assaults on the "rigged system" and the president.

By contrast, vigils and protests flared up across the country the day after the election, as opponents of President-elect Trump displayed their anger and rage over the election results, highlighting continued division in the country and that the election was not over and the country was far from united. The Trumps got to view the protests up front and close, as thousands of protesters marched up Fifth Avenue toward the Trump Tower in midtown Manhattan, which was surrounded by giant garbage trucks filled with sand, armed police, and security guards. A crowd of thousands gathered in front of the president-elect's building with angry demonstrators chanting: "Fuck your tower! Fuck your wall!" Several blocks of Fifth Avenue were blocked off from traffic, making New York appear a city under siege.

Elsewhere in the country, protestors held marches and sit-ins from sea to shining sea on election night and in some cases for days thereafter. College students gathered in spontaneous marches and asked university leaders to schedule meetings to assure students of color, Muslims, women, and others denigrated and threatened by Trump and his followers that they would be protected. Following Trump's victory speech, more than 2,000 students at the University of California, Los Angeles, gathered on campus and marched through the streets of Westwood. There were similar protests at the University of Southern California in Los Angeles, with rivals UCLA and USC united in their horror of Trump. Other campuses in the University of California system in Berkeley, San Diego and Santa Barbara held protests, as did other Universities throughout the country.

High school students also stormed out of class and held raucous anti-Trump demonstrations. Students walked out of classes in Arizona on election day to protest Trump and notorious Sheriff Joe Arpaio, infamous for his aggressive anti-immigrant policies and draconian treatment of prisoners (Arpaio lost his bid for re-election and is under criminal investigation for his policies). On Facebook, a page titled "Not My President" called for protesters to gather on Inauguration Day, Jan. 20, in the nation's capital. "We refuse to recognize Donald Trump as the president of the United States, and refuse to take orders from a government that puts bigots into power. We have to make it clear to the public that we did not choose this man for office and that we won't stand for his ideologies."[49]

Thousands of anti-Trump protesters took to the streets all over the country to protest on election night, and the day after the election, there were major demonstrations with protestors marching and chanting "not my president," while shutting down roadways, freeways, and downtown areas in major cities like Los Angeles, New York, Washington DC, and Philadelphia. Other demonstrations, fueled by social media, took place in Seattle, Portland, Oakland, Denver, Minneapolis, Milwaukee, Portland, Oakland, and dozens more US cities. While the demonstrators were mostly peaceful, there were effigies of Trump burned, a piñata of Trump beaten to shreds close to Trump Tower, small fires in the street and broken windows in some cities that featured clashes between demonstrators and police. The King Of Nasty Tweets was not happy with the demos and protests, writing:

Donald J. Trump

✓ @realDonaldTrump

Just had a very open and successful presidential election. Now professional protesters, incited by the media, are protesting. Very unfair!

6:19 PM – 10 Nov 2016[50]

The protesters were not "professional," but just ordinary people, and they were not "incited by the media," but were protesting Trump's campaign and the horrors of a Trump administration. Protests were planned in the weekend following Trump's election and a major anti-Trump movement seemed to be in the making, as the political establishment and media which he had mocked was normalizing Trump, as if it was business as usual, and just another transition in the hallowed history of American democracy which Trump had mocked as rigged. Against media and establishment forces normalizing Trump, there were forces all over the country protesting and insisting: "He's not my president!" On Saturday, November 12, 2016, there was a large demonstration of at least 10,000 marching through downtown Los Angles, while on the other side of the country, thousands marched down Fifth Avenue, surrounding once again Trump Tower, as Trump and his associates tried to prepare their transition team and government, for which insiders said they were woefully underprepared (apparently Dumbass Donald is superstitious and didn't want to talk about who would be in his administration until after the election).

What would Trump do as President? The first days after the election, he was playing the national unity card and trying to appear presidential. However, it was known that vengeful destructiveness was one of Trump's defining personality traits, and there were fears he'd go after his enemies. One of Trump's inner circle, Omarosa Manigault, who had been an *Apprentice* contestant the first season and then joined the Trump organization as a token black, revealed to the media that Trump indeed had an "enemies list," suggesting that Trump had picked up another tactic from Richard Nixon, who had been impeached in part for his zeal in pursuing enemies.[51]

The New York Times and *The Washington Post* had reported some weeks before that "Trump allies are actively laying plans to punish the GOP leadership for failing to fully embrace Trumpism" – and, crucially, to keep Trumpism's legacy very much alive as a malevolent and disruptive political force inside the Republican Party. *The Times* notes that Trump campaign CEO Stephen Bannon is intent on forcing out House Speaker Paul Ryan, while other leading Congressional supporters of Trump are warning the GOP leadership not to dare moderate on immigration, which could stir the great Trumpian masses to rise up in rage."[52]

However, now that he had won the election, perhaps Trump would turn to the Republican elite and work with them, although he had long threatened to oust the House Congressional Leader Paul Ryan who had not really supported Trump. Would Trump work with Ryan and those Republicans who had constantly insulted him and refused to support his candidacy? Would Trumpism become the dominant ideology of the Republican Party and would he be an authoritarian leader who would govern by the force of his will alone as he had done successfully during the primaries and the general election?

And would Trump work with the Democrats, the party he had once belonged to and helped finance, or would he caucus with Republicans who controlled the House and Senate to push through an aggressively rightwing agenda, destroying Obamacare, as he had promised to do, and undo all of the progressive measures of the Obama years? Would he and the Republicans pursue Hillary Clinton and her alleged crimes and continue decades of investigation of the Clintons? Would he block or allow criminal investigations concerning his previous campaign manager Paul Manafort, whose business connections and ties to Russia were allegedly the subject of an FBI investigation?

There were also allegations that a group of computer scientists claimed that a server at the Trump Organization was covertly communicating with a Russian bank that is tied to Vladimir Putin's government. While the purpose of the server is unclear, *Slate*'s Franklin Foer reported that the communications appear to resemble "the pattern of human conversation" and took place during normal working hours in both New York and Moscow. Foer acknowledges in his piece that "what the scientists amassed wasn't a smoking gun," but contained "suggestive" evidence.[53] Would the FBI or U.S. intelligence uncover compromising information of unsavory connections between the Trump campaign and the Russians that could cause nightmares of his own for Trump and his underlings?

How would Trump resolve his legal problems and would one of the most litigious businessmen in U.S. history be constrained from suing his enemies as he had done for decades? Trump University had been revealed as a complete con, and students who were ripped off by Duplicitous Donald had sued him and won. Trump had attacked the Judge in the case as biased – because he was a Latino and all Latinos allegedly hated Trump's plan to build a wall along the Mexican border and put together a deportation force, according to Trump's biased reasoning as to why a Mexican-American judge *must* be biased. On November 14, 2016, lawyers for Trump filed papers requesting that the trial against Trump University should be postponed until after the inauguration, and an Op. Ed. appeared in the *Los Angeles Times* arguing that all of the 75 plus litigations that Trump was involved in, as well as any future litigation, should be postponed until after his term as president.[54]

Over the weekend of November 12–13, 2016, the Trump transition team announced that Republican National Committee Chairman Reince Priebus would be Trump's Chief of Staff, and Steve Bannon, the alt-right flamethrower who had been one of the key advisors in Trump's campaign, would be "Chief Strategist." These appointments made it clear that the Trump Administration would comprise an unholy mixture of hardcore establishment Republicans and alt-right extremists, and Bannon's appointment ignited a firestorm of protest and critique of Trump's poor judgment in selecting an alt-right extremist as one of his key advisors.

And what effect would Trump's election have on the American people? No President-Elect had in my lifetime inspired such terror and anger as Donald J. Trump. Many people of color were in fear of racist hate crimes, while Latinos were in fear of deportation, Muslims were in terror of repression and exclusion, and women feared an increase in sexual assault with the president a well-documented sexual predator with little respect for women. Women who depend on Planned Parenthood were worried about losing birth control devices and abortion rights. People who depended on Obama-care were in fear of losing medical coverage, perhaps life-preserving or threatening. Gays and lesbians were in fear of losing hard-gained civil rights like gay marriage and laws making attacks against them a hate crime. While Trump himself had apparently not discriminated against gays and lesbians, his Vice President Mike Pence was perhaps the most anti-gay member of the

U.S. political establishment. As Governor of Indiana and member of Congress, Pence had consistently attacked gay marriage, had signed laws making it legal for businesses to discriminate against gays and lesbians in the name of "religious freedom," and had even voted for federal funds to carry out controversial and widely-declaimed "gay conversion" therapies, outing this "small government conservative" as a raging homophobe.

There were generalized fears of wars and increased societal violence, and the perhaps catastrophic effects of climate change exploding to apocalypse under a Trump administration. Economists feared that a bungling and incompetent Trump administration would crash the U.S. and perhaps even global economy,[55] and apocalyptic visions of a Trump administration were creating wide-spread fear and anxiety of a degree never before apparent in my life-time after a presidential election that usually people are happy to be over with and content to see where the new administration takes the country.

As the demonstrations against Trump continued, and as the Trump team begin to focus on who would be in their administration and what they would do, it was clear that Trump's posture as an anti-establishment figure was a con. While Trump was swept to power by a largely white working-class authoritarian populist movement which claimed to represent the voices and interests of forgotten people, and to oppose big business and Wall Street, in his transition to power, it was clear that the Trump team represented the same interests as the lobbyists and figures from big business and the financial and political establishment of the past. As Eric Lipton wrote:

> An organizational chart of Trump's transition team shows it to be crawling with corporate lobbyists, representing such clients as Altria, Visa, Coca-Cola, General Electric, Verizon, HSBC, Pfizer, Dow Chemical, and Duke Energy. And K Street is positively salivating over all the new opportunities they'll have to deliver goodies to their clients in the Trump era. Who could possibly have predicted such a thing?

> The answer is, anyone who was paying attention. Look at the people Trump is considering for his Cabinet, and you

won't find any outside-the-box thinkers burning to work for the little guy. It's a collection of Republican politicians and corporate plutocrats – not much different from who you'd find in any Republican administration.[56]

Trump's campaign which had posed itself as anti-establishment, and which had attacked and delegitimated the ruling political, economic, and media establishment, was now bringing into its administration exactly the same establishment forces it had attacked. These establishment politicians, lobbyists, business sector, and military figures would no doubt defend dominant economic and political interests, as had all Republican and most Democratic regimes, and would continue to exploit, oppress, and manipulate the voters and citizens.

Moreover, there had been reports of an increase in racial violence and violence in schools during the election, as there had been after Brexit. Katherine D. Kinzler had warned how during the election, there were alarming reports of students and young people engaging in increased bullying and discriminatory talk and behavior,[57] and after the election where was a wave of hate crimes against Latinos, Muslims, and other minorities, and bullying in schools in the name of triumphant Trumpism.

Indeed, throughout U.S. society, there has been a dramatic increase of reported incidents of violence and hate crimes since Trump's election. The Southern Poverty Law Center has documented 701 hate crime incidents across the United States from election day to the end of November,[58] with new hate crimes cited every day. There have been reports of racist graffiti, of attacks against Mosques, of Muslim women having their hijabs yanked off, of anti-Trump protestors getting beaten, and of racist incidents against African Americans by Trump supporters.[59] There have also been attacks on Trump supporters and fights between pro- and anti-Trump groups in an alarming escalation of societal violence.

As a reaction against rising and future Trumpian repression, state and local governments have promised to provide "safe zone" from Trump's policies. California, and indeed the entire West Coast, had strongly repudiated Trump, and elected officials, politicians, political groups, and others were talking of refusing to follow any noxious policies that Trump might inflict on specific groups. In particular, it was important to affirm and protect existing rights for Latinos and people of color, women, gays and lesbians, Muslims, and other groups vilified by Trump and his followers who could be the victims of his policies. Anti-Trump demonstrators after the election were making these demands, and politicians, police, and city officials were promising to work with citizens to protect everyone from potential noxious effects of Trumpism.

Yet there were limits to safe zones as Trump and the Republican majority could overturn any number of progressive national policies that will make it harder to protect local zones of liberalism, social justice and protection of rights.[60] Once again, major problems with the Electoral College and the entire system of presidential elections were all too apparent as Clinton's popular vote rose and, as with Al Gore, the candidate with the most popular votes would lose.[61] Because of the peculiar features of the Electoral College, heavily populated states like California and states with large urban populations are underrepresented, while smaller states with largely rural populations are overrepresented. This electoral system provides advantages to candidates like Donald Trump who appeal to rural voters, deploying anti-establishment populism that plays on fears and resentments toward elites, urban and multicultural populations, and the West and East coastal more liberal populations and regions, an issue I address later in the text.

DRAIN THE SWAMP: THE ALLIGATORS OF WALL STREET, BILLIONAIRE SNAKES OF CORPORATE AMERICA, SWAMP CREATURES OF WASHINGTON, AND MILITARIST GENERALS

After naming Republican National Committee Chairman Reince Priebus Chief of Staff, and alt-right extremist Steve Bannon as his "Chief Strategist," the Trump transition team started announcing would-be cabinet appointments and key officials for a Trump administration. While John F. Kennedy's Harvard brain trust of key appointments were labeled "the brightest and the best," Trump's motley crew of rightwing extremists, cranks, campaign loyalists, billionaires, and assorted Republican hacks could be called "the stupidest and the worse," as many of his appointees had no previous experience in their assigned fiefdom under the reign of King Donald the Dumbass. Moreover, many of his appointees, were opposed to the previous policies of their assigned fiefdom, and even in some cases opposed the very existence of the cabinet position to which they were assigned and had called for its abolition.

In the 19th century, Karl Marx described a rapidly expanding form of market capitalism in which economic forces were coming to control more and more the state, the legal and judicial system, the educational and cultural system and even forms of consciousness. In the 20th century, a group of theorists known as "The Frankfurt School" described the rise of monopoly state capitalism in which powerful corporations and the capitalist state came to control more and more dimensions of society and the polity, culminating in the fascist regimes which in World War II ignited a global war in which the survival of freedom and democracy were at stake. A hero of World War II, General Dwight D. Eisenhower became president of the United States from 1953–1960 and in his oft-cited "Farewell Address" warned of the growth of a military-industrial complex controlled by corporations, the military, and authoritarian politicians.

In putting together his transition team, cabinet, and administration, Donald J. Trump went further in confirming Marx's view of capitalism and embodying Eisenhower's warning against the military-industrial complex than any president in modern U.S. history, choosing an assortment of generals, billionaires, rightwing ideologues, and cronies for top positions in his government, often without qualifications in the area in which they were chosen to serve. They also included the worst racists, Islamophobes, sexists, homophobes, and creatures of the swamp imaginable, suggesting that rather than draining the swamp, Trump was constructing a morass of swamp creatures who were likely to create an era of unparalleled nastiness, conflict, crisis, and warfare that would put U.S. democracy to its most severe test in its history.

Trump started by choosing Senator Jeff Sessions (R-Ala.) for attorney general and Representative Mike Pompeo (R-Cal.) for CIA director. Sessions had been the first Senator to endorse Trump's candidacy, and became a strong supporter for Trump's hardline positions on immigration and law and order. As leader of the Justice Department, Sessions would have significant power to enforce a hardline position on immigration and make American white, Christian, and conservative again. The rightwing Alabama Senator has long been accused of racism, and in 1986, Sessions was denied a federal judgeship after former colleagues testified before a Senate hearing that he had made racist remarks frequently over the years and even joked about the Ku Klux Klan, saying he thought they were "okay, until he learned that they smoked marijuana." The National Association for the Advancement of Color People (NAACP) put out a statement noting: "Senator Sessions was denied appointment as a federal judge in 1986 for a slew of racist comments, including calling the work of the NAACP and ACLU 'un-American.' He has also repeatedly spoken out against the federal Voting Rights Act."[62]

Nominated by Trump as his CIA Director, Mike Pompeo was first elected to the House of Representatives in 2010 as part of the initial wave of so-called Tea Party lawmakers. While serving on the House Permanent Select Committee on Intelligence, Pompeo was a vocal critic of the Obama administration's nuclear accord with Iran and a champion in prosecuting Hillary Clinton on Benghazi. Just before his offer to become CIA Director, Pomey tweeted: "I look forward to rolling back this disastrous deal with the world's largest state sponsor of terrorism," suggesting that another area of chaos could be unleashed in the Middle East with renewed U.S. military aggression. In addition, Pompeo is a longtime ally of the Koch Brothers and champion of surveillance and the re-establishment of government collection of telephone, email, and other forms of personal communication, paving the way for a Leviathan Surveillance State.

The choice of two hardcore rightwing Republicans from the swamp of Washington, Sessions and Pompeo, was supplemented by Trump's decision to offer the position of national security adviser to retired Lt. General Michael T. Flynn. A close advisor to Trump on military affairs during the campaign, Flynn, a militarist and Islamophobic general with a record of incendiary statements about Muslims, would be a strong advocate for aggressive military policy in the Middle East and elsewhere, as well as a supporter of extreme anti-Muslim policies. Flynn was "retired" as director of the Defense Intelligence Agency in the Obama era after reportedly clashing with superiors over his allegedly chaotic management style and a loose relationship with facts, leading his subordinates to refer to Flynn's repeated dubious assertions as "Flynn facts."[63]

Flynn also distinguished himself with floating conspiracy theories, ranging from stories that Hillary Clinton "is involved with child sex trafficking and has 'secretly waged war' on the Catholic Church, as well as charges that Obama is a 'jihadi' who 'laundered' money for Muslim terrorists."[64] When a young man shot up a pizzeria in Washington that was allegedly a source of Clinton-related sex slavery, Flynn's son, who was serving as an advisor to his father, and who had been retweeting and spreading the story about the Clinton sex slave ring, was fired from a Trump administration position, and people were raising questions whether Flynn was qualified himself to serve as national security adviser.[65]

Later reports claimed that during his time in Afghanistan Flynn, mishandled classified information. While during the presidential race, Flynn campaigned vigorously for Donald Trump and drew attention for his scalding attacks against Democratic opponent Hillary Clinton for mishandling classified material, *The Washington Post* reported that: "A secret U.S. military investigation in 2010 determined that Michael T. Flynn, the retired Army general tapped to serve as national security adviser in the Trump White House, "inappropriately shared" classified information with foreign military officers in Afghanistan, newly released documents show."[66]

Flynn was also one of a cadre of close Trump associates who had fond relations with Vladimir Putin and the Russians, as pictures circulated of Flynn next to Putin in Moscow at an event celebrating Russian Television (RT). Given that Republicans had been Cold War super-adversaries of Russian Communism, it was highly bizarre to see so many of Trump's inner circle and Trump himself so enamored of Putin and the Russians.

By mid-November, Trump Tower had become a media circus as suppliants for jobs in his administration appeared one after the other, including Mitt Romney, who had sharply attacked Trump in the Republican primaries, and who was rumored to be a candidate for Secretary of State. It was as if Godfather Trump was forcing his allies and enemies alike to come to his Tower to pledge obeisance and to audition or plead for a job in his administration. Palace intrigue was feverish with reports that Governor Chris Christie had been removed as head of Trump's transition team, perhaps because when Governor of New Jersey, Christie had prosecuted and jailed Jarod Kushner's father, and Vice President-Elect Mike Pence was brought to head the transition team. Kushner was married to Trump's beloved daughter Ivanka and was said to be one of Trump's closest advisors, for whom he had requested national security clearance so that could be present at meetings with foreign leaders or important intelligence or military personnel.[67]

Along with Christie, several of his close allies were removed from the Trump transition team, leading one of the purged Christie allies to complain of a "Stalinesque purge" going on in Trump Tower.[68] After making cabinet choices that would please his hard right supporters, Trump turned to the billionaire class to assure representation for the nation's wealthiest, a status Trump himself had long sought. His surprise pick of Betsy DeVos for Secretary of Education placed a billionaire, who was long a critic of public schools and who favored charter schools and vouchers, in charge of the nation's public education system to the shock and dismay of my fellow educators. As Kate Zernike noted: "For nearly 30 years, as a philanthropist, activist and Republican fund-raiser, she has pushed to give families taxpayer money in the form of vouchers to attend private and parochial schools, pressed to expand publicly funded but privately run charter schools, and tried to strip teacher unions of their influence."[69] Educators were outraged, writing:

> "The president-elect, in his selection of Betsy DeVos, has chosen the most ideological, anti-public education nominee put forward since President Carter created a Cabinet-level Department of Education," said American Federation of Teachers president Randi Weingarten. "In nominating DeVos, Trump makes it loud and clear that his education policy will focus on privatizing, defunding, and destroying public education in America."

> Lily Eskelsen-Garcia, president of the National Education Association, said DeVos "has consistently pushed a corporate agenda to privatize, deprofessionalize, and impose cookie-cutter solutions to public education."[70]

Trump himself had pledged a $20 billion voucher program during his campaign to undercut public education, so the selection of DeVos suggests a major attack on public education will take place during the Trump administration. A member of a prominent Republican fund-raising family, DeVos' husband Dick is heir to the Amway fortune, "a retailer found guilty by the FTC of price-fixing and making exaggerated income claims in 80s, and more recently had to pay over $50 million in a class action settlement to plaintiff's alleging the corporation committed fraud, racketeering, and functioned as a pyramid scheme."[71] De Vos' brother Erik Prince is founder of the notorious Blackwater corporation, whose private security firm was accused of war crimes in Iraq and elsewhere. The De Vos family was one of the major funders of the Republican Party, and "The Dick & Betsy DeVos Foundation is also one of three conservative foundations responsible for funding the Citizens United U.S. Supreme Court ruling that created the current

Super PAC system for campaign financing that allows for unlimited political contributions–like those made by Students First PA."[72]

Continuing to enhance the billionaire reactionary sector of his administration, Trump named investor Wilbur Ross as commerce secretary. Ross is known as the "king of bankruptcy," a kingdom that Trump himself has explored,[73] for buying distressed businesses with the potential to extract profits from their restructuring and resale. A key economic advisor to Trump's campaign, Ross was one of the few financiers to bail Trump out when he was going bankrupt with his Atlantic City casino fiasco in the 1990s. More recently, Ross supported Trump's hardline stance on the need to renegotiate – or even withdraw from – "free trade agreements," like NAFTA, and he shares Trump's America First nationalist line.

Ross made his billions by buying failing companies that were once at the heart of U.S. industry, such as steel mills, coal mines and textile factories, investing in them to modernize and up their value, and then selling them, piling up billions of dollars along the way. While Ross was at one time credited as saving manufacturing jobs in the steel industry by the United Steelworkers, since then the steel industry has declined in the face of cheaper steel from foreign countries, like China, and Ross sold his steel conglomerate in 2004 for about $4.5 billion. Further:

> Ross applied a similar strategy to other industries as well. His metallurgical coal company was headquartered in West Virginia, cobbled together from the remnants of bankrupt mining company Horizon Natural Resources and smaller coal companies. Shortly after the company went public in 2005, an explosion at its Sago Mine in West Virginia killed a dozen people. Ross sold the business to Arch Coal in 2011 for $3.4 billion.[74]

As Deputy Secretary of Commerce to Ross, Trump choose Todd Ricketts, co-owner of the Chicago Cubs, whose family made their fortune through a discount brokerage firm. One of Trump's earliest supporters in the business community, Ricketts had no political qualifications or experience, adding another crony capitalist and certified swamp creature to his cabinet of horrors.

Trump continued to augment his collection of the 1% billionaire class by adding Wall Street and Hollywood insider Steven Mnuchin as Secretary of the Treasury. An early supporter of Trump, he became the campaign's national finance chairman after Trump won the New York primary. A son of a Goldman Sachs partner, Mnuchin joined the firm after graduating from Yale, and worked there for 17 years, rising to oversee trading in government securities and mortgage bonds, ran a hedge fund, and went to Hollywood to finance popular movies like *X-Men* and *Avatar*. Liberal groups attacked Trump's Treasury candidate as one of the Wall Street sharks who "'purchased a bailed-out bank for pennies on the dollar and then aggressively foreclosed on tens of thousands of families,' Jon Green, a spokesperson for the Take on Wall Street campaign, said in a statement. 'Anyone concerned about Wall Street billionaires rigging the economy should be terrified by the prospect of a Treasury Secretary Mnuchin.'"[75]

The critique was apparently referring to "Mr. Mnuchin's role in 2009 in a group that bought the failed California mortgage lender IndyMac from the government. He became the chairman of the company, renamed OneWest, which was ultimately sold to CIT, the nation's largest small-business lender, in 2015 for more than twice the price the group had paid. During Mr. Mnuchin's tenure, OneWest faced allegations that it had foreclosed improperly on some borrowers. Fair-housing groups also filed a complaint with the federal government, claiming that OneWest was not meeting its legal obligation to make loans in minority neighborhoods."[76]

Trump turned to another top Wall Street banker, JP Morgan's Jamie Dimon, to lead "outreach" between the sharks of the business world and the swamps of Washington. Dimon, the chairman and CEO of JPMorgan Chase, is set to become chairman next year of the Business Roundtable, one of the most powerful lobbying organizations in the country. A member of Trump's economic advisory team, Dimon will connect business groups with the Trump administration projects, like lowering corporate taxes and rolling back environmental, financial and other regulations issued by the Obama administration.

In addition to choosing billionaires, rightwing militarists, and hardcore loyalists, Trump made some Machiavellian choices for his cabinet that allowed him to brag of diversity. Choosing Republican insider Elaine Chao as transport secretary, Trump forged an inside link to Mitch McConnell, Senate Majority Leader, who was married to Chao. The daughter of a shipping magnate, Chao made more than $1 million from serving on the boards of Rupert Murdoch's News Corp, and scandal-ridden bank Wells Fargo, Ingersoll Rand and Vulcan Materials. Chao was perceived as an anti-labor Secretary of Labor under George W. Bush, suggesting that the Trump administration would not be the champion of labor that it had promised to its working class voters, in line with Trump's longtime adversarial relations to workers and labor unions. Chao's critics argued that as labor secretary she had inadequately protected employee rights, and the Center for American Progress called her selection an "ominous sign for workers."[77]

Chao's husband, Mitch McConnell, found himself in a potential scandal, however, when a *Washington Post* story published on December 10, 2016, revealed that McConnell blocked release in a report that documented how Russian-sponsored hacking interfered and may have decisively influenced, the U.S. presidential election.[78] There was a consensus among U.S. intelligence services, which Trump refused to accept, that Russian intelligence, connected to WikiLeaks, had released during the primaries and presidential election material hacked from the Democratic National Committee and then the Clinton campaign that was embarrassing to the Democrats and the Clinton campaign team which may have swung the election to Trump. Obama had appointed a high level commission to release the material concerning the Russian interference in the election before the end of his term in office and had convened a bi-partisan meeting of the leaders of the Democratic and Republican party to sign off on a release of this information. Protecting the interests of the Russians and their connections to the Trump campaign, McConnell blocked the release, which has become a major post-election contention that I will discuss further below.

Trump's selection of South Carolina governor Nikki Haley to be the US ambassador to the United Nations was at first surprising, since she had opposed him in the campaign and had no diplomatic experience, yet her leaving South Carolina gave the governorship to Henry McMaster, a Trump ally, and coopted Halley, a rising

Republican star who might have emerged as a strong critic of the Trump administration, as she had been of Trump during the primaries.

Trump's cabinet and other job selections produced the daily media spectacle of suppliants coming in for jobs in the Trump administration at Trump Tower, or one of his golf courses, and the rolling out of his team for the media. The major drama concerned who Trump would pick for the key role of Secretary of State. Among those called to Trump Tower for an interview for the job was Mitt Romney who had strongly opposed Trump in the Republican primaries, criticizing him as unfit for office. But after a well-publicized dinner with Trump in Trump tower, Romney told reporters that Mr. Trump "continues with a message of inclusion and bringing people together, and his vision is something which obviously connected with the American people in a very powerful way."

Other candidates for Secretary of State included Former New York mayor Rudy Giuliani, who was perhaps Trump's most loyal spokesperson during the campaign, perhaps alone defending Trump's treatment of women after the *Access Hollywood* tape revealed Trump's attitude toward women as sex objects. And while woman after woman accused Trump of improper sexual harassment, Rudy continued to dismiss the charges and defend Trump's comments as "locker room talk." Yet Giuliani's complex web of foreign connections during his career as a lobbyist raised questions about his fitness for the job, and made Trump Tower a site of palace intrigue as various factions battled for their favorite candidates to help Trump rule the world.

Clearly, Trump's billionaire cabinet was one of the wealthiest administrations in history and was filled with 1% tycoons who will likely do nothing to fulfil Trump's promise of helping working-class Americans and of serving as champion of the working class. Trump's Big Money administration was appearing to be set to replay the 1980s era of Ronald Reagan, with tax cuts for the rich, deregulation, and an administration catering to the rich and powerful while celebrating unrestrained capitalism, greed, and the amassing of wealth.[79]

Another category of Trump appointee comprised rightwing ideologues who opposed the departments and area of government they were chosen to lead, or destroy as the case may be. Republican congressman from Georgia, Tom Price, was selected as health and human services (HHS) secretary. An orthopedic surgeon, Price staunchly opposed Obamacare, leading the Senate's incoming minority leader, Sen. Charles E. Schumer (D-N.Y.) to note: "Congressman Price has proven to be far out of the mainstream of what Americans want when it comes to Medicare, the Affordable Care Act, and Planned Parenthood," Schumer said in a statement. "Thanks to those three programs, millions of American seniors, families, people with disabilities and women have access to quality, affordable health care. Nominating Congressman Price to be the HHS secretary is akin to asking the fox to guard the hen house."[80] In addition, Price is a strong opponent of abortion rights, and was co-sponsor of a bill that would grant fetuses equal protection rights under the 14th Amendment.

The choice of his former campaign rival Ben Carson to be housing secretary also positioned a conservative ideologue to undermine the agency he was put in charge of. A retired neurosurgeon, Carson became a conservative star after attacking Obamacare, and ran for president with no experience or qualifications whatsoever. Carson seemed more interested in selling his self-promoting books than campaigning, and expressed a sweeping opposition to many government programs devised to end poverty, which he said had replaced church-based and other community initiatives. And so a man who repeatedly proclaimed that "It's not the government's job" to provide healthcare, housing, or any other public service, and who days before his appointment insisted that he was not interested in the job because he had no experience in managing a federal bureaucracy, was put in charge of an agency that was supposed to help provide low and middle-income housing.

Beefing up the cadre of militarists in his cabinet, on December 7, Trump nominated retired Marine Gen. John F. Kelly for Secretary of the Department of Homeland Security (DHS), bringing a border security hawk into his administration. Kelly's main challenge would be to build Trump's Wall along the U.S.-Mexico border to keep out illegal immigrants. Although Trump has claimed that constructing a border wall would be easy, experts have replied that the structure would face environmental and engineering problems, as well as fights with ranchers and others who would resist giving up their land.

Kelly clashed with the Obama administration over the President's plans to close the prison at Guantanamo Bay, and defended the treatment there of detainees against criticism of their treatment by human rights groups which Kelly dismissed as "foolishness." Kelly criticized the Pentagon's order to open for the first time all jobs in combat units to women, and took an extremely hawkish position on the war against radical Islam, a position compatible with Trump.

Further reinforcing the military phalanx in his administration, Trump also selected retired Marine General James N. Mattis (aka Mad Dog) for defense secretary, while retired Army General David H. Petraeus was under consideration for secretary of state. In letting slip out at one of his victory tour rallies that he had chosen Mad Dog Mattis as Secretary of Defense, Trump took great delight in repeating "Mad Dog" over and over, claiming that Mattis was the toughest general since Patton. Although Mattis seemed to be respected in military and political circles, he would need a waiver from Congress to become defense secretary as he has not been retired from the military for the requisite seven years, and some Senators argued that the principle of civilian control of the military was important and that it could be dangerous to have a military man in charge of the complex tangle of rivalries in the Pentagon. More worrisome, Mattis had been fired by the Obama administration because he had pushed so hard for war in Syria and Iraq, suggesting that the Trump/Mad Dog duo could wreak havoc in the Middle East as well as elsewhere.

The profusion of generals chosen by Trump for top positions in his administration intensified worries that the Trump administration would be shaped disproportionately by military commanders. Although during the campaign, Trump insisted he knew more about ISIS than "the generals," when it came to choosing his cabinet, he seemed to think that generals were what his government needed. This predilection for strong military figures suggested that Trump would go for a big military build-up and militarist policies, although he had claimed he was against an interventionist foreign policy and the "regime change" politics of recent Republican presidents like the Bushes.

Senate Democrats worried about the reliance on generals running key segments of the civilian government, with Senator Chris Murphy

(D-Conn.), a member of the Foreign Relations Committee: "I'm concerned. Each of these individuals may have great merit in their own right, but what we've learned over the past 15 years is that when we view problems in the world through a military lens, we make big mistakes."[81]

In another bizarre selection, Trump choose wrestling impresario Linda McMahon to head the Small Business Administration. A former chief executive officer of World Wrestling Entertainment (WWE), Trump added another billionaire to his collection of the 1% rich and infamous. Trump himself was involved in WWE hi-jinx, sponsoring wrestlers and participating in publicity stunts with McMahon and her husband, who were among his biggest campaign donors. Hence, with the McMahon appointment, Trump is bringing more of his campaign financiers and cronies into the inner circle of his administration.

Indeed, one of Trump's main critiques of "Crooked Hillary" was that "she's totally controlled by Wall Street and all these people that gave her millions," yet "by Christmas Trump has stocked his Cabinet with six top donors – far more than any recent White House, Linda McMahon was one of the biggest contributors giving $7.5 million to a super PAC backing Trump."[82]

Moving from the merely scandalous to the horrific, Trump picked Scott Pruitt, Oklahoma attorney general, to run the Environmental Protection Agency (EPA). Critics see Pruitt as a tool of the oil and gas industries, which is not surprising in Oklahoma, where oil and gas are dominant industries who fund and control politicians. Pruitt is indeed a fervent champion of the fossil fuel industry, attacking Obama's signature global warming policy, the Clean Power Plan, as a "war on coal." In an editorial against the choice in the *New York Times,* its editors wrote:

> Since becoming Oklahoma's top legal officer in 2011, Mr. Pruitt has been a bitter opponent of the E.P.A., joining in one lawsuit after another to kill off federal environmental regulations. He has challenged standards for reducing soot and smog pollution that cross state lines. He has fought protections against mercury, arsenic and other toxic pollutants from power plants. He has sued to overturn an

E.P.A. rule modestly enlarging the scope of the Clean Water Act to protect streams and wetlands vital to the nation's water supply.

More recently – and of greater interest to the world community – he has joined with other states in a coordinated effort to overturn the E.P.A.'s Clean Power Plan, the centerpiece of President Obama's regulatory efforts to reduce carbon pollution. If approved by a federal court, the plan could transform the electricity sector, close down hundreds of coal-fired power plants and encourage the growth of cleaner energy sources like wind and solar.[83]

Pruitt is also a climate change denier, committed to overturning President Obama's pledge in global agreements to reduce America's overall greenhouse gas emissions by 26 percent to 28 percent below 2005 levels by 2025. Environmentalists and climate change scientists warn that if there is not a global effort to keep atmospheric warming from rising, an apocalyptic future would involve rising sea levels, extended droughts, and other devastating consequences. Should a Trump administration step back from that commitment, other nations could follow suit, rendering previous environmental agreements irrelevant and driving the world toward irreversible climate change.

Pruitt was the third of Trump's nominees who have major philosophical differences with the missions of the agencies they have were chosen to run. As Chris Mooney, Brady Dennis and Steven Mufson noted: "Ben Carson, named to head the Department of Housing and Urban Development, has expressed a deep aversion to the social safety net programs and fair housing initiatives that have been central to that agency's activities. Betsy DeVos, named education secretary, has a passion for private school vouchers that critics say undercut the public school systems at the core of the government's mission."[84]

In another shocking choice, Trump named Andrew Puzder, the chief executive of the company that operates fast food restaurants Carl's Jr. and Hardee's, as labor secretary. Puzder has been an outspoken opponent of a meaningful increase in the federal minimum wage, which is $7.25 an hour and which the majority of workers and many politicians want to see raised. Moreover, Puzder has been a scathing critic of efforts by the Obama administration to update the rules for overtime-pay eligibility, which have not been fully adjusted for inflation since the mid-1970s. While the Secretary of Labor is supposed to protect workers, Puzder has been an enemy of workers his entire corporate life and in fact is a big fan of automation to replace workers because machines were "always polite, they always upsell, they never take a vacation, they never show up late, there's never a slip-and-fall or an age, sex or race discrimination case."[85]

In an editorial affirming "Andrew Puzder Is the Wrong Choice for Labor Secretary," the editorial board of *The New York Times* declared, in relation to the record of Puzder's fast food restaurants: "When the Obama Labor Department looked at thousands of complaints involving fast-food workers, it found labor law violations in 60 percent of the investigations at Carl's Jr. and Hardee's, usually for failure to pay the minimum wage or time and a half for overtime."[86]

TV news programs announcing Puzder's designation as labor secretary pointed out that his companies were notorious for presenting ads with scantily dressed models caressing their almost naked bodies with his giant greasy triple-burgers, suggesting a disrespect for women and diet and health. Puzder explained: "'I like beautiful women eating burgers in bikinis,' he told Entrepreneur magazine. 'I think it's very American.... I used to hear, brands take on the personality of the CEO. And I rarely thought that was true, but I think this one, in this case, it kind of did take on my personality."[87] Obviously, the Puzman was a Donald J. Trump Sexist Soul Brother and Junk Food Fan.

Joining former Goldman Sachs honchos Steve Bannon and Steven Mnuchin in key roles of the Trump administration, Trump appointed Goldman Sachs executive Gary Cohn to lead the national economic council, a group which coordinates economic policy across government agencies. Cohn is a longtime Goldman commodities trader who moved through bond trading, broader securities, and, eventually, became co-president in 2006. Filling up his government with Goldman Sachs executives is particularly hypocritical as Trump attacked Ted Cruz for his Goldman Sachs connections during the Republican primaries and attacked Hillary Clinton for giving paid speeches to Goldman, implying this made her a patsy of the Wall Street establishment which Trump had belatedly embraced after making demagogic critiques of the industry throughout his campaign.

Trump confirmed that ExxonMobil CEO Rex Tillerson was under consideration for secretary of state and on December 13, 2016 formally made the announcement. The Tillerston nomination raised great worries in that Tillerston was one of three powerful positions within the Trump/ Putin administration that had especially close relations with Vlad the Slayer Putin and the Russians. In over 30 service with ExxonMobil, Tillerston had especially warm relations with Putin and the Russians, cutting big business deals, becoming a personal Friend of Vlad, and even receiving Russia's Order of Friendship. Typical anti-Russian Republicans were worried about the too cozy relationship between Tillerston and the Russians: "Let's put it this way: If you received an award from the Kremlin, order of friendship, then we're gonna have some talkin'. We'll have some questions," Senator Lindsey Graham (Rep.-S.C.) said upon hearing Tillerston was going to be Trump's choice for the key Secretary of State office. "I don't want to prejudge the guy, but that's a bit unnerving."[88]

It was unnerving to many because not only was Trump himself excessively well-disposed toward Putin, but Michael Flynn, Trump's national security adviser was enamored of Putin and the Russians as was Tillerson. The nomination was especially unnerving because the major story of the week of Tillerson's designation to lead state was an uproar over the Russian's hacking the 2016 election, and a story in the *Washington Post*, that the Russians had intervened to help Donald Trump get elected. Trump himself totally denied that the Russians had hacked the Democrats and released selected information to help Trump and hurt Clinton, whereas major figures in both parties, the U.S. intelligence services, and media were all convinced that Russia had intervened in the U.S. election, and President Obama had just announced a commission that would put out a report on the Russian intervention as soon as possible.

Of course, it would be wrong to claim that the United States was an innocent who had never intervened in foreign elections in the light of an entire history of the U.S. incursions in foreign elections, starting in a post-War Italy where the CIA did everything in its power to make sure the Christian Democrats beat the Italian Communist Party.[89] During the Reagan era, William Casey's CIA intervened in a number of Latin American countries, and after failing to oust the Nicaraguan Sandinistas through the electoral process funded an illegal Contra war that embarrassed the Reagan administration and destroyed the careers of some of its officials when it was uncovered that an illegal deal selling arms to Iran was funding the Contra war.[90]

The nomination for secretary of state of Rex Tillerson, was also worrisome because although as chief executive of ExxonMobil, he had worked extensively around the globe and built relationships with such leaders as Russian President Vladimir Putin, there was concern that he had no real diplomatic experience, had been his entire life in private industry, and might put the interests of oil corporations and big business before the interests of the American people. Further, Tillerson was an extreme doctrinaire capitalist ideologue who idolized Ayn Rand.[91]

According to James Hohmann, "Tillerson and Trump had no previous relationship, but the Texas oilman and the New York developer hit it off when they met face to face. One of the things that they have in common is their shared affection for the works of Ayn Rand, the libertarian heroine who celebrated laissez-faire capitalism." Further: "The president-elect said this spring that he's a fan of Rand and identifies with Howard Roark, the main character in *The Fountainhead*. Roark, played by Gary Cooper in the film adaptation, is an architect who dynamites a housing project he designed because the builders did not precisely follow his blueprints. 'It relates to business, beauty, life and inner emotions. That book relates to ... everything,' Trump told Kirsten Powers for a piece in *USA Today*."[92]

In addition, "Andy Puzder, tapped by Trump last week to be secretary of labor, is an avid and outspoken fan of Rand's books. One profiler last week asked what he does in his free time, and a friend replied that he reads Ayn Rand. He is the CEO of CKE Restaurants, which is owned by Roark Capital Group, a private equity fund named after Howard Roark. Puzder, who opposes increases in the minimum wage and wants to automate fast food jobs, was quoted just last month saying that he encouraged his six children to read *'Fountainhead'* first and *'Atlas Shrugged'* later." Moreover: "Mike Pompeo, who will have the now-very-difficult job of directing the Central Intelligence Agency for Trump, has often said that Rand's works inspired him. 'One of the very first serious books I read when I was growing up was *Atlas Shrugged*, and it really had an impact on me,' the Kansas congressman told Human Events in 2011."

Hence, key members of Trump's cabinet are Randists, as is Paul Ryan,[93] and other members of his administration: "Trump has been huddling with and consulting several other Rand followers for advice as he fills out his cabinet. John A. Allison IV, for example, met with Trump for about 90 minutes the week before last. "As chief executive of BB&T Corp., he distributed copies of *'Atlas Shrugged'* to senior officers and influenced BB&T's charitable arm to fund classes about the moral foundations of capitalism at a number of colleges," the Journal noted in a piece about him. "Mr. Allison's worldview was shaped when he was a college student at the University of North Carolina-Chapel Hill and stumbled across a collection of essays by Ms. Rand.'"

Hence, it is apparent that Trump is not turning just to billionaires and cronies to fill his cabinet and administration, but to a cabal of hardcore Randists, suggesting that Rand's *The Virtue of Selfishness* will be the manifesto of the Trump administration.[94] These swamp creature also embody Adam Smith's warning that: "All for ourselves and nothing for other people, seems, in every age of the world, to have been the vile maxim of the masters of mankind."[95] Trump's masters of mankind, however, were more interested in ruling the world than protecting the environment.

Continuing his war against the environment, the Trump transition teach announced that they were to choose climate skeptic Cathy McMorris Rodgers for Department of Interior. The oil and gas cartel, poised to run the Trump administration and the world, was thrilled that climate skeptic Rodgers would run interior and were exultant about the dream team for the oil industry with Pruitt at the EPA, Exxon's Tillerston at state and McMorriss at Interior. This set of climate skeptics and supercapitalists set off dreams of opening up parklands, tribal lands, and areas from the Arctic to the Gulf of Mexico for energy production, turning from conservation promoted by many Secretaries of the Interior to Sarah Palin's manta "Drill, Baby, Drill!"

A slight glitch appeared briefly in the oil companies dream of running the world when Donald Trump Jr. bonded over hunting with Rep. Ryan Zinke (R-Mont.) and told Daddy Trump that his new bro love would be a better choice for Interior. Zinke is a star of the crackpot right "who told voters in 2014 that Clinton was "the real enemy" – "'the Antichrist.'"[96] Yet Zinke would probably go along with the oil cartel to help rape, pillage, and destroy the environment while he and Donald Jr. satisfied their blood lust with shooting animals.

Keeping with the pro-oil and corporate nominations for his cabinet, Trump picked Rick Perry, Ex-Governor of Texas as Energy Secretary. Choosing a representative of an oil-rich state as Energy Secretary is another move toward reverting to fossil fuels as the basis of the energy system and favoring the interests of Big Oil and Big Energy over the environment, consumers, and a future with a new more sustainable and environmental friendly energy system. Ironically, Perry will become in charge of a federal agency that he could not remember its name when during a televised debate in 2011 as he was seeking the Republican nomination, Mr. Perry started to list the federal departments that he would eliminate. Famously, he could not remember the Department of Energy ("Ops!") which he could now destroy along with Housing, the EPA, and other agencies where Trump had named individuals who wanted to eliminate, or destroy.

Revealingly, before Trump named Perry to head up Energy, his transition team has issued a list of 74 questions for officials in Energy Department, asking them there to identify any department employees and contractors who have worked on forging an international climate pact as well as domestic efforts to cut the nation's carbon output – which critics saw as a potential hit list.[97] The union and workers refused, calling it a potential witch-hunt, and so far it appears Rick Perry will have to do his own research on who in the energy department does not function as a tool of big energy and conservative ideology. It was also reported that with the fear that the climate skeptic

Trump administration would disappear decades of crucial climate measurements and data, scientists have been attempting to copy reams of government climate change research onto independent servers to safeguard it from distortion or destruction.[98]

Appealing to his conservative Congressional base, Trump named Mick Mulvaney (R-S.C.) as his director of the Office of Management and Budget, signaling his intent to slash spending and address the deficit as president. Elected to Congress in 2010 as part of the Tea Party movement, Mulvaney has been an advocate for spending cuts and reducing the deficit. To the delight of rightwing conservatives, Mulvaney will lead Trump's charge to drastically cut taxes for the rich, but doing this and slashing the budget will require what George H.W. Bush called "voodoo economics" or divine intervention since the "Committee for a Responsible Federal Budget estimated Trump's tax plan would cost more than $5.3 trillion over the next decade. Even after factoring in faster economic growth, Trump's proposals are expected to add at least $2.6 trillion to the debt over the next decade, according to the nonpartisan Tax Foundation."[99] How the rightwing ideologue Mulvaney, devoid of government management experience, will perform this miracle has economic conservatives worried.

In addition to the nomination of cabinet members, Trump continued to choose controversial key members of his administration, such as his choice for the ambassador to Israel, his longtime lawyer and friend David Friedman. Friedman was on the far right spectrum of American Jews, supporting extremist policies, vilifying progressive American Jewish groups, such as a liberal US group J Street which supports a two state solution, which Friedman denounced as "far worse than kapos" (i.e Jews who turned in fellow Jews in the death camps). Further, Friedman and Trump's son-in-law Jared Kushner support far-right and illegal religious settlements on the West Bank, with Friedman and Kushner serving as volunteer fundraisers for American Friends of Beit El Institutions, which funnels money to illegal Israeli settlements. Judy Maltz of Haaretz reports, "Among the institutions that benefit from the organization's fundraising efforts is a yeshiva headed by a militant rabbi who has urged Israeli soldiers to disobey orders to evacuate settlements and who has argued that homosexual tendencies arise from eating certain foods."

Friedman also supports Trump's rash campaign promise to move the US embassy from Tel Aviv to Jerusalem, and some fear that Trump's policies with Friedman as his point man on Israel could greatly endanger Israel and alienate it and the US from our Arab allies.

Continuing his efforts to recruit creatures from the nether-regions of the swamp into his administration, Trump chose swamp creature Donald McGahn to be his White House counsel. Although the White House counsel operates out of the public eye, it performs that important task of providing the president with legal advice and of steering the president clear of conflicts of interests. As a commissioner at the Federal Election Commission, however, McGahn was a largely negative force, blocking all attempts to fight corruption and dirty money in politics, according to a fellow commissioner Ellen L. Weintraub who claimed: "Even though the Supreme Court resoundingly endorsed the benefits of disclosure in *Citizens United*, McGahn blocked all attempts to rein in unreported dark-money spending."[100]

Even more outlandish, Trump chose 80-year old investor Carl Icahn as special adviser to the president on regulatory reform. The billionaire investor can serve as poster old dude for Conflict of Interest King. Having over the years invested billions in sundry and shady capitalist enterprises, Icahn has set himself up as an icon for anti-regulatory policies, ranting and raving against regulations for decades, and putting him in position to kill regulations that inhibit his own corporate interests and investments. Hence, regulatory reform for the Trump administration obviously will involve a slice-and-dice approach as long as the old regulation slasher Icahn has his hands on the kill-the-regulations weapon which should delight fans of the American Horror genre of "slash the regulations!"

As so into December, the reality show of the Trump Transition Spectacle continued with daily pilgrimages to Trump Tower for job suppliants to kiss the Godfather's ring and beg for a position in his Media Circus and Spectacle of the Swamplands. While Trump Tower continued to be surrounded by police and giant trucks filled with sand, Trump continued receiving and making phone calls to world leaders.

These calls inevitably led Trump to bring up business interests of his in the country in question, often leading him to ask foreign leaders to intervene in problems his organization was having in their countries, leading to criticisms of the morass of conflict of interests Trump and the United States were getting embroiled in with the first billionaire president.

CONFLICTS OF INTEREST AND FAMILY NEPOTISM, FAKE NEWS AND TELEPHONE DIPLOMACY

While the Media Circus swirled around Trump's transition team and appointments, criticism intensified of Trump's conflicts of interest. Trump's initial response was that conflict-of-interest laws generally do not apply to the president, but critics continued to bring up laws and clauses in the constitution. Critics argue that if Trump does not divest his business interests, he would be at risk of violating the Constitution's emoluments clause, which bars U.S. officeholders from taking anything of value from foreign governments. Trump continued into December and the new year in his refusal to release his tax returns and other relevant documents concerning his business interests which means that the public has a very incomplete picture of the scope of his interests, and possible involvement of foreign banks, oligarchs, and corporations that might hold blackmail power over Trump.

While Constitutional lawyers and White House ethics counsellors from Democratic and Republican administrations warned Trump that his presidency might be blocked by the electoral college if he does not give up ownership of at least some of his business empire,[101] Trump balked and bragged that "The brand is certainly a hotter brand than it was before," and indeed it appeared that his election victory had been good for Trump's businesses. Trump proclaimed that he was giving up his Organization to his children who would run them while he ran Washington. Critics pointed out that the Trump organization was a family company and that he and his children had worked together for years, so it was improbable that the kids would suddenly take over without dad playing a big league role in the family enterprises.

Indeed, the Trump organization was already profiting from his ascendency to the presidency. Trump's new Washington hotel was often half-full, even at steep discount prices, during the fall election season after it opened and it appeared that Trump was losing the election. Yet, following his surprise victory, foreign delegations have been booking the hotel for celebrations and business dealings, with top prices for its rooms overlooking Pennsylvania Avenue for the inauguration on January 20.

The conflict of interests whirling around the Trump International Hotel alone are staggering. Trump leases the Old Post Office Building site of his Washington hotel from the General Services Administration (GSA) which prohibits any elected official of the U.S. government from being part of the lease or deriving any profit from it. Yet Trump appoints the head of the GSA, and it is not beyond imagination to conjure that the new GSA head will have promised sweet-heart deals for the Trump organization as part of his job. As *The Guardian* points out: "Other government agencies also play a role in the hotel's conflict-of-interest saga, such as the National Park Service, which recently took steps to help approve a tax subsidy worth up to $32 million for the Trump Organization. Last month, the National Labor Relations Board – an independent federal agency tasked with investigating unfair labor practices – ruled against the Trump International Hotel Las Vegas for refusing to bargain with the union representing much of its staff. Now, President-elect Trump will be tasked with appointing new members to the five-person oversight board. Immediately, that will mean filling two vacant seats that have been empty for most of the Obama years due to deep partisan divides over the role of the NLRB."

Since the election, there has been one story after another concerning how the Trump family and organization has already been cashing in on its victory, beginning with Ivanka Trump's jewelry company using the family's post-election interview appearance on "60 Minutes" to sell a $10,800 diamond and gold bangle which she wore in the interview. *The Washington Post*'s Editorial Board summed up early conflicts of interests in Trump's activities right after the election:

> Then came the president-elect's private meeting with three Indian business partners who are building a Trump-branded luxury complex in India. Mr. Trump's newest hotel, on Pennsylvania Avenue, held a reception for foreign diplomats. As *The Post*'s Jonathan O'Connell and Mary Jordan reported, many diplomats duly took the hint that they should book rooms there to curry favor with the new administration. In his first meeting with British politicians, Mr. Trump urged them

to campaign against offshore wind farms – which Mr. Trump has opposed because he believes they will blight the view from a golf resort he owns in Scotland.

And so it goes, and so it will go unless Mr. Trump divests. The magnitude of the problem was underscored by a report from The *Post's* Drew Harwell and Anu Narayanswamy showing that at least 111 Trump companies have done business in 18 countries and territories across South America, Asia and the Middle East. This Trump empire will be both a potential vehicle for foreign influence and a potential target of terrorist attacks.[102]

Trump announced that after the election, he phoned Argentinian president Mauricio Macri, and following the conversation, an Argentinian associate of the Trump organization, Felipe Yaryura, announced that construction would start next year on the planned Trump Tower Buenos Aires, and that the zoning restrictions which had stalled the project for years would soon be swept away.

Although Trump claims that he will hand over the day-to-day running of the Trump Organization to his children, he has so far retained his ownership stake and those same children are sitting in on his meetings with foreign leaders. Ivanka Trump, for example, was in the room with the president-elect's first meeting with a foreign leader, Japanese prime minister Shinzo Abe. Ms. Trump had been negotiating a licensing deal with the Japanese apparel giant Sanei International, the largest shareholder of which is the Development Bank of Japan, that is wholly owned by the Japanese government. Hence, Invanka appears to be pursuing her private business interests in meetings with her father and foreign leaders, opening new unexplored realms of conflict of interest and potential scandal.[103]

In addition, days after Trump's election victory, a news agency in the former Soviet republic of Georgia reported that a long-stalled plan for a Trump-branded tower in a seaside Georgian resort town was now back on track. In 2012, Trump announced in the Black Sea resort town of Batumi that a new luxury Trump Tower would be erected in the country. However, "the project was delayed by an economic downturn, a local land planning dispute and, some analysts said, the electoral defeat of then-Georgian President Mikheil Saakashvili, a personal friend of Trump's who had championed the deal."[104] Yet in recent months, these roadblocks were removed and the Trump Organization was told that the project could now proceed.

The Trump Organization also has interests in Turkey, including the Trump Towers Istanbul and his partner in the deal is one of Turkey's biggest oil and media conglomerates, which has been a strong supporter of Turkey's increasingly repressive regime. Such conflicts explain why presidents usually put their assets in a "blind trust" to avoid problems. Further: "Trump's other business interests range from sprawling, ultraluxury real estate complexes to one-man holding companies and branding deals in Azerbaijan, Indonesia, Panama and other countries, including some where the United States maintains sensitive diplomatic ties. Some companies reflect long-established deals while others were launched as recently as Trump's campaign, including eight that appear tied to a potential hotel project in Saudi Arabia, the oil-rich Arab kingdom that Trump has said he 'would want to protect.'"[105]

As noted, many of Trump's business connections involve licensing the Trump name, which, for the time being at least, is an even more valuable commodity when Trump becomes president. Moreover, many of Trump's properties, are financed by loans, through foreign banks and institutions, including banks in China and Deutsche Bank, which is currently negotiating what could be a multibillion-dollar settlement over housing-crisis-era abuses with the Justice Department, whose leaders will be Trump appointees.

Further, Trump's advisers, including Michael Flynn, the controversial lieutenant general chosen to become White House national security adviser, also faces conflict of interests issues. Flynn's consulting firm has been hired to lobby on behalf of a group tied to the Turkish government, which is increasingly involved in the latest version of Terror War and Middle East politics. In addition, Flynn and chief White House strategist Steve Bannon have close ties and affinities to extremist movements in Europe that have fascist overtones. Trump's aides deny that Flynn had met with Heinz-Christian Strache, the leader of the far-right Austrian Freedom Party, as Strache had claimed. Yet Europe's far right has clearly been empowered by Trump, and Bannon "has spoken favorably of the 'women of the family Le Pen,' meaning Marine Le Pen, the presidential candidate of the nationalist and anti-immigrant."[106]

While Trump was assembling his cabinet and administration and deflecting stories concerning his family conflicts of interests, the President-elect engaged in some shocking telephone diplomacy. In these conversations, Trump would engage in family business issues during some of the calls from foreign leaders, would praise brutal dictators, and in some cases would engage in dangerous policy shifts without really thinking through the issues.

The most consequential example of telephone diplomacy involved Trump speaking with the president of Taiwan on December 2, 2016, constituting a major break with decades of U.S. policy on China that adhered to a "One China" policy. Since formally breaking off relations with Taiwan in 1979, as the U.S. formalized relations with China, the U.S. had not formally recognized Taiwan as an independent country, even though the U.S. provided substantial military support to Taiwan, engaged in significant trade, and had friendly relations with the island. The call between Trump and Taiwanese president Tsai Ing-wen was the first known contact between a U.S. president or president-elect with a Taiwanese leader and sent shock waves through Asia. China considers Taiwan a province, and news of the official outreach by Trump is likely to infuriate the regional military and economic power.

Trump's telephone diplomacy came at a particularly tense time between China and Taiwan, which earlier this year elected a president, Tsai Ing-wen, who has not endorsed the notion of a unified China. Her election angered Beijing to the point of cutting off all official communication with the island government. However, it was not really clear whether Trump intends a radical shift in U.S. relations with Taiwan or China, or just picked up the phone to chat with a well-wisher after his election victory. Trump's handlers claimed that the president-elect and Tsai simply congratulated each other on winning their elections, and note "the close economic, political, and security ties

... between Taiwan and the United States," according to a statement released.

Yet, China was miffed and it's foreign minister, Wang Yi, called Trump's conversation a "petty action" that "cannot change China's standing in international society." The breach of protocol will "not change the One China policy that the U.S. government has supported for many years," he said. Later, China lodged an official complaint with the United States over the Trump chat with Tsai.

A debate then merged in the media and political circles whether Trump did or did not know about the long-standing U.S. policy toward Taiwan when the call occurred. While one Trump senior adviser claimed that Trump innocently took a call and didn't really know the ramification for U.S. policy, his forked-tongue spinner Kellyanne Conway chirped: "He's well aware of what U.S. policy has been." Conway insisted that Trump was properly briefed before the call on U.S. policy, and deploying her usual strategy of deflecting questions she didn't want to pursue, she asked coyly why President Obama did not receive similar queries about his knowledge of foreign affairs, a rather silly remark. Then moving from spin and snark to straight-out lie, Conway stuck out her chin and asserted: "President-elect Trump is fully briefed and fully knowledgeable about these issues... regardless of who's on the other end of the phone."

Yet the phone call continued to elicit controversy. Some pundits believed the president-elect's call was planned in advance and that Trump took the call on purpose as a move in a calculated switch in relations toward China and Taiwan. Trump's advisers include "several people who have been strong supporters of Taiwan in Republican administrations, including Stephen Yates, deputy national security adviser under Vice President Richard B. Cheney, who was reported to be visiting Taiwan when the call occurred, and John Bolton, neo-con hawk who had allegedly been to Trump Tower just before the call and may have briefed him to take a pro-Taiwan stance. Further, Trump himself had been considering hotel investments in Taiwan earlier this year. The mayor of Taoyuan said last month that a representative from the Trump Organization had visited and was interested in constructing hotels in the northwestern Taiwanese city, according to China Times. Trump has said he will separate himself from his businesses before he is inaugurated."[107]

The Democratic National Committee said the call may mean the businessman is "prioritizing his personal fortune over the security interests of the nation," claiming: "Donald Trump is either too incompetent to understand that his foolish phone call threatens our national security, or he's doing it deliberately because he reportedly wants to build hotels in Taiwan to pad his own pockets," said DNC spokesperson Eric Walker. Indeed, Trump's Taiwan phone call was preceded by hotel development inquiries in Taiwan by the Trump organization.[108]

During the same period, Trump reportedly had a telephone call from Philippine President Rodrigo Duterte who had been slaughtering people in the street in a violent drug war. Trump reportedly extended an invitation for Duterte to visit the United States next year, marking a startling turnabout for a foreign leader who famously called Obama a "son of a whore", and bragged how he had personally killed drug dealers. Yet Duterte had named a business associate of Trump's as Phillipine trade representative and so Trump's business interests took priority over human rights and decency.

Trump had been taking phone calls from all over the world, from allies and enemies alike, and had causally invited many leaders to "come on over and visit," setting off worries for the diplomatic corps which needs to carefully organize and prioritize state visits. Trump's phone calls also set off foreign policy repercussions like the Taiwan-China call and a call between Trump and Pakistani Prime Minister Nawaz Sharif. Pakistan released an account of the conversation that has Trump heaping praise on Sharif as "a terrific guy" and Pakistanis as "one of the most intelligent people." When Sharif invited Trump to visit Pakistan, he replied that he would "love to come to a fantastic country," setting off worries from India that had complex relations with Pakistan, as did the U.S. which tried to cultivate relations with Pakistan as an ally in the struggle with radical Islam, when Pakistan itself provided, trained, and funded Jihadhi groups, some with support from the Pakistan military.

Most worrisome, however, concerned the Pakistani account of Trump pledging partnership that could suggest favoritism in Pakistan's long-running rivalry with India – with both armed with nuclear weapons. According to the Pakistanis, Trump told Sharif he would "play any role you want me to play to address and find solutions to the country's problems," which caught the attention of not just India but also China, North Korea, Russia, and other regional powers who had complex relations with Pakistan. Trump was likely not aware in the least of the complexity of these relations and was just shooting off his mouth and being manipulated by a more cunning statesman, demonstrating the costs of having a buffoon in the White House.[109]

Yet Trump's telephone diplomacy also displays an inexperienced foreign policy team that cannot handle Trump's uniformed and off-the-top of his head twittering and blabbering that might have serious foreign policy consequences. Dumbass Donald's diplomatic inexperience and weak team makes it easy to manipulate Trump, whether setting him off with wild Tweets, or making offhand uninformed comments. Part of foreign diplomacy is framing issues and relations according to a rational foreign policy agenda, and so far Trump and his team has proved itself highly inept in this field.

Interestingly, in the multiplying collection of stories documenting Trump's business interests and conflict of interests that his many properties might involve, Trump shut down several of his companies tied to Saudi Arabia in mid-December after questions were raised concerning the too close relations his business interests in Saudi involved in a country with dicey connections with global terrorism. As questions concerning links between Trump's business interests and his role as president became a major story of the day, Trump cancelled the press conference on December 15, 2016, when he was supposed to discuss how he was distancing himself from his business interests and other questions that he'd promised to address, such as his taxes which he had yet to release.

Also in mid-December, it was announced that Ivanka Trump would have an office in the West Wing and assume many First Lady functions as Melana Trump planned to stay in New York so her son Baron could continue in school (a dicey story, but we'll leave this one to the tabloids). Ivanka continued to market her name for profit and family prestige in one of her brother Eric's charities which offered a coffee-with-Ivanka date for the highest bidder until the Trump family was told that the First Family could not use their names for private charities.[110] This episode suggests that the Trump administration will consist of continuing conflicts between nepotism and the law, with the avaricious Trump family trying to use all their new political power to enhance their business empire.

The next week, Trump's sons Donald Jr. and Eric got into trouble when it was announced that they were part of a post-inauguration gambit where contributors of $500,000 to one million dollars could have face-time and a photo-op with the president after the inauguration, or for more cash, go on a hunting trip with the presidents sons who seemed to think that killing animals was a good way to start their tenure as First Sons. Someone in the Trump transition team became aware of this pay-to-play scam, and his sleazy sons pictures were taken off of the Opening Day Foundation charity website that had organized the "event," but they were still on the Board of Directors of the purported "charity" that had planned the event.

Shortly thereafter, it was announced that Donald Jr. would close down his own foundation to avoid conflict of interests and just before Christmas, Donald Sr. announced that he was closing the Trump Family Foundation for the same reasons. However, the New York Attorney General who was investigating the Trump Foundation for financing improprieties, including using Foundation funds for private Trump family interests like the alleged purchase of a larger than life portrait of the Donald with foundation funds.

From this perspective, the Trump family is best seen as an elaborate con, a family of hustlers, grifters, and con artists, who use the family name to promote their brand and increase their wealth and power. The Trumps license their name to an array of disparate merchandise from hotels to vodka and steaks to Ivanka's fashion line. Interestingly, the Trump campaign presented the Clinton's as a crime family with their pay to play foundation, and insisted that Hillary Clinton was the most corrupt politician ever, a branding that helped work to defeat her in the 2016 election. In fact, the Trump family is a con and grifter family whose Big League cons put the small time Clinton foundation fund-raising and access to shame. Everything about Donald Trump is a con from his business career from the time he stopped building buildings and went bankrupt with his failed Atlantic City casinos to his selling his name to different enterprises, some of which themselves were cons that cost investors their savings.

Trump's brave new world is shaping up as a world in which his role as the U.S. president, family Capo de tutti di capi of his private family enterprises across the globe, his relationships with foreign business partners and the leaders of their governments, his secret network of advisors and partners, selected tentacles of his best bro Vlad's private and public agencies, and US intelligence agencies could all become intertwined, and Trump could rule his enterprise as an amalgam of private and public interests, encompassing the local, national, and global empire of a new world order that for now we can call *TRUMPLAND*.[111]

Every day after the election, Trumpland becomes more powerful and adds connections, pushes forward past deals, and expands the global reach of his brand which goes up in value every day. No doubt the rising value of Trumpland also enriches his domestic and overseas partners, and strengthens their clout in their home countries, making them useful conduits to business and political interests in their home country and beyond as well. Trumpland realizes the fantasy of the president of the television corporation in the 1975 movie *Network* in which the news corporation president Jensen, played by Ned Beatty, tells his TV anchorman Howard Beal (Peter Finch) the truth about the system and who runs the world. Beal, in a Trumpian mode, screamed on-air "I'm mad as hell and I'm not going to take it anymore," and became the voice of a populist movement of angry (mostly white people) who Jensen informs:

> Jensen: You have meddled with the primal forces of nature, Mr. Beale, and I won't have it!! Is that clear?! You think you've merely stopped a business deal. That is not the case. The Arabs have taken billions of dollars out of this country, and now they must put it back! It is ebb and flow, tidal gravity! It is ecological balance!

You are an old man who thinks in terms of nations and peoples. There are no nations. There are no peoples. There are no Russians. There are no Arabs. There are no third worlds. There is no West. There is only one holistic system of systems, one vast and immane, interwoven, interacting, multivariate, multinational dominion of dollars. Petro-dollars, electro-dollars, multi-dollars, reichmarks, rins, rubles, pounds, and shekels.

It is the international system of currency which determines the totality of life on this planet. That is the natural order of things today. That is the atomic and subatomic and galactic structure of things today! And YOU have meddled with the primal forces of nature, and YOU WILL ATONE!

Am I getting through to you, Mr. Beale?

You get up on your little twenty-one inch screen and howl about America and democracy. There is no America. There is no democracy. There is only IBM and ITT and AT&T and DuPont, Dow, Union Carbide, and Exxon. Those are the nations of the world today.

What do you think the Russians talk about in their councils of state – Karl Marx? They get out their linear programming charts, statistical decision theories, minimax solutions, and compute the price-cost probabilities of their transactions and investments, just like we do.

We no longer live in a world of nations and ideologies, Mr. Beale. The world is a college of corporations, inexorably determined by the immutable bylaws of business. The world is a business, Mr. Beale. It has been since man crawled out of the slime. And our children will live, Mr. Beale, to see that perfect world in which there's no war or famine, oppression or brutality – one vast and ecumenical holding company, for whom all men will work to serve a common profit, in which all men will hold a share of stock, all necessities provided, all anxieties tranquilized, all boredom amused.

Trumpland, like MobilExxon, whose CEO Rex Tillotson Trump choose to be Secretary of State, knows no national loyalties and recognizes no transcendent or democratic values beyond power and profit. Trumpland is post-truth and lives on the propagation of fake news. For Donald Trump himself, discourse serves the interests of Trumpland and has no relation to truth and falsity. While there was an uproar after the election with the discovery of Fake News sites that had claimed Hillary Clinton sold arms to ISIS, was part of a child sex slavery ring and the like, while claiming that Donald Trump was supported for president by the Pope, Denzel Washington, and the like, the media did not recognize that Donald J. Trump ran an entire campaign on Fake News and continues with his Twitter feed and post-campaign speeches and interviews to promote Fake News. During the campaign, Trump continually spread rumors, false news, and outright lies on his Twitter feed and in his campaign speeches where he would usually provide a fraudulent take on stories of the day and add his Fake News stories to the media mix, without much commentary or critique from the media that he castigated for the few times he was called out on his lies and fabrications of reality.[112]

Trump Fake News continued after the election via his Twitter Feed and victory tours where Adulation Addict Donald continued to travel around the country making speeches and making up reality, refusing for instance, to recognize that Russia hacked the DNC and Clinton's campaign manager John Podesta, and that this helped Trump win what was looking like one of the most scandalous elections in U.S. history. By mid-December, the Russian hacking story, and Trump's denial of it, was becoming a major issue, as Obama kicked in during his last press conference and explained why he hadn't dramatized the issue earlier. Obama claimed that he did not want to appear overly partisan, did not want to bait Russia to hack the actual voting machines, and did not want to de-legitimize the electoral process and give Trump an opportunity to contest the legitimacy of the election and wreak political havoc.

Trumpland Fake News trumpeted that Donald the Great and Powerful had persuaded Ford Motors not to move its Louisville, Kentucky plant abroad when Ford had no intention of doing so anyway.[113] Donald the Trumpet presented Masayoshi Son, one of Japan's richest billionaires in person at Trump Towers, and bragged that son was going to invest $50 billion in the U.S., as if Donald the Magnificent had persuaded him to do so, tweeting that the company would never have done "had we [Trump] not won the election!" In fact, Mr. Son had already announced he was investing the big bucks in the states in October before the election and would no doubt have done so if Hillary had won.[114]

Trump's daily Fake News reports continued into December on his feverish Twitter account and continued "victory tour." When controversy emerged concerning Russia's hack attack during the election and Russia's support of Trump against Clinton, Trump attacked President Obama for not raising an alarm about Russian interference in the US election earlier, when in fact on October 7, 2016, the Obama administration issued an official statement accusing the Russians of being behind the cyber attack.

On what he claimed was his last "thank you tour" before his inauguration, during a rally in Alabama on December 17, 2016, Trump reviewed the highlights of his campaign, bragging over and over what a great victory he won, going through state after state in which he was predicted not to win, and then crowed about how he had foiled these predictions and won a great victory. Trump continued to attack the media, like John King of CNN, who on his blackboard claimed night after night that Trump had no path to victory. He attacked Third Party candidate Evan McMullin, and even John Kasich, showing that the Vindictive Donald never forgets, never reaches out to those he has defeated, and delights in ridiculing his enemies and those he has vanquished.

Yet as the days until inauguration reached 30, the hacked election was becoming increasingly de-legitimized as the Clinton campaign moved from blaming FBI Director James Comey for illegitimately intervening in the election process, by also blaming Vladimir Putin and the Russians for the outcome. In a speech at "thank you" party for those who donated millions to her presidential campaign at the Manhattan Plaza Hotel, once owned by Donald Trump, Clinton claimed that Putin hacked the Democrats to get revenge on her for criticizing Russian elections, when as Secretary of State she raised questions about Putin and the Russian electoral process which she claimed Putin had rigged.[115]

In any case, the Russian hack was one of the great scandals in U.S. election history and there would debates into the Trump presidency concerning what had happened and how to address the problem, which pertains to key issues of national security concerning election sovereignty and cybersecurity. There were calls for the Obama administration to declassify as much as possible concerning what is known about the Russian hack, and calls by both Democratic and Republican members of the senate to investigate the alleged Russian intervention in Election 2016. There were calls for Congress to authorize a far-reaching, bipartisan independent investigation modeled on the 9/11 Commission to find out exactly what happened, why, and what can be done to prevent future attacks. There were also calls to investigate the FBI "to determine why the FBI responded overzealously in the Clinton case and insufficiently in the Russian case. The FBI should also clarify whether there is an ongoing investigation into Trump, his associates and their ties to Russia. If ever there were a case of 'intense public interest,' this is it. What's broken in the FBI must be fixed and quickly."[116]

TRUMP AT WAR: MEDIA, CORPORATIONS, ORDINARY CITIZENS, AND THE U.S. INTELLIGENCE SERVICES

In early modernity, the philosopher Thomas Hobbes postulated that without a strong monarchy and state, humanity lived in a state of nature where "life is nasty, brutal, and short." Hobbes posited the need for a "leviathan" authoritarian state to keep unruly impulses and conflicting forces in check, and political philosophy for centuries thereafter has debated the scope of state power, its limitations and restraints, and the way that the state can make human life better, while criticizing excessively authoritarian regimes, state repression, and degenerate forms of the polity like fascism. Donald J. Trump and his administration seems poised to take us back to the good old days of the 1600s where a Leviathan state and an absolute ruler exist in a state of warfare. This time, however, it is the authoritarian leader Donald J. Trump who, since his surprise election, has been in a state of warfare against corporations that have aroused his ire, the media, critics and citizens who have spoken out against his proposed policies and cabinet and even, perhaps for the first time in history, has inaugurated an all-out war against the CIA before even assuming the presidency.

Making it clear to the mainstream corporate media in a private meeting with major heads of networks, newspapers, and journalists that he was not pleased with the coverage of his campaign, Trump allegedly railed at the corporate media elite, and demanded better coverage of his presidency. For months after the election, Trump did not carry out a public news conference, although in a "thank you tour" (aka victory tour), Trump continued to rehash the story of his fabulous campaign and victory, and continued to attack the media contingent assigned to cover him.

One of Trump's first major post-election actions was a mano-a-mano battle with the Carrier factory in Indiana, which had during the election announced its decision to outsource jobs to Mexico, thus becoming a punching bag for Trump's campaign theme that jobs were leaving the U.S. for Mexico and other developing world countries and that he would get them back. In a highly publicized stunt on the weekend of December 3, 2016, news was dominated by Trump's claim that he had personally persuaded Carrier to keep a number of the jobs scheduled for Mexico in the U.S. (although the specific number would be in question).[117]

Indiana Governor Mike Pence was Trump's partner in the deal and it turned out that the state agreed to give Carrier $7 million in tax incentives over 10 years, while the company has agreed to invest $16 million in Indiana. There was also speculation that Carrier's parent company United Technologies had been threatened with the loss of lucrative defense contracts, and corporations began worrying that Trump would resort to blackmail to force his deals. Whatever, the details of the deal Trump made it a PR victory as he toured the plant in Indianapolis and shook hands with workers on an assembly line. Some yelled, "Thank you Mr Trump!" and "Thanks, Donald," as he greeted them, *Reuters* reported.

Economic analysts pointed out that deals like the one at Carrier are unlikely to stem the job losses caused by automation and cheap foreign competition, and that the agreement is unsustainable on a big scale and could set a worrying precedent for companies looking for tax concessions. Conservatives thought it was a bad precedent when politicians intervened in the market to influence decisions of a specific corporation, and that businesses should not make decisions to please politicians. On the left, Senator Bernie Sanders wrote scathingly in an op-ed for the *Washington Post*: "Trump has endangered the jobs of workers who were previously safe in the United States. Why? Because he has signaled to every corporation in America that they can threaten to offshore jobs in exchange for business-friendly tax benefits and incentives."[118]

When Chuck Jones, the president of the local chapter of the United Steelworkers union that represents Carrier employees in Indianapolis, informed the *Washington Post* that Trump exaggerated the number of jobs he claims to have saved, twenty minutes after an appearance on CNN telling the story, which put Trump's veracity in question, the president-elect began attacking him on Twitter. Jones received threatening phone calls and had his fifteen minutes of media fame, while cable news spent days debating whether it was appropriate for the President of the United States to attack an ordinary citizen on Twitter, with most commentators seeing the episode as exemplary of Trump's propensity for bullying and all-too-quick Twitter finger.

In early December, *Time Magazine* crowned Trump "Person of the Year," an award also received by Hitler and Stalin. The cover referred to the president-elect of the 'divided states of America," leading querulous Donald, in an interview on NBC's *Today* show, to insist: "I didn't divide them … They're divided now. I'm not president yet, so I didn't do anything to divide!" Refusing to acknowledge his divisive role in the election, Trump then claimed that he is actually "very restrained" on social media, showing a constitutional inability to recognize the truth or an advanced state of delusion.

Since winning the election on November 9, Trump continued his war against the media, corporations, ordinary citizens, and even the CIA and U.S. intelligence service. He continued to attack the media on a daily basis on his Twitter feed, and organized meetings with broadcasting executives, *The New York Times*, and various media figures to criticize their performance during the primaries and election, where Trump believed he was not taken seriously and presented negatively. His deep animus and resentment against the media is weird because even if he was negatively presented or criticized on the media, he got far more coverage and attention than any other candidate which helped him immensely in his victory in the Republican primaries where he got more coverage alone than the entirety of the other mass of candidates all together.

During the primaries, Clinton received relatively little coverage on cable news, and Bernie Sanders almost none, with Trump massively dominant in amount of news coverage. Moreover, in the national election, Trump received far more coverage than Clinton with almost all of his daily events covered by cable news, often broadcasting full speeches live, and his daily campaign event was then dissected in the evening by both cable and network news. Thanks to Twitter, Trump dominated new media throughout the campaign season. Indeed, without such massive coverage, Trump would have had little chance in either the primaries or the general elections.

After securing the Republican nomination and then winning the general election, Trump took to attacking major corporations. Throughout his campaign, Trump made Carrier a punching-bag during his anti-globalization election crusade, before bribing them to keep some jobs in their Louisville plant to give Trump a bragging rights that he was going to save jobs. After cutting the deal with Carrier, Trump made Boeing aircraft a target for his Twitter rants, claiming that its announced $4 billion price tag for developing an advanced presidential Air Force One plane was big league excessive. Keeping up his attacks on the airline industry, Trump tweeted on December 12, 2016, that costs for Lockheed Martin's F-36 fight-jet program were way "out of control."

This daily use of Twitter to promote a political agenda is a new form of presidential power, perfectly suited for an authoritarian like Trump. His supporters saw this as a smart bargaining weapon to cut better "deals" with the corporation or individual under attack, but it showed a propensity to govern by fear and bullying, and made nastiness a part of everyday political life. In addition, Trump continued attacking ordinary citizens on his Twitter feed, as well as the media, other political figures, corporations, and his critics. Chuck Jones of Carrier was for some time in November the Everyman who suffered the wrath of Trump's Twitter feed but anyone who dared criticize Delicate Donald could be the target of Trump's new tech bully pulpit.

Yet the most astounding Trump Twitter War took place in December 2016 in an all-out battle against the CIA. Needless to say, few politicians ever criticized head-on the CIA and never had any president-elect waged such a bizarre war on the CIA. In a blockbuster story published December 9, 2016, the *Washington Post* reported that the CIA concluded in a secret assessment that Russia intervened in the 2016 election to help Donald Trump win the presidency, rather than just to undermine confidence in the U.S. electoral system.[119] In October, it was widely reported that when the DNC and Clinton campaign manager John Podesta had their email account hacked and WikiLeaks began publishing them Russia was involved in the hacks,[120] and since then U.S. intelligence agencies have identified individuals with connections to the Russian government who provided WikiLeaks with thousands of hacked emails. The officials described the individuals involved in hacking as actors known to the intelligence community and part of a wider Russian operation aiming to boost Trump and hurt Clinton's chances.

Twit Tweeter Trump immediately responded in typical fashion mocking the CIA and claiming: "These are the same people that said Saddam Hussein had weapons of mass destruction. The election ended a long time ago in one of the biggest Electoral College victories in history. It's now time to move on and 'Make America Great Again.'"[121] This response is amazing for many reasons. First, Trump is denouncing the CIA and siding with Russia and Putin, who denied the hacking, as more credible sources than U.S. intelligence services. Never has a president been so openly hostile and contemptuous of U.S. intelligence services, and valorized the Russians, the U.S. enemy in the Cold War and in global geopolitical struggles up to the present. Secondly, it was not one of the "biggest Electoral College victories in history" by any measurement and in fact ranked #46 out of 58 elections; moreover, Trump lost the popular vote by almost 3 million.[122]

During the same period, Trump had revealed that he was not going to the daily presidential briefings from U.S. intelligence experts that are usually part of a presidential-elect's preparation for the challenges of the office. An irate Trump told Chris Wallace in a *Fox News* interview that he "was smart," didn't need the repetitive briefings, and would listen to the briefers if they had something important to report. U.S. intelligence figures and politicians who had been regularly given such briefings insisted that they were an important dimension of government, and were stupefied that Trump didn't want to take the briefings and had resisted them for weeks. This was especially concerning in that Trump was the least informed and most inexperienced president-elect in modern history.

Indeed, as a second reason why Trump did not want to take daily briefings from U.S. intelligence, and ultimately why he did not want to address and blithely dismissed the CIA claim that the Russians had intervened in the U.S. election to help Trump win, was that in Trump's view: "The election ended a long time ago in one of the biggest

Electoral College victories in history." As noted, Trump's Electoral College victory was middling, and he had lost the popular vote, by almost 3 million votes, raising serious questions about the Electoral College and providing a strong argument why the U.S. should adopt a popular vote mandate in presidential elections. Trump's comment also again raised the issue as to whether Trump was delusional, actually believing he won "one of the biggest victories in history."

During a presidential debate, when the issue of the Russians hacking the DNC and John Podesta was brought up, Trump repeatedly said he didn't believe this and that there was no proof, while Clinton insisted that 13 separate U.S. intelligence agencies claimed that Russian did the hacking. After the *Post* reported that the CIA had concluded that Russia tried to help Trump win, Trump denounced this as "ridiculous," repeating his earlier mantra: "I don't believe it."

Democrats and the Clinton campaign team, in their first public stance after the election, called the report of Russian intervention in the election a scandal and called for congressional investigations, a call reluctantly supported by Senate Majority Leader Mitch McConnell and other top Republicans, while Trump and his advisers continued to push against the claim and to try to deflect the story. Foreign policy experts claimed that "Russia's efforts to interfere in the U.S. elections are unprecedented in American history," as Michael E. O'Hanlon, a senior fellow in foreign policy at the Brookings Institution, put it, adding: "Never before has technology allowed such widespread, semi-clandestine, and semi-deniable effects." He added, "Whether one thinks they swayed the outcome or not, whether Vladimir Putin thinks we try to do the same thing to influence elections in pro-democratic ways in countries like Ukraine or not, all Americans should be alarmed. And that puts it mildly."[123]

THE HACKED ELECTION, THE SWAMP OF SCANDAL, AND CONSTITUTIONAL CRISIS

Election 2016 was appearing to be one of the most scandalous elections in U.S. history. Never before had the FBI Director, or an official in the U.S. intelligence apparatus, publically intervened with bombshell announcements so close to the election that slowed down the momentum of a candidate leading by as many as ten points in some polls and raising questions about the suitability of the candidate, Hillary Clinton, by placing her in yet another email scandal. Never before, as far as we know, had a foreign government hacked into one party's email servers and released information calculated, first, to raise questions concerning DNC bias toward one candidate (i.e. Clinton), and efforts to negatively impact the campaign of her surprise competitor Bernie Sanders in the Democratic Party primaries. In the general election campaign, the Democrats were hacked again with a drip drip drip of embarrassing emails raising questions about the Democratic candidate Hillary Clinton.

It was especially outrageous when the CIA announced – eventually getting the FBI and other U.S. intelligence agencies to agree – that it was Russia who was in charge of the hacking in an effort to defeat Hillary Clinton and elect Donald Trump. It was also outrageous that throughout the election season Trump had made positive comments about Vladimir Putin, the former KGB agent who had become de facto dictator of Russia and was seen by most in the U.S. intelligence and political establishments as the U.S. major strategic enemy. No one knew if the Russian hacking scandal had directly affected the outcome of the election, but it was significantly close enough that the Russian hack was at least one of the major reasons for Trump's victory.

It was also outrageous that Trump had called for the Russians to hack Clinton's email to find the allegedly missing email that she had not turned over the government agencies investigating problems with her private email server. Trump also denied the CIA and U.S. intelligence service consensus that the Russian had hacked the

Democrats and intervened in the election, calling the allegation "ridiculous." By December, many members of Congress were calling for investigations, special prosecutors, and the like, but the damage was done and Trump was preparing for the inauguration.

On December 19, 2016, the American Horror Show was officially ratified as electors in the 50 states met and certified Trump's win in the Electoral College, sealing his presidential victory – even though he lost the national popular vote by nearly 3 million votes. Although there had been feverish attempts to persuade Trump electors to flip, and while there were demonstrations in many state capitals to protest Trump and the Electoral College, once the votes were tallied, only a handful of Trump and Clinton electors chose alternative candidates.

Yet the final tallies showed a close election and no real mandate for Trump. Although Trump continued to claim he had won in a "landslide," and in another case claimed he had "won one of the biggest Electoral College victories in history," once the final tallies were added up (they would be certified in Congress on January 6, 2017), it appeared Trump was delusional. Trump had lost the popular vote by almost 3 million votes racking up the second biggest loss of the popular vote in history by a president who had won the electoral college. Moreover, polls showed that Trump had the lowest presidential popularity rating of any president-elect in modern history and only 29% considered that he had a popular mandate for governing.[124]

Trump's victory in the Electoral College and massive defeat in the popular votes, combined with the general view that he is completely unqualified to be president and has confirmed this by the choice of his cabinet and other major jobs in his administration, makes it clear that the Electoral College is completely outdated and should be eliminated as a vestige of peculiar compromises made centuries ago by the Founding Fathers. To begin, in the contemporary era, the Electoral College is completely unfair with its biases against states with high populations and undemocratically marginalizes urban and nonwhite voters. Conservatives say the Electoral College serves as a necessary bulwark against big states, preventing states like California and New York from having more power in selecting a president (California has bragging rights current of siding with Clinton by a vote margin of four million, or 30 percentage points). Yet the opposite argument is equally valid, that small rural states that go conservative have an unfair advantage over bigger states with larger populations.

In addition, the Electoral College's (largely) winner-take-all design provides excessive focus on battleground states as sectors of the East Coast and the entire West coast are reliably blue (i.e. Democratic Party strongholds), while the South and rural states are increasingly red (i.e. Republican). Trump had a major advantage in the traditional battleground states because most are whiter, less educated, and more rural and conservative than the country as a whole.

The Editorial Board of *the New York* Times penned an op-ed "Time to End the Electoral College," arguing:[125]

> By overwhelming majorities, Americans would prefer to elect the president by direct popular vote, not filtered through the antiquated mechanism of the Electoral College. They understand, on a gut level, the basic fairness of awarding the nation's highest office on the same basis as every other elected office – to the person who gets the most votes.

> But for now, the presidency is still decided by 538 electors. And on Monday, despite much talk in recent weeks about urging those electors to block Donald Trump from the White House, a majority did as expected and cast their ballots for him – a result Congress will ratify next month.

> And so for the second time in 16 years, the candidate who lost the popular vote has won the presidency. Unlike 2000, it wasn't even close. Hillary Clinton beat Mr. Trump by more than 2.8 million votes, or 2.1 percent of the electorate. That's a wider margin than 10 winning candidates enjoyed and the biggest deficit for an incoming president since the 19th century.

> Yes, Mr. Trump won under the rules, but the rules should change so that a presidential election reflects the will of Americans and promotes a more participatory democracy.[126]

Further, the Times's Editorial Board notes that the Electoral College is connected with the country's "original sin" i.e. Slavery, and provided a compromise with the Southern states, counting salves as three-fifths of a white person, which ended up giving the slave states more electoral votes. Yet perhaps the greatest vulnerability and argument for its abolition is the absolutely arbitrary nature of the actual voting by the Electors who can in fact vote for anyone they choose and are not really bound in any significant way to represent the regions that choose them to participate in the obsolete ritual of the Electoral College.

By Monday evening, there were at least nine faithless electors who voted their conscience against the state tallies and candidates they were supposed to support, with Washington State tallying four faithless electors as part of a stop Trump "Hamilton Electors" movement. While the movement was named after Alexander Hamilton who helped shape the role of the electoral college in the Federalist Papers, Hamilton himself was a fierce proponent of the Electoral College, writing in the *Federalist Paper* No. 68 that the meeting of the electoral college "affords a moral certainty, that the office of President will never fall to the lot of any man who is not in an eminent degree endowed with the requisite qualifications." In fact, an elitist sector of the Founding Fathers worried about the results of popular democracy choosing a radical, and constructed the Electoral College to make sure each state choose some of its best people who would reliably vote for the candidate chosen by the voters in the state. Now selection of the electors is random and "faithless electors" could reverse a vote that went against electoral results. A record nine electors in 2016 appeared to have gone against their state vote, and in a close election it is plausible that a handful of Electors could reverse the decision made nationally by voters in the election day voting, showing the utter obsolescence and disfunctionality of the Electoral College.

Various remedies to reform the College have been proposed with the *NYT* Editorial Board proposing: "There is an elegant solution: The Constitution establishes the existence of electors, but leaves it up to states to tell them how to vote. Eleven states and the District of Columbia, representing 165 electoral votes, have already passed legislation to have their electors vote for the winner of the national popular vote. The agreement, known as the National Popular Vote interstate compact, would take effect once states representing a majority of electoral votes, currently 270, signed on. This would ensure that the national popular-vote winner would become president."[127]

I'm inclined after Election 2000 and Election 2016 to advocate the complete abolition of the Electoral College, and to go with a direct democracy popular vote system, following the model of most Western democracies. The Electoral College is totally obsolete, is deeply flawed, and is perhaps the single most problematic aspect of the U.S. presidential election system. Hopefully, citizens of the future will see this and the U.S. can emerge from the crisis of democracy under which we have suffered throughout the contemporary era.

AMERICAN NIGHTMARE AND THE DISASTER
OF ELECTION 2016

As Christmas weekend approached, Donald Trump gave the world an early Christmas nightmare, by asserting in a tweet that he would expand the U.S. nuclear arsenal, upending a reduction course set by presidents of both parties over the past four decades. Further, rather than wrapping Christmas presents, Trump tweeted against a pending U.N. resolution that criticized Israel's settlements policy. The Obama administration, fed up with Israel's refusal to seriously negotiate with the Palestinians to give them the state they deserved, and angry with Israel's continuing West Bank illegal settlements in territory allocated to the Palestinians, abstained from the UN condemnation of Israel's colonization of Palestinian territory, assuring that Israel would throw a temper tantrum.

Indeed, Israeli Prime Minister Benjamin Netanyahu claimed "iron-clad information" from sources that reveal the Obama administration drafted the UN document that condemned Israel for building illegal settlements and pushed the motion through the UN, claims that the Obama administration denied. Netanyahu replied he would give the evidence to the Trump administration, and with his new fake hairpiece, bulging pot-belly, bluster, and propensity for conspiracy theories, no doubt Netanyahu could join Putin in Trump's best-bro authoritarian club.

Trump and Netanyahu exchanged bro-love tweets with Trump assuring Bibi that all would be well when he assumed office, telling Israel to hang tight in the meantime. Trump's tweeting was getting serious people alarmed. Arms control experts worried that "Trump's willingness to Tweet about nuclear weapons raises the possibility of Trump doing the same as president – and more to the point, the possibility of him doing so *amid some species of international crisis or escalation.*" Experts pointed out that Twitter was a blunt and aggressive means of communication, especially in Trump's sweaty and small hands, and could escalate in a crisis to trigger nuclear war.[128]

Another Christmas delight, providing some clues to the emergent type of Trumpian political discourse in the coming era, came from Carl Paladino, the co-chair of Donald Trump's New York state presidential campaign who spouted about Michelle Obama "being a male" who should be "let loose in the outback of Zimbabwe" to live "in a cave with Maxie, the gorilla." Earlier, the Trumpian comedian had barked out a fake news headline: "[Barack] Obama catches mad cow disease after being caught having relations with a Her[e]ford." Paladino had visited Trump Tower earlier in December, spending an hour with the president-elect, and meeting with Mike Pence, Reince Priebus, Stephen Bannon, Jared Kushner, and Michael Flynn, who would be leading the way to take the U.S. in 2017 into the Swamps of Trumpland.

However, yet another swamp creature mysteriously disappeared from Trumpworld. Jason Miller, who had been a loyal spin doctor and communication advisor for Trump throughout the primaries and campaign, had been appointed before Christmas to the high-level post of overseeing White House communications strategy. Yet, one day later, on Christmas Eve, Trumpworld announced that Miller wouldn't be taking the post after all, and that he wanted to go home and focus on his family – a code word suggesting that Miller had been a bad boy and was now shunned from Trumpworld. Jilted Jason thus provided another example of how Trump discards his most loyal subjects with regal impunity, and that there can be no less secure employment in the land than working for King Donald the Fire Demon. Meanwhile, Trump campaign manager Kellyanne Conway had announced she was not taking a White House job so that she could spend more time with her young children, but through December and into the New Year, she continued to appear frequently on television, trying to present a cheerful demeanor to spin Trump's latest absurdities. Yet her Mission-Impossible was taking its toll as the once-perky and pert Kellyanne was becoming increasingly haggard and wizened, as if the daily lying and spinning were turning the media princess into a witch.

As the year 2016 came to its inevitable end, Donald the Twitter King kept those inappropriate tweets coming. In response to Democrat and Republican calls for official investigations of the Russian hacking, Trump tweeted, Bah humbug, investigations: "I think we ought to get on with our lives." As President Obama prepared to impose sanctions on Russia for hacking, Donald Trump, the Twitter Technology Philosopher King tweeted: "I think that computers have complicated lives very greatly. The whole age of computer has made it where nobody knows exactly what's going on" – expanding on his initial tweet/response to allegations of Russian hacking, that it could be anyone, "somebody sitting on their bed that weighs 400 pounds, OK?" When Obama retaliated for the Russian hacking that may have changed an election and given Trump the presidency, Trump's bro Vlad the Slayer Putin uncharacteristically announced he was not going to retaliate in kind, leaving President-Elect Trump to tweet: "Great move on delay (by V. Putin). I always knew he was very smart!"

For those who believed a kind and gentler Trump would emerge during the New Year and surprise everyone with his wisdom and beneficence, Donald J. tweeted an end-of-year Greeting:

Donald J. Trump

✓ @realDonaldTrump

Happy New Year to all, including to my many enemies and those who have fought me and lost so badly they just don't know what to do. Love!

5:17 AM – 31 Dec 2016

Donald just cannot control his malignant aggression syndrome and shout out to his enemies, to kick them in the face and insult them, especially when they are down, and then out of the fullness of his being wish everyone: Love! Curiously, Trumpspeak had become the political lingua franca of the New Era. While Putin declined to respond to the U.S. expelling Russian diplomats and shutting down some Russian luxury spy nests for the hacking of the Democrats in the election, Russian spokeswoman Maria Zarakhova tweeted that "the Obama team are embittered and dimwitted foreign policy losers, [and] humiliate Americans with anti-Russia sanctions," while the Russian embassy in London tweeted out a picture of a duck emblazoned with the word "lame" (see illustration below). While during the Cold War, the U.S. and U.S.S.R. would call each other names, the current

 **Russian Embassy, UK** ✓
@RussianEmbassy

President Obama expels 35 ▬ diplomats in Cold War deja vu. As everybody, incl 🇺🇸 people, will be glad to see the last of this hapless Adm.

RETWEETS	LIKES
1,170	834

12:09 PM - 29 Dec 2016

© Twitter Russian Embassy UK

discourse had a Trumpian inflection and suggested that Trumpspeak would be the language of the new era.

The Trump Inauguration brigade, however, was having trouble getting celebrities to show up for the inauguration, which would be a mournful event for over half of the nation and most of the civilized world. After every A and B list celebrity refused the Trumpsters, they bragged that they had bagged the Rockettes for the inauguration, but there soon was dissent among the Radio City Music Hall dancing troupe, and their manager said performing at the inauguration would be voluntary. Although Alec Baldwin joked that he had offered to play Trump at the inauguration and sing "Highway to Hell," his performance had not been confirmed. And most insulting, of the former presidents invited, only Jimmy Carter had allegedly sent his RSVP.[129]

Trump gamely tweeted that he wanted the people and not celebrities to celebrate his inauguration, but this is another Big Lie as no individual on the face of the earth had been more celebrity-besotted than Donald J. Trump, and the refusal of A, B, and even C and below list celebs to entertain at his inaugural is no doubt causing sleepless nights, temper tantrums, and fantasies of Big League Revenge in the sweaty beds of Trump Tower.

While Team Trump worried about the paucity of celebrity response to their invitation to the fast-approaching inauguration, pundits did their annual reflection on the past year and many saw it as the worst year in recent memory. Comedian Dave Barry opened the year with "Dave Barry's Year in Review: Trump and the 'hideous monstrosity' that was 2016" in the *Washington Post* and went through the horror show of 2016 month by month.[130] My hometown *Los Angeles Times* featured a hilarious "Fake News History of 2016" by David Horsey starting with January: "Donald Trump shoots someone in the middle of 5th Avenue. The NRA immediately endorses him. His poll numbers soar."[131] Yet one of the best yearly reviews of 2016 was the *New York Times* who in an editorial opined: "Take a Bad Year. And Make it Better." The *Times* Editorial Board recognized that 2016 was pretty bad, writing:

> Let's pretend we're in some cosmic therapist's office, in a counseling session with the year 2016. We are asked to face the year and say something nice about it. Just one or two things.
>
> The mind balks. Fingers tighten around the Kleenex as a cascade of horribles wells up in memory: *You were a terrible year. We hate you. We'll be so glad never to see you again.* The silence echoes as we grope for a reply.
>
> The Cubs?

Looking back on the last 12 months, those who feel miserable and afraid have plenty of justification. For many it was the election of a president unfit for the job. He seems to want to run the country like some authoritarian game-show host, but we don't really know what he'll do, and uncertainty worsens the sickening feeling.

Yet so many bad things happened, from the unthinkable to the horrifying to the merely shocking. Things fell apart. Tyrants and terrorists trailed blood and rubble across the Middle East and Europe. Refugees drowned in the Mediterranean. Right-wing extremism and xenophobia were on the march. The American election let loose old racial hatreds. The planet got hotter; the Arctic went haywire. The world was burning or smoldering or blowing up or melting.[132]

However, *The Times* Editorial Board also recognized in 2016 "the power of unity, of drawing close, and of speaking out. Of the strength that solidarity wielded in 2016, over and over."[133] They recalled the disparate struggles throughout the country to raise the minimum wage and the more than two dozen states and localities that have enacted legislation to produce higher wages for workers. While immigrants and refugees were demonized by the Trump campaign and globally by resurgent right-wing nationalist movements, there were also examples of the embrace of refugees by families and communities, and many major cities, states, and localities have pledged themselves to protect immigrants and to resist any mass acts of repression by the Trump administration. It was a year that recognized Black Lives Matter with a national protest movement against police violence directed at people of color; there were movements by Native Americans and their allies, including veterans, to protect Native Lands against the oil industry; a global movement fought to protect the earth and an important climate change agreement was made in Paris. Cures were found for the Zika virus and there was progress for an effective Ebola vaccine. And, I would add, the Bernie Sanders movement, building on the Occupy movements of 2011, show a radicalized youth struggling for progressive social change and transformation.[134]

It is certain, however, that U.S. politics in the Age of Trump will involve permanent war in Washington among different political groups, and a war of Washington against liberal and enlightened sectors of the U.S. society and polity, which could unleash significant forces of resistance. Upon Trump's election, there had already been a week of demonstrations and sit-ins protesting his presidency and there were plans for demonstrations on his inauguration day and the following day a Women's March was planned in Washington and in cities throughout the country and world.

Hence, while the Trump administration may be an American Horror Show, forces of resistance and solidarity may enable us to make it through the Trump era which promises to be one of intense conflict and repression. If we make it through to a new era, it will take intelligence, courage, solidarities, and the hard political work of mobilizing, organizing, and fighting the reactionary forces gathered around Donald Trump and his political allies and supporters. U.S. politics run in cycles, and it is highly possible that there could be immediate reaction against the horror show of a Trump administration, that his regime will implode and self-destruct in a morass of in-fighting, scandal, scissions, and intense opposition, all of which will help us make it through the nightmare and into a new dawn of democracy.

As 2017 unfolded, Trump continued assembling his administration and while he had promised to "drain the swamps," his selection of cabinet members and other high officials came out of the swamps of the billionaire class, rightwing militarists and ideologues, and the dank nether regions of Wall Street, Goldman Sachs, and other big corporations against which candidate Donald J. Trump had railed and claimed that Hillary Clinton was the tool of these corporate and political interests. Hence, in the next section, based on the pre-Inauguration events of January 2017, I will tongue-in-cheek describe the King of the Swamps Donald J. Trump assembling his Swamp Creatures and preparing the fields of Washington for swamps of corruption, cronyism, militarism, and craziness, such as the still-stunned nation and dangerous world had never yet observed.

SWAMP KING

For the New Year's holiday, the Swamp King gamboled and putted around one of his mansions, in the Royal Resort of Mar-a-Lago in the swamplands of Florida. The King was pictured at his holiday swamp resort with Don King, a fight promoter of yesteryear who had stomped an associate to death, and done some prison time. On New Year's Eve, the Swamp King was pictured with his old pal Joey No Socks Cinque, an ex-felon with mob connections, who, as head of a phony American Academy of Hospitality Sciences, had bestowed their Star Diamond awards upon the Swamp King that he proudly displayed in his royal mansions. New Year's video showed the Swamp King and Joey No Socks standing next to each other in front of a crowd of revelers who cheered rapturously as the King promised to slash Obamacare and build a wall along the Mexican border, with Joey pumping his arms up and down with glee as the crowd roared.

Meanwhile, in the Swamps of Washington, the most immoral Swamp Creatures of the House labored mightily, in secret, to gut the Office of Congressional Ethics, set up after their fellow Republican Swamp Monsters had committed crimes so grievous that the more refined denizens of the Congressional Swamp were embarrassed and set up an independent agency to monitor the most unacceptable actions and crimes of the Swamps of Congress.[135] The Republican charge to destroy the Office of Congressional Ethics was led by Rep. Robert Goodlatte (R.-Va), and angry denizens of his fiefdom stormed his office to give him a New Year's card offering greetings to the Swamp Thing, with Goodlatte's body replaced by a photo of the movie monster.[136]

But Lo and Behold!, the Swamp King himself sent out a tweet admonishing the Swamp Creatures of Congress to invest their energies into more profitable enterprises, such as creating tax cuts for the richest members of the Swamp, that would most benefit the King and his cronies, or build a giant wall along the deserts of Mexico to keep people of color out of the United White States of Swampland. And Behold! The Twitter of the King sent the Swamp

Creatures of Congress scurrying into the secret chambers of the Swamp House, and they decided after all not to put aside their Office of Congressional Ethics, at least for the time being, as it had angered the Swamp King and his followers on social media who wanted the swamps drained.[137]

The war between the Swamp King and his intelligence services seemed to continue apace, however, as the King declared that his intelligence briefing over the Russian hacking into the election had been postponed until Friday, January 11, which the King found "strange," while the intelligence officials insisted that the briefing had always been scheduled for the date, so either the King was confused, or hadn't learned to check with the authorities before sending out his tweets.

The Swamp King's war with U.S. intelligence services took another weird – really strange!- turn on January 4, 2017, when following an appearance by WikiLeaks founder and international fugitive from justice Julian Assange on Fox's *Sean Hannity Show* (the most fawningly pro-Trump show on TV), the Swamp King tweeted respectful quotes from Assange, accepting his judgement (lie?) that the Russian didn't do the WikiLeaks hack and that a 14-year-old could have hacked the Democrats. Hence, the Swamp King is allying himself with Assange, deemed a traitor by members of the Obama administration and U.S. intelligence services, against U.S. intelligence services that had concluded that it was the Russians who had hacked U.S. politicians and parties and selectively distributed the results through WikiLeaks. TV networks embarrassed the Swamp King by playing footage from 2010 when the King described WikiLeaks as "disgraceful" and said that his new buddy Assange should be subject to "the death penalty."

The next day there were Republican-led hearings on the Russian hacking, and while the Swamp King had announced over the New Year's weekend that he was a "smart guy" and "knew things" about the Russian hacking that ordinary people did not have access to, the intelligence chiefs and Senators seemed to think that the Swamp King was neither so smart or well-informed, and his advisors hoped that the intelligence chiefs set to brief him the next day would set him straight about the Russian hacking and attendant dangers to his Kingdom from foreign cyberhackers.

The Swamp King also dredged in early January a Swamp Creature from the Swamp of Wall Street by announcing that he was to nominate Wall Street lawyer, Jay Clayton, to head the Securities and Exchange Commission (SEC). Clayton, who had dutifully done work for Goldman Sachs – who Trump had vilified during the campaign but now is using key members of the firm for his economic team –, is tasked with playing a key role in the Swamp King's efforts to usher in a period of deregulation. The King's priming the Swamp includes undoing parts of 2010's financial reform legislation, known as the Dodd-Frank Act, so that Wall Street can return to the depths of the Swamp of Corruption and Speculation that led to the spectacular crashes of 2007–2008, and that had justified the regulation that the Swamp King was planning to undo, hence signaling to the Wall Street Swamp Creatures that once again they could do their predatory worst.

Sadly, if confirmed by the Senate, Clayton would replace the Honorable Mary Jo White, who, known for her intelligence and fairness, had strengthened the SEC's enforcement efforts over the last three years, "pushing for more companies to admit guilt and taking more cases to trial. And during her term, the SEC has been a central player part of the Obama administration's effort to rein in big banks following the 2008 financial crisis and prevent future taxpayer bailouts of the industry. The agency has pushed for more oversight of hedge funds and other asset managers and has established rules that make it more difficult for big banks to make risky bets on the markets."[138]

Continuing to draft Goldman Sachs people into his administration, guaranteeing that they would largely determine a Wall Street and Billionaire-friendly economic agenda, Trump appointed Dina H. Powell, a Goldman partner who heads impact investing, as a White House advisor. In addition, Trump choose Anthony Scaramucci, a Goldman Sachs alumunus who founded SkyBridge Capital, to have a general advisory role with his economic team.

The Swamp King continued into January selecting brackish Swamp Creatures to help him extract maximum wealth and exert dirty power within the Swamp. The King and his minions chose

Robert Lighthizer to be America's next chief trade negotiator who would work with Swamp Hawk and Ideologue Peter Navarro as trade adviser. Lighthizer has advocated increasing tariffs and repeatedly criticized China for failing to adhere to international trade practices, saying tougher methods were needed to change the system. Swamp ideologue Navarro had previously described China's government as a "despicable, parasitic, brutal, brass-knuckled, crass, callous, amoral, ruthless and totally totalitarian imperialist power."[139] Putting anti-China Swamp Creatures in charge of trade antagonized the Kingdom of China, who drawing on their ancient cultural traditions warned: "May the arrogant Americans realize that the United States of America is perhaps just a shooting star in the ample sky of history."[140]

Former Indiana Senator and Vice President Dan Quayle was considered the dimmest light bulb in the room during his undistinguished time as the butt of media "deer in the deadlights" jokes. So it is perhaps not surprising that the Swamp King would choose Quayle's "protégé" Senator Dan Coats (R-Ind) to succeed James Clapper as director of national intelligence. Not only is Coats not the brightest light bulb in Washington, but he is a fan of NSA surveillance, suggesting that the Swamp King wants to build a National Surveillance State. Coats is a detractor of Edward Snowden, an advocate of torture, and opposed to closing Guantanamo Bay (which, by the way, is part of Cuba), and would be dedicated to focusing intelligence on doing the most frightening and anti-democratic activity that the King and his Swamp Creatures can dream up.

In 1984, George Orwell drew an unforgettable portrait of a totalitarian state where "Big Brother is Watching You!" through omnipresent television sets dedicated to state propaganda. Barack Obama's intelligence services have given the Swamp King an unparalleled apparatus of surveillance to monitor email and social media, telephone, and other technologies of communication which give the state unparalleled power to monitor all aspects of individual life. What will the Swamp King and his minions do with this apparatus and what will happen to privacy? Orwell's regime in 1984 was also post-truth where the state defined what was true and what was false, just like the Swamp King in his relentless tweets and rants to the public.

Meanwhile, the Swamp King continued his war against the current U.S. intelligence services who had concluded that the King's Best Bro Russian President Vladimir V. Putin had directed a vast cyberattack aimed at denying Hillary Clinton the presidency and installing the King in the Oval Office. In a Senate Hearing, top Senators of both parties accepted the report's findings, but the King was skeptical, even after getting a two-hour briefing at Trump Tower in New York with the top leaders of America's intelligence agencies.

Soon after leaving the meeting, intelligence officials released the declassified, damning report that described the sophisticated cyber campaign as "part of a continuing Russian effort to weaken the United States government and its democratic institutions. The report – a virtually unheard-of, real-time revelation by the American intelligence agencies that undermined the legitimacy of the president who is about to direct them – made the case that Mr. Trump was the favored candidate of Mr. Putin. The Russian leader, the report said, sought to denigrate Mrs. Clinton, and the report detailed what the officials had revealed to President Obama a day earlier: Mr. Trump's victory followed a complicated, multipart cyberinformation attack whose goal had evolved to help the Republican win."[141]

The day of the briefing, however, the Swamp King used his Twitter account to tell the nation the really important news of the day: "Wow, the ratings are in and Arnold Schwarzenegger got 'swamped' (or destroyed) by comparison to the ratings machine, DJT… So much for being a movie star–and that was season 1 compared to season 14. Now compare him to my season 1. But who cares, he supported Kasich & Hillary." The Swamp King was referring to the TV-show *Celebrity Apprentice* that the King had produced and starred in for years, and still served as Executive Producer, since being President is not so important or prestigious for a Swamp King as being affiliated with a reality-TV show. And while former body-builder and California Governor Arnold Schwarzenegger had been chosen to take-over as host for him, Arnold had not supported the King's political endeavors, and when he got poor ratings during his inaugural show as host, the Swamp King used his Twitter venom against Arnold who responded:

4:42 AM – 6 Jan 2017 Arnold

✓ @Schwarzenegger

I wish you the best of luck and I hope you'll work for ALL of the American people as aggressively as you worked for your ratings.[142]

It was incredible how much the Swamp King was twittering as his inauguration day approached. He had attacked car companies (Toyota and General Motors being his latest targets for building auto plants in Mexico and elsewhere rather than the U.S.). Trump also attacked airplane manufacturers and other key sectors of industry in his daily multiple tweet tirade, many of which companies suffered decline in the stock market after being attacked by the King, creating a great fear among the Titans of Industry that their company could be the next target of Trump's Great Twitter Wrath.[143] Analyzing his tweet-barrage over the Christmas holidays, astute former anchorman Keith Olbermann, forced by TV-severance agreements to stay off of the medium of TV news, circulated a YouTube that through a close reading of seven of the Swamp King's recent tweets concluded that Donald J. Trump was not a well man and that dangerous times lay ahead for his Kingdom.[144]

Meanwhile, as The Swamp King fought his multiple daily Twitter wars, his sleazy son Donald Jr. worked to make it easier to buy gun silencers so that shooters like himself could fire their weapons more silently.[145] Earlier in the year, the Sleazy Son was forced to take his name off of a website that promised a hunting trip with the son and a meeting with the Swamp King if fellow shooters donated a substantial sum to charity. While this was deemed unseemly for the First Swamp Family, Jr.'s behavior suggested that there would be a lot of shooting and love for guns during the King's Reign.

There would also be intense and protracted war between the Swamp King, Hollywood, and the media during his realm. A preview of the contempt with which the creative community of the Kingdom looks upon the Donald was viewed by the world in a speech by Hollywood Royalty Meryl Streep at the 74th Golden Globes in

Beverly Hills, California. After receiving the Cecil B. DeMille Award for lifetime achievement, Ms. Streep made a plea for empathy, press freedom, and opposing bigotry and intolerance, telling the audience which was on its feet giving her a standing applause:

Please sit down. Thank you. I love you all. You'll have to forgive me. I've lost my voice in screaming and lamentation this weekend. And I have lost my mind sometime earlier this year, so I have to read.

Thank you, Hollywood Foreign Press. Just to pick up on what Hugh Laurie said: You and all of us in this room really belong to the most vilified segments in American society right now. Think about it: Hollywood, foreigners and the press.

But who are we, and what is Hollywood anyway? It's just a bunch of people from other places. I was born and raised and educated in the public schools of New Jersey. Viola was born in a sharecropper's cabin in South Carolina, came up in Central Falls, Rhode Island; Sarah Paulson was born in Florida, raised by a single mom in Brooklyn. Sarah Jessica Parker was one of seven or eight kids in Ohio. Amy Adams was born in Vicenza, Italy. And Natalie Portman was born in Jerusalem. Where are their birth certificates? And the beautiful Ruth Negga was born in Addis Ababa, Ethiopia, raised in London – no, in Ireland I do believe, and she's here nominated for playing a girl in small-town Virginia.

Ryan Gosling, like all of the nicest people, is Canadian, and Dev Patel was born in Kenya, raised in London, and is here playing an Indian raised in Tasmania. So Hollywood is crawling with outsiders and foreigners. And if we kick them all out you'll have nothing to watch but football and mixed martial arts, which are not the arts.

They gave me three seconds to say this, so: An actor's only job is to enter the lives of people who are different from us, and let you feel what that feels like. And there were many, many, many powerful performances this year that did exactly that. Breathtaking, compassionate work.

But there was one performance this year that stunned me. It sank its hooks in my heart. Not because it was good; there was nothing good about it. But it was effective and it did its job. It made its intended audience laugh, and show their teeth. It was that moment when the person asking to sit in the most respected seat in our country imitated a disabled reporter. Someone he outranked in privilege, power and the capacity to fight back. It kind of broke my heart when I saw it, and I still can't get it out of my head, because it wasn't in a movie. It was real life. And this instinct to humiliate, when it's modeled by someone in the public platform, by someone powerful, it filters down into everybody's life, because it kinda gives permission for other people to do the same thing. Disrespect invites disrespect, violence incites violence. And when the powerful use their position to bully others we all lose. O.K., go on with it.

O.K., this brings me to the press. We need the principled press to hold power to account, to call him on the carpet for every outrage. That's why our founders enshrined the press and its freedoms in the Constitution. So I only ask the famously well-heeled Hollywood Foreign Press and all of us in our community to join me in supporting the Committee to Protect Journalists, because we're gonna need them going forward, and they'll need us to safeguard the truth.

One more thing: Once, when I was standing around on the set one day, whining about something – you know we were gonna work through supper or the long hours or whatever, Tommy Lee Jones said to me, "Isn't it such a privilege, Meryl, just to be an actor?" Yeah, it is, and we have to remind each other of the privilege and the responsibility of the act of empathy. We should all be proud of the work Hollywood honors here tonight.

As my friend, the dear departed Princess Leia, said to me once, take your broken heart, make it into art.[146]

The celebrity-worshipping Swamp King struck back immediately, dismissing Queen Streep as "a Hillary lover," and noting he was "not surprised" that he had come under attack from "liberal movie people." Still seething, Trump tweeted in deranged fury the next day, denouncing Streep as "one of the most over-rated actresses in Hollywood" and "a Hillary flunky who lost big." The King did not respond to the fact that the entire Golden Globes show featured attacks on him, starting with host Jimmy Fallon who assured the country that the Globes were awarded according to "the popular vote" (a point hitting a sore spot for the King who lost the popular vote by almost 3 million), who referenced Russian hacking, Trump's troubles booking performers for his inauguration, and compared Trump with King Joffrey on "Game of Thrones" (a reference that I didn't get). I did get Hugh Laurie's witticism, during his remarks after winning for his work in the TV-mini-series drama *The Night Manager*, that he assumed this would be the last Golden Globes celebration because the organization "has Hollywood, Foreign and Press in the title. And I think to some Republicans, even Association is slightly sketchy." The crowd wildly applauded every critical reference to the Swamp King, with Meryl Streep getting standing applause. Henceforth, U.S. entertainment culture would strive to see who could make the most-cutting jokes, the most sharp take-down, and the most compelling critique of the Swamp King, his minions, and his policies, guaranteeing that the cultural wars would be of unprecedented scope and interest during the Swamp King's reign.

Senate Hearings were to begin on six of the Swamp King's most controversial choices for his administration on January 10, 2017, and the King himself was to give his first press conference in months the next day. However, some of the King's billionaire nominees had not filled out proper ethics and financial disclosure forms so some Senate Hearings for his Swamp Creatures were delayed.

DONALD J. TRUMP: USEFUL IDIOT OR
PUTIN'S POODLE?

As the political class prepared for the Congressional Hearings vetting of DJT's Swamp Creatures on January 9, 2017, a bombshell revelation was dropped concerning how Intelligence chiefs had briefed Trump and Obama on unconfirmed claims Russia has compromising information on the president-elect. CNN reported only that a two-page summary of the report "was presented last week to President Barack Obama and President-elect Trump [and] included allegations that Russian operatives claim to have compromising personal and financial information about Mr. Trump." The dossier cited "multiple U.S. officials with direct knowledge of the briefings," and said the FBI was investigating. *BuzzFeed* published what it said was the full report "compiled by a person who has claimed to be a former British intelligence official."

The dossier was reportedly composed by a former British spy named Christopher Steele who "had served undercover in Moscow in the early 1990s and later was the top expert on Russia at the London headquarters of Britain's spy service, MI6. When he stepped down in 2009, he started his own commercial intelligence firm, Orbis Business Intelligence." He was reportedly hired by first Republican and then Democratic Party political operatives to assemble a dossier of incriminating material concerning the connections between Donald Trump and Russia. His report had been allegedly circulated among political operatives, the media, and U.S. and U.K. intelligence services when *Buzzfeeed* decided to print it, even though no one had proved the allegations, many salacious, to be true.[147]

The dossier began with descriptions of Trump's allegedly salacious behavior during a trip to Russia where it was claimed that Russian security agents watched Trump engaging in "perverted sexual acts" that were "arranged/monitored by the FSB," the Kremlin's leading spy agency.[148] The FSB, it said, "employed a number of prostitutes to perform a golden showers (urination) show in front of him."[149] Not only that, according to the report's anonymous Russian sources, Trump deliberately chose for his escapade "the Ritz Carlton hotel, where he knew President and Mrs. Obama (whom he hated) had stayed on one of their official trips to Russia and defiling the bed where they had slept."[150] More incriminating, the dossier was full of material suggesting that there had been ongoing contacts between members of Trump's inner circle and representatives of Moscow during the election and that Moscow was exerting itself on behalf of Trump's presidential campaign.

Trump quickly denied the report in a Twitter post without referring to its details. "FAKE NEWS – A TOTAL POLITICAL WITCH HUNT!" he shouted out. In succeeding posts, he assailed the U.S. intelligence services for putting such salacious fare in an appendix to an official report, and in his-long awaited press conference on January 13, 2017 claimed that such a release of slanderous documents was "something that Nazi Germany would have done and did," thus comparing U.S. intelligence services to Nazi Germany."[151] Intelligence experts said that no president or presidential-elect had so insulted U.S. intelligence services, and that the breach between Trump and the intelligence establishment appeared to be massive, endangering U.S. national security that required reliable intelligence and good relations between the executive branch and the intelligence services to protect the nation, thus dramatizing again the danger of the Swamp King presidency.

In his press conference, Trump insisted that the story about the Russian prostitutes could not possibly have been true because he is a well-known "germaphobe." In addition, the Swamp King went into great detail about his knowledge of how Russians bugged hotel rooms of those they wanted to compromise with "small cameras" everywhere. Trump also savaged the media in his press conference and refused to answer the question of CNN's Jim Acosta because "your organization is terrible" (CNN had discussed the Buzzfeed Trump/Russia dossier), concluding his anti-CNN rant with the royal proclamation: "You are fake news."

This little twist showed how Trump was able to turn around a critique aimed at him and his supporters of manufacturing fake news to help him win the election into an attack on his critics. It was also the first time media critics could remember a president-elect attacking the news media with such vigor before he had even taken office. Yet another spin of this amazing media spectacle is possible. Trump's first press conference in six months was initially organized so that Trump could tell how he was going to divest himself of his business interests before assuming the presidency, and at the event Trump announced, as anticipated, that his sons were going to run his businesses and that he was in no way divesting himself of his business interests – as had Vice-President Nelson Rockefeller, one of the richest people in America, and everyone else who assumed the offices of Vice President or President, including those that had modest interests, such as Jimmy Carter who sold his peanut farm, and Barack Obama who put his modest financial interests in a blind trust.

Trump dutifully assigned a PR flack to announce his "divestment plan," and pointed to boxes on a table behind her that had divestment documents in them (reporters who peaked in the boxes found some empty). Yet by focusing his news conference on his tirade against CNN and attack on the media, Trump diverted attention from the fact that he, allegedly the richest president-select in modern times, had not taken the divestment steps that had been previously taken by major politicians at the top of the political hierarchy. Nor had Trump released his taxes as had every president and candidate since Richard Nixon, nor did anyone really know the scope of Trump's business interests, what and where they were, how much debt he owed and to whom, nor did the public know who might have compromising information on him. Hence, any decision Trump made as president could involve a conflict of interest, and guaranteed that his administration would be trapped in a morass of scandal. From this perspective, Trump's assault on the media and the *Buzzfeed* dossier could be a diversion to switch media focus from problems with his business conflicts of interest to an assault on the media that positioned him as a victim.

Friday the 13th was not a lucky day for Donald J. Trump as footage was released of an interview with civil rights icon John Lewis who said that he was going to boycott the presidential inauguration since he believes that Trump was "not a legitimate president" because of election meddling by the Russians "and others." In an interview for the Sunday edition of *Meet the Press*, footage showed a pained Lewis questioning the legitimacy of the president, and when asked by interviewer Chuck Todd what people should do about it, Lewis evoked the memory of Martin Luther King and told people to speak out and protest.

Never before in my lifetime had the legitimacy of the presidency been so questioned, nor had a president-elect had lower ratings in the days before his inauguration. Since the accusations of Trump's all-too-cozy relations with the Russians and failure to divest his businesses, release his tax forms, and show a willingness for transparency, Trump's approval poll numbers have been going down,[152] and he has responded with increasingly aggressive Twitter blasts raising questions about his stability and ability to govern. Curiously, it was Trump himself who throughout the primary and then the general election was claiming that the system was "rigged" if he lost a primary, or fell behind in polling in the general election. Further, Trump refused to commit to accepting the results of the election if he did not come out ahead, thus putting in question the system's legitimacy.

In addition, the FBI's legitimacy was now in question as the Obama administration announced that the Inspector General would investigate FBI Director James Comey's interventions in the election by making public pronouncements concerning Hillary Clinton's emails and then announcing a new investigation into Clinton's email nine days before the election, while failing to note that there were investigations of relations between the Trump campaign and the Russians, connections that Congress and other government entities were now investigating. On Friday the 13th, FBI Chief James Comey met behind closed doors with Congressional leaders to brief them on FBI investigations, but Comey would not discuss investigations into connections between the Trump campaign and administration and the Russians, angering Democratic members of Congress, and leading Maxine Waters (Rep. Cal) to declare after the meeting that "The FBI Director had no credibility."

A battle between Republican Congressional Trump flacks and the federal government erupted after Walter Shaub Jr., director of the

Office of Government Ethics, "issued a stern and unusually public rebuke of President-elect Donald Trump's business separation plans. Rep. Jason Chaffetz (R-Utah), chairman of the GOP-led House Oversight and Government Reform Committee, summoned Shaub to come to the House to answer questions about his comments. The summons 'was viewed by ethics experts as a veiled threat to the budget of the Office of Government Ethics unless its director changes his rhetoric and approach.'"[153]

There was also a flap about a report that Lt. Gen. Michael T. Flynn, appointed to be Trump's national security adviser, spoke with Sergei I. Kislyak, the Russian ambassador to the United States, the day before President Obama imposed sanctions on Russia for election hacking, raising questions as to whether the Trump administration was feeding government information to Moscow to curry favor; Flynn had already been pictured as friendly with Putin, had appeared on *Russia Today (RT)*, the Kremlin's TV station, and was a key part of Trump's pro-Russian coterie.[154] Trump flacks insisted that Flynn was just trying to arrange a phone call between President Vladimir Putin and Trump once he becomes president, although obviously Trump and his bro Putin could call each other anytime without arranging a call weeks in advance.

Indeed, there was speculation in discussions on CNN and MSNBC on Friday the 13th whether Trump was a "useful idiot" of the Russians or a "Manchurian candidate" manufactured to serve as a Russian puppet, or as Putin's Poodle.[155] Trump couldn't say enough nice things about Vlad Putin, angering Republican allies who correctly see Putin as a thug and dictator. Further, Trump's position on NATO, Syria, his endless praise of Putin, and his constant calls for friendly relations with Russia certainly serve Putin's and Russia's interests. To top it off, Trump's appointment of Rex Tillerson as Secretary of State, a man who accepted a Russian Order of Friendship award given to him personally by Putin in 2013, after Tillerson cut big league oil deals with Russia, correspond completely with Russia/Putin's interests. With investigations underway into connections between the Russians and the Trump campaign, this issue was not going to fade away.[156]

Taking on the bizarre and mind-boggling connections between Trump and his circle and Russia, and the incredible Russian hacking of DNC emails that has to be one of the most surreal and perhaps consequential crimes against the Republic in US history, Malcolm Nance addressed these issues in his astonishing *The Plot to Hack America. How Putin's Cyberspies and WikiLeaks Tried to Steal the 2016 Election*, obviously published before the election. With a strong background in intelligence and counterterrorism, Nance explores the Russian connections of Trump and his associates, and the ways that Russia traditionally recruits agents and manipulates useful idiots. Nance demonstrates that Putin and the Russians launched a major operation to hack DNC and other email in the U.S. to intervene in the 2016 election, a story that has yet to unfold completely, but that is starting to peep through the dark curtain of Russian deception and to raise frightening questions about Donald Trump and his associates.

So far, there is no incriminating evidence that Donald Trump or any member of his inner circle are Russian agents. Yet following Nance's analysis, it is clear that it is in Russia's interests to promote a candidate who would carry out Trump's policies, and Trump himself has run a campaign, and assembled a transition team, cabinet, and administration, that could undermine and even destroy U.S. democracy and diminish the U.S. position in the world. Trump's campaign divided the country with his attacks on Mexicans, immigrants, Muslims, women, the disabled, the media, and whoever dared criticize him. He attempted to destroy his Republican opponents, and then Hillary Clinton, rather than just to beat them, with nasty names, innuendo, personal attacks, and a daily barrage of Twitter insults. Twitter, in Trump's hands, is itself a weapon to undermine democracy which requires dialogue, debate, deliberation, compromise, and consensus. Trump's Twitter attacks by contrast polarize, inflame, alienate, and divide.

Having clearly divided U.S. society and polity through his campaign and his transition period, Trump is set out to destroy many key elements of the liberal democratic polity that has been developed since the New Deal. Trump's proposed Attorney General Jeff Sessions "was denied appointment as a federal judge in 1986 for a slew of racist comments, including calling the work of the NAACP and ACLU 'un-American.' He has also repeatedly spoken out against the federal Voting Rights Act."[157] Hence, Sessions, if confirmed, could undo decades of progressive civil rights and voting rights legislation, thus weakening the Justice Department.

Secretary of Education, Betsy DeVos is a sharp critic of public schools who has favored charter schools and vouchers, and could undermine the U.S. system of public education that has served us well, despite its flaws, for decades. The environment will be under assault with climate change denier and enemy of environmental regulation, Scott Pruitt appointed to run the Environmental Protection Agency (EPA). With Ben Carson appointed to head the Department of Housing and Urban Development, Trump has chosen someone who has expressed opposition to social safety net programs and fair housing initiatives and could undermine public housing initiatives and programs. Andrew Puzder, nominated as Trump's labor secretary, has been an outspoken opponent of a meaningful increase in the federal minimum wage, and has been a critic of efforts by the Obama administration to update the rules for overtime-pay eligibility. And Rick Perry, a tool of Texas oil interests, named to head Trump's Department of Energy, has called for the elimination of the very department he has been asked to head and generally opposes oil and energy regulation (see above).

Trump's billionaire cabinet, chosen from Goldman Sachs and the Swamps of Wall Street and Big Corporations, will support income tax cuts for the super wealthy, and could dramatically increase income inequality. The rightwing Republicans that serve his administration are deeply committed to destroying the Affordable Care Act and have talked of privatizing Medicare, Social Security, and other government programs. Taken cumulatively, the Trump administration thus constitutes a clear and present danger to U.S. democracy and could seriously weaken the country.

Of course, Trump, his family, and many in his administration are highly scandal prone and burdened with conflicts of interests. An example of Trump family conflict of business interest broke on Friday the 13th with revelations on *The Rachel Maddow Show* that Donald J. Trump had bailed out a South Carolina company owned by Donald Jr. which had subsequently gone bust. It turns out the company's site was seriously polluted, and South Carolina was in a quandary whether it was a good idea to sue the President and his son for a big environmental mess they'd dumped on South Carolina.[158]

Trump started out Martin Luther King holiday weekend with a Twitter attack on John Lewis, who had marched with King and was an icon in the civil rights movement, and who in an interview the same week called in question the legitimacy of the Trump presidency and announced that he would skip the coming inaugural ceremony. Trump exploded in Twitter Rage tweeting: "Congressman John Lewis should spend more time on fixing and helping his district, which is in horrible shape and falling apart (not to mention crime infested) rather than falsely complaining about the election results. All talk, talk, talk – no action or results. Sad!"

The media, Democrats and even many Republicans exploded in fury at Trump's attack on Civil Rights icon John Lewis. Ben Sasse, a Republican senator for Nebraska, tweeted: "John Lewis and his 'talk' have changed the world." Further, "Conservative commentator Bill Kristol posted: 'It's telling, I'm afraid, that Donald Trump treats Vladimir Putin with more respect than he does John Lewis.' Evan McMullin, a former CIA officer who ran as an independent conservative in the presidential election, said: 'While you avoided the draft, John Lewis risked his life for equality in America. You'll never even dream of such selfless patriotism, Donald.'"[159] And Charles M. Blow wrote: "Stop and think about what you just read: A lecher attacking a legend; a man of moral depravity attacking a man of moral certitude; an intellectual weakling attacking a warrior for justice. This on Martin Luther King Jr. weekend, no less."[160]

Throughout the Martin Luther King holiday weekend, criticisms of Trump's nasty Twitter assault on John Lewis continued to mushroom. Trump's comment that Lewis' "district, … is in horrible shape and falling apart (not to mention crime infested)" was easily disproved with footage of nice and well-kept neighborhoods in Lewis' district, attesting that Trump operates with a racist stereotype of African-American neighborhoods as crime-ridden and run-down. Over the weekend, at least 23 members of Congress announced that they would not be attending Trump's inauguration, some noting that their absence would be a response to Trump's comments on Lewis. Hence, once again Trump revealed a deep-rooted insensitivity to the African-American community and people of color (the inauguration boycott number of Lewis' congressional colleagues would rise to one-third of House Democrats, the largest inauguration boycott ever).

Trump's poll approval numbers continued to go down with only 44% approving of Trump's behavior during the transition according to a Gallup poll, while a Quinnipiac University poll showed only 37% approval. By contrast, previous Gallup polls had scored a 68% approval of Bill Clinton just before his taking office, 61% approved of George W. Bush, "and a whopping 83% approved of Barack Obama."[161] In a *Washington Post-ABC* poll, only 40 percent of those polled had a favorable impression of Trump, while 54 percent view him unfavorably and 41 percent have "a strongly unfavorable impression of him." Consequently, "President-elect Donald Trump will take the oath of office Friday as the least popular incoming president in at least four decades."[162]

Further, Trump freaked out European leaders when he said in an interview with major European media that he thought the European Union was bound for a break-up and that NATO was obsolete. Ignorant Pundit Trump opined that the 28-nation European Union (whose number of member countries Trump got wrong) was a vehicle for German interests and that he was indifferent to the bloc's fate, while expressing skepticism about NATO. Europe was already deeply alarmed as anti-immigrant and Euroskeptic leaders continued to gain popularity and now had Trump as a champion. It appeared that the U.S.-Europe alliance which had kept the peace and guaranteed 60-plus years of stability was threatened for the first time as Vladmir Putin and Trump's Russian and pro-Russian comrades chortled with glee.

As the inauguration approached, Washington opinion leaders got increasingly nervous with predictions of disaster for the coming Trump administration. On January 17, 2017, the headline story read that and six Op-Ed pieces on the *Washington Post* website read=Opinions

Trump's presidency is doomed

- By Richard Cohen

Trump's troubles have just begun, Post-ABC poll shows

- By Jennifer Rubin

A parting gift from Obama's most trusted: A Donald Trump survival guide

- By Jonathan Capehart

Media, don't play Trump's game of divide and conquer

- By Katrina vanden Heuvel

Just when you thought Trump's ethics disaster couldn't get worse, it did

- By Richard Painter and Norman Eisen

Trump gets no respect. That's because he hasn't earned it.

- By Dana Milbank[163]

There was speculation concerning whether protests would outstrip and overshadow the inauguration. Although presidential inaugurations have traditionally been star-studded affairs with Beyoncé and Kelly Clarkson performing at Barack Obama's second inauguration in 2013 and Aretha Franklin singing at his first in 2009, major celebrities had refused to participate in Trump's inauguration events, although many planned to protest, including Scarlett Johansson, Katy Perry, Amy Schumer, Julianne Moore, and Trump's longtime adversary Cher who planned to protest in the Women's March on Washington on 21 January, the day after the inauguration. And during the ceremony itself, other A-listers will be hosting a live telethon – officially called a "Love-a-thon" – to raise money for Planned Parenthood and the American Civil Liberties Union.

On January 17, 2017 Pootie Poot Putin[164] kicked in on the publication of the dossier of his friend Donald's alleged indiscretions and corrupt relations with the Russians published in *Buzzfeed*, and said that those who published such dreck were "worse than prostitutes." Putin couldn't help noting, in a Trumpian mode, however, that Russian hookers were "the best in the world." Pootie Poot also insisted that any allegation that Trump was essentially a Russian intelligence asset was nonsense, marking the first time that a Russian leader had ever publically denied that a U.S. president was a Russian asset. Yet Putin's intervention raised the question whether Trump was Putin's poodle as he continued to push Putin's anti-Nato agenda and details were being negotiated for Putin's trip to the U.S.

THE AMERICAN HORROR SHOW: DONALD TRUMP BECOMES 45TH U.S. PRESIDENT

Heading for pre-Inauguration festivities, the Trump entourage left Trump Tower in New York on January 19, 2017 in a motorcade that took them to an airplane to fly down to Washington – a back and forth that would define the Trump presidency as it was expected that Trump's wife Melania and his ten-year old son Baron would stay in New York, while Trump would wreak havoc in Washington for a few days and then fly away for long weekends in Florida, a Trump golf course, or Trump Tower to consult with his sons over business deals to get away from Washington where only 4% of the population had voted for him.

Once the Trump entourage landed in Washington, they went to the Capital's most important new destination that would be the heart of their social life and perhaps financial and political life – the Trump International Hotel. At a dinner for the superrich donors, some of whom he insulted in a "welcoming" speech for sending him big checks the day after the election, Trump gushed that the ballroom was a "fabulous" space and "a genius must have designed it." After inspecting his Washington property, Trump crossed the Potomac for a wreath-laying with Vice President-elect Mike Pence at the Tomb of the Unknowns at Arlington National Cemetery. Trump and Pence Inc. and their spouses and family then drove to the Lincoln Memorial for a pre-Inauguration concert. As the small crowd waited restlessly for the Great Man and his entourage to arrive, downbeat bars of the Rolling Stones "You Can't Always Get What you Want," (inexplicably Trump's campaign anthem), were played over and over, finally giving way to the Stones' "Heart of Stone" as the Great Man arrived to the mournful intonation of Mick Jagger singing "Heart of Stone, Heart of Stone," as Trump tramped across the stage waving at the crowd, a strange lyric to define the new President-to-be.

78 year-old Jon Voight, the only actor in Hollywood that would participate in Trump's (not)Gala, played master of ceremonies for the B and C list groups that entertained the Trumps and the crowds.

Trump gamely tried now and then to move with the music, but his wife Melania stood as a frozen statue of beauty, while Son-in-law Jarod Kushner, who with his wife Ivanka, were rumored to be the powers behind the throne who Trump often consulted before major decisions, stood rigid and dazed as he listened to the no-doubt unfamiliar country music, the military brass bands, the crazed piano dudes, and the jarring heavy metal act, wondering what cauldron of culture and populism he was now trapped in.

The network pundits themselves seemed dazed and not able to conceptualize what was happening as Trump made rambling remarks that the mike didn't pick up too clearly. A fireworks display gave Trump a chance to escape, and the iconography of the multicolored fireworks exploding over Washington created an eerie spectacle of the Capital under attack and exploding in an apocalyptic signaling of a New Era of World History, or maybe just the End of America as we once knew it, as." And then: "As Trump and his wife, Melania, descended the monument's steps at sunset, the president-elect saluted the marble statue of President Abraham Lincoln, flashed a tight smile and pumped his fist in the air to the roar of the crowd and the Rolling Stones' 'Heart of Stone' playing from the speakers."[165]

After this fiasco of a Bad Culture Event, the Trump Gang hurried to the now-familiar space of Trump's new Washington hotel for a pricey dinner for the super donors where he became unhinged and made a rambling speech, pointing out Republican dignitaries, donors, and other emerging pillars of the New Order, as he kept congratulating himself on what a great campaign he'd run, what a great victory it was, and what great things he'd do for the country to Make America Great again, a phrase he just couldn't stop repeating, along with evocation of The Trump Movement: "It's a movement like we've never seen anywhere in the world, they say." Trump also gushed that "[W]e have by far the highest IQ of any Cabinet ever assembled," although many of his cabinet nominees had done poorly in initial Congressional Hearings, providing comic montage for both news and late night television that would keep a worried nation entertained and perhaps assured that this Trump Clown Show wouldn't suddenly become the American Horror Show, as many feared.

The Day of Dread arrived on January 20, 2017, and believe it or not, Donald John Trump was sworn in as the 45th president of the United States. The TV day began with Trump and his wife Melania Trump attending a service at St. John's Episcopal Church near the White House, continuing an inauguration-day tradition. One of the ministers speaking was Robert Jeffress, a Southern Baptist minister and pastor of a Dallas megachurch, who had made inflammatory condemnations of both Mormonism and Islam in the past.

As the political class assembled for the inauguration ceremony on the Capital steps a poignant split screen showed Obama and Trump standing next to each other talking, while on the other screen Bill and Hillary Clinton arrived for the ceremonies, looking dejected and forlorn. A colleague appeared and talked to Hillary, and she appeared to cheer up, and as she went down the steps for the inauguration ceremony that could have been hers, greetings from colleagues brought back her winning smile.

Other former presidents assembled and walked down the steps to the ceremony with the announcer calling out the number of the presidents with 39 Jimmy Carter and his wife Rosalynn still standing strong and proud, followed by 42, Bill and Hillary Clinton, and 43 George W. and Laura Bush. With all the luminaries assembled on the steps of the capital, a subdued Donald John Trump took the oath of office and became the 45th president of the United States.

When Trump began his inaugural address, the grey sky opened up and rain started falling, serving as tears of grief for the dark vision of Trump's inaugural address which mobilized the greatest hits of his campaign, focusing on the anti-Establishment populist thrust of putting himself and the people against Washington politics. Repeating the sinister and pessimistic vision of his RNC speech, Trump spoke of an "American carnage" with "mothers and children trapped in poverty in our inner cities; rusted-out factories scattered like tombstones across the landscape of our nation; an education system, flush with cash, but which leaves our young and beautiful students deprived of all knowledge; and the crime and the gangs and the drugs that have stolen too many lives and robbed our country of so much unrealized potential."

Reaching the crescendo of his dark vision, Trump thundered: "This American carnage stops right here and stops right now." The carnage would end and everything would change, Trump assured his hardcore followers and true believers (for whom the speech was fashioned), and henceforth Trump would put the people first and the "forgotten men and women" could once more be proud of their country and would be the focus of government. Taking a clue from Hollywood, Trump insisted that "we are transferring power from Washington DC and giving it back to you, the people," repeating a line from the villainous demagogue Bane in the film *The Dark Knight Rises*.

Trump also reprised his "American First" theme,[166] saying that this would be the guiding principle of his administration and that every decision would put American interests and people before any other consideration, playing the card of authoritarian populism. Yet while Trump excoriated wasted trillions on foreign wars, he talked of strengthening old alliances and forging new ones (presumably with his pal Putin) in the goal of destroying Islamic terrorism, wiping it off the face of the earth, evoking the specter of a global Terror War with frightening consequences.

Trump's nasty speech was especially insulting to Barack Obama and all the assembled members of his administration, who were, in effect, accused of leaving the country in a *Mad Max* apocalyptic collapse of civilization. Yet Trump's attack on Washington aimed as well at George W. Bush and Republicans who had worked for his administration and in some cases were still active, leading Bush to narrow his eyes in anger during Trump's tirade. Indeed, the speech was an insult and attack on Washington itself, reflecting the dark desires of Steve Bannon and the Breibart Wild Bunch who wanted to destroy Washington.[167] Trump implied that all previous politicians had served themselves and their own interests and not the people, and that Trump alone would end the "carnage" and that for the first time the government would be for the people.

Trump's followers cheered as rain kept falling while Trump concluded that he would make America strong, wealthy, safe, proud, and GREAT AGAIN, obviously the major idea of his campaign and inauguration address, although he did not give one clue as to how this would happen. Hence, Trump's dark, twisted, and threatening inauguration speech, quickly labeled the worst in history by TV pundits, and receiving sharp criticism from all except his fanatic followers, announced that Donald J. Trump would henceforth be the Demon of Carnage, wreaking havoc everywhere, starting with Washington and the political establishment, making his dark vision a possibly prophetic American Horror Show.

Upon the speech's conclusion, Trump walked over and shook hands with Obama and Joe Biden and studiously ignored Bill and Hillary Clinton, although Bill tried to get his attention. The Pences escorted the Bidens to a car that would take them to the train station to return to Delaware, while the Trumps escorted the Obamas to the Air Force Helicopter that would take them to Joint Base Andrews where they would catch a plane to fly to Palm Springs, California, to safely vacation in the Golden State where Hillary Clinton had beaten Trump by four million votes. Trump and Obama exchanged smiles and small talk, while Michelle Obama looked detached and rather stoic as the couples clumsily exchanged kisses and farewells (a montage that night on *The Daily Show With Trevor Noah* showed Michelle Obama looking devastated as Trump spoke and then interacted with them).

And so the Obama era was over as their helicopter flew one last time over the White House and now Donald Trump would open a new era fraught with dangers and uncertainties. The nation got a preview of the New (dis)Order as Trump and his minions strode to the Oval Office, like a coven of Princes of Darkness led by their Demon King. As promised, one of Trump's first signed documents attacked executive orders that Obama had promulgated to encourage environmental preservation and protection, and another ambiguous Executive Order set in motion a process of ending the Affordable Care Act. As Trump signed official documents approving his cabinet nominations, who would be vehicles of the Carnage, Trump joked about his appointments with assembled members of Congress, giving Democrats in the room pens used to nominate Department Heads bent on destroying the gains and progress of the previous administration. Hence, Trump and his Demons of Carnage were dead set on destruction of liberalism and government actions to protect the environment, civil liberties, and minority groups. The White Men of Privilege now ruled and Whiteness of Skin Privilege and Darkness of Vision and Destruction were the ethos of the New Order which the New Maximum Leader would implement.

The rest of the day followed the usual formalities with Trump and establishment politicians and his Big Donors attending a congressional luncheon in the Capitol with not a worker or peasant in sight. The New Maximum Leaders and their families went to watch the inaugural parade from a reviewing stand outside the White House and planned to attend three official inaugural balls in the evening. Yet behind the scenes, the Trumpsters began their carnage, taking aim at the progressive accomplishments of the Obama administrations. As William Rivers Pitt notes: "A fair roadmap of the days and weeks to come can be found on the White House website, which was transformed into a factory for terrible ideas moments after Trump took the oath. All references to climate change, meticulously compiled by the Obama administration over the years, have been scrubbed with no explanation given. An energy plan that received a 'Zero' score from the Sierra Club is touted. As for the criminal justice system, the new Trump administration minces no words: 'The dangerous anti-police atmosphere in America is wrong. The Trump Administration will end it.'"[168]

The coronation spectacle of King Carnage and his Demons of Darkness had its traditional moments of pomp and circumstance, suggesting that the Republic had never freed itself completely from trappings of monarchy, and now had a Demon King of Carnage who would no doubt attempt to strengthen Executive Power and weaken democracy at every turn. Yet King Donald was coming in as the least popular president in history, his inauguration was one third less the size of Obama's first inauguration,[169] the parade was the shortest and most sparsely attended in recent history, with many bleachers almost empty, and the concerts, the balls, and other events were the most paltry and pathetic in memory, as major celebrities, artists, and performers were all boycotting the ceremonies.

Furthermore, there were copious protests and disruptions in Washington, as throughout the city, groups of people protested the inauguration with signs, chants, and tweets against the Trump presidency. In Washington, protest groups gathered at each of the 20 security checkpoints where attendees entered the Mall and some got in to protest. Anarchists and angry young people smashed Starbucks windows and attacked a limo, burned trash, and fought with police leading to many arrests. On the whole, however, protest in Washington and elsewhere was peaceful but defiant with RESIST emerging as the keyword for opposition to Trump.

Throughout the country, there were large marches and demonstrations in every major city and part of the country with thousands marching through driving rain in Los Angeles, angry masses gathered in John Lewis' Atlanta outraged at Trump's racist remarks about their city, and defiant groups gathered in state capitals from Austin to Madison, representing a diversity of issues and groups, as part of a week of anti-Trump protests of diverse kinds. As Emily Eakin reports: "On Wednesday night, several hundred demonstrators sang and shimmied their way through the D.C. neighborhood where Vice-President-elect Mike Pence is temporarily residing, as part of a travelling 'queer dance party' to protest Pence's lack of support for L.G.B.T.Q. rights."[170]

The big demonstration, however, was scheduled for Saturday the day after the inauguration, and already tens of thousands women were descending on Washington for the Women's March. Charter buses began arriving from around the country, and joined by husbands, boyfriends, children, and male protestors, women demonstrators occupied terrain around the National Museum of the American Indian. March organizers, who originally sought a permit for a gathering of 200,000, said that they now expect as many as a half million participants – dwarfing Trump's inaugural crowd. Indeed, as Saturday arrived and protestor's swarmed in for the Women's March by mid-morning Washington authorities were predicting that over 500,000 were assembled, making it one of the largest DC protests in history.

Hence, while on Saturday morning, Trump attended a traditional national prayer service at Washington National Cathedral, looking bored throughout the droning sermons, the energy was on the Mall and the streets as protestors poured into the heart of the capital city to listen to speeches, to march, and to begin a resistance movement against Trump to oppose his every move and block whatever of his programs that they could. The demonstrations reminded me of the 1972 anti-Nixon inauguration demonstration that I participated in at the height of the Vietnam War. Interestingly, in his RNC speech and campaign, Trump often invoked Richard Nixon and the "silent majority" who he claimed he represented. Trump was probably the most Nixonesque candidate since Nixon's disgraceful demise (in the bad paranoid, dark, conspiratorial, and unhinged sense). Indeed, as I watched the anti-Trump demonstrations unfold, I recalled that Nixon was forced to resign during the Watergate Hearings that investigated his many crimes, around 18 months after his second inauguration, and I wondered how long the scandal-ridden Trump would avoid investigation and possible prosecution and impeachment.

Meanwhile, back at the Women's March, Ashley Judd did a spell-binding "nasty woman" routine, playing off of Trump's nasty comment to Hillary Clinton during a presidential debate. Yes, Trump was Poster Boy for Nasty Man and one wondered how his nasty Twitter finger would respond to the verbal assaults on him during the demonstration with Gloria Steinem, Madonna, Scarlett Johansson and others making strong speeches, while Cecile Richards, head of Planned Parenthood, assured the crowd: "My pledge today is our doors stay open" (to abortion clinics that conservatives want closed). Placards read: "Minority president", "Women roar" and "I'm afraid," while many women wore pink hand=knit "pussy hats" – a rebuke to Dirty Donald, once caught on an *Access Hollywood* video boasting: "Grab them by the pussy."[171]

In addition, millions of people gathered in cities around the world as part of an international day of action in solidarity with the Women's March on Washington and other protests in the U.S. Estimates indicated that over 400,000 demonstrated in New York, with a crush of demonstrators surrounding Trump Tower. An equal amount of marchers was estimated showing up in a boisterous rally in Los Angeles, and March organizers estimated that there were many other Women's March events taking place in the U.S. with more than 670 related demonstrations taking place throughout the world.

While millions of people protested against Trump, he visited the CIA headquarters and then met with the press telling a group of media and CIA officials assembled after his meetings with top officials that he loved intelligence and the CIA. Yet Trump quickly veered to an attack on the media for underestimating the amount of people who had attended his inauguration and bragged of his "running war with the media," who he said were among "the most dishonest human beings on Earth". Trump rambled on for 18 minutes of self-aggrandizement and bragging about his election, how smart he was, the number of times he appeared on the cover of *Time* magazine, and how everyone in the room voted for him, clear signs of his intense narcissism and insecurity. Astonishingly, he also revealed his distance from shared social reality and his life in an alternative reality when he recounted how when he began his inauguration address, suddenly the rain stopped and the sun shined on all (a claim counter to the images I saw on TV of rain falling on Trump and the audience as he began his speech and the audience began putting on ponchos, including George W. Bush who made a mess of his).[172]

Always conscious of backdrop, Trump had chosen the CIA Wall of Heroes as the site of his live-televised remarks, but former CIA chief John Brennan complained of Trump using the sacred CIA space of the Wall of Heroes to promote himself without a word about the sacrifice of CIA agents, leading CNN news commentators covering the event and other media sources to note how angry some CIA leaders were that Trump had so insulted the agency and U.S. intelligence for weeks and then showed up to blather and brag. Through a former aide, John Brennan noted that he was "deeply saddened and angered at Trump's despicable display of self-aggrandizement" in front of the memorial wall, leading Trump's spinsters to attack Brennan.

Trump also used the first day to send out his hapless press secretary Sean Spicer who read a carefully and nastily written attack on the media for misrepresenting the amount of people who had attended Trump's inauguration, and threatened that the media would be held responsible for their lies and distortions. Spicer correctly argued that the Federal Parks Service did not do crowd estimates, but falsely claimed that many more people took the Metro the day of Trump's inauguration than on

Obama's inauguration and provided what turned out to be completely false numbers in his false claim that Trump's inauguration was the biggest in history. The D.C. Metro quickly released inauguration day rider statistics for the Trump and Obama events, and reported that many more took the Metro the day of Obama's inauguration, thus leading CNN and other media to report that the Trump administration began its reign with bald-faced lies on its first day in office, and had launched an attack on the media for allegedly lying, while available statistics and facts indicated that the media had in fact basically told the truth about comparative crowd size, Metro usage, and comparative pictures of the Obama and Trump administration inaugurations which showed that many more attended the former.[173]

On Sunday morning more evidence emerged that the Trump administration had gone full out post-factual as President Donald tweeted: "Wow, television ratings just out: 31 million people watched the Inauguration, 11 million more than the very good ratings from 4 years ago!" The still functioning media quickly pointed out, however, that:

> Nielsen reported Saturday that 30.6 million viewers watched inaugural coverage between 10 a.m. and 6 p.m. on Friday. That figure is higher than Obama's second inauguration in 2013, which drew 20.6 million viewers.

> But it's lower than that of Obama's first inauguration in 2009, when 38 million viewers tuned in, according to Nielsen. The record is held by Ronald Reagan, when 42 million watched his inaugural festivities in 1981.

The same morning, on *Meet The Press,* the Trumpsters multiple and multiplying by the minute misrepresentations of inauguration numbers were cited by moderator Chuck Todd who asked Kellyanne Conway, counselor to the president: "Why put him [i.e. Press Secretary Sean Spicer] out there for the very first time, in front of that podium, to utter a provable falsehood? It's a small thing, but the first time he confronts the public, it's a falsehood?" Conway responded: "Don't be so overly dramatic about it, Chuck. You're saying it's a falsehood, and they're giving – our press secretary, Sean Spicer, gave alternative facts to that. But the point really is –" Todd jumped in and retorted: "Wait a minute. *Alternative facts!?* Alternative facts!? Four of the five facts he uttered ... were just not true. Alternative facts are not facts; they're falsehoods."

The Trumpsters have obviously come to believe that they can define facts and reality and that if the media doesn't validate their truths, Trump and his post-factual brigade of media flacks will take them on, presenting a challenge to the media to subject every word of Trumpspin to rigorous scrutiny and if necessary critique. It will be interesting to see how long Trump's minions will continue to tell bold and brazen lies that they and their media critics and informed audiences know to be untrue.[174] Henceforth Conway will be referred to as AF Conway (as in "alternative facts") and Spicer will be known as 4L4M (as in "four lies four minutes") Spicer, and everything they say should be subjected to the same rigorous scrutiny and criticism that should be applied to the ultimate source and King of Lies, Donald John Trump.

4L4M Spicer riled the media by his aggressive hectoring tone, threats that the media would be held responsible for its lying reporting, and then after loudly and aggressively repeating his litany of lies, he shouted: "And that's what you should be reporting!" The media does not like to be told what to report any more than politicians and their spinners like to be confronted with alternative facts that trump their facts. Democracy requires a separation of powers and the press serves classically as the "fourth estate" to provide part of a system of checks and balances against excessive, misused, or corrupt state power, including speaking truth to lying liars. In the first full day of the Trump administration, King Donald bragged of his "running war against the media" in front of CIA employees and sent his flunkeys out to battle the press, but the barrage of ridicule, criticism, and anger they stirred up suggest that Trump and Co. lost the battle of Day One.

Of course, Trump's daily twitters, that he promised to continue despite contrary advice, and his "running" war against the media, could be a distraction in the real war to push through a rightwing and militarist agenda while the press is distracted chasing down the Daily

Lies and shooting down fake news and alternative facts that are the epistemological novum of the newly-minted Trump administration; i.e. never had an administration run on a daily dosage of fake news and alternative facts as the Trumpsters.

As the Trumpsters trudged into their offices on the administrations first full work-day on Monday, January 23, 2017, the new comers saw a lot of empty desks and it appeared that the Trump administration was woefully understaffed. As the *New York Times* Editorial Board notes:

> An incoming president is expected to fill about 4,000 positions. Nominees for more than 1,100 of them must be confirmed by the Senate. It is impossible for any president to fill all these positions by Day 1. But transition veterans recommend that a new president have a White House team assembled – 450 people who don't require Senate confirmation – and have nominees for the top 100 positions that must be Senate-confirmed.

> Mr. Trump is not even in the ballpark. There are no nominees for three-quarters of the top 100 jobs. His White House staff, some 30 of whom were sworn in on Sunday, is light on governing experience. Yet many of those, like the former "Apprentice" and "Celebrity Apprentice" contestant Omarosa Manigault, the assistant to the president and director of communications for the Office of Public Liaison, carry the titles that rank highest.[175]

The State of the Union was not good as the Donald J. Trump White House Reality Show moved into its first week in office. The stock market had declined for five days straight before the inauguration and lost all of its gains for the year and continued to go down, although there would be no doubt roller coasters to come. The Earth's temperature had risen to all-time highs for the third year in a row and an administration full of climate deniers and contemptuous of science would no doubt continue to heat things up. Inauguration weekend had seen extreme weather events from coast to coast as heavy rain continued to pound California after a severe five-year drought, tornados and extreme storms ripped through the country, and ocean temperatures were on the rise while the Artic sea ice continued to melt. No one could predict what forms the Donald Trump American Horror Show would take although there was plenty to be worried about.

RIGHTWING BILLIONAIRE
AUTHORITARIAN – NOT POPULIST

During his first 30 days in office, Trump proved himself to be an authoritarian, but not a populist. Stacking his cabinet and administration with billionaires, rightwing ideologues, and cronies who had contributed to his campaign, Trump pursued a hardright agenda to primarily aide the billionaire class while eliminating regulations and programs that helped working people.[176] Signing daily Executive Orders, Trump and his cronies attacked government regulations protecting workers, consumers, animals, and the earth itself. Representing the kleptocracy of the billionaire class, Trump promised his fellow billionaires tax cuts that would "make you happy" and, he hoped, would make them like and support him. He signed Executive Orders that would undo Obama's legacy of liberalism and progress and return America to the Swamps of Hardright Reaction.

As Trump and his executors signed papers to destroy social programs, his militarist wing decided to carry out a military intervention, ordering an attack in Yemen on a well-guarded brick house in a remote village in a mountainous area of Yemen that supposedly contained a treasure trove of al Queda documents and leaders who they could kill. Trump's first foray into militarism was a total debacle, although he and his Ministers of Truth proclaimed it a success, demonstrating again that Orwellian language rules in the White House (i.e. War is Peace, Slavery is Freedom, etc).[177] Believing that there were major al Queda leaders and documents in the site, instead children and civilians were killed, while a U.S. Special Operations forces member died of injuries suffered when occupants of the house, and neighboring houses, including women with guns, started firing back. Three other American troops, members of a Navy SEAL unit, were wounded in the operation.[178]

The Trumpsters claimed that the Obama administration had planned the raid, although high-ranking Obama officials quickly retorted that the claim was erroneous, and in any case the Trumpsters had initiated the fiasco. Yet Trump and his minions continued to insist on its success, even though apparently nothing of interest was retrieved from

159

the house. The first batch of documents released from the site, which were supposed to prove the value of the intelligence found, turned out to be documents that had been released a decade before! Continued insistence on the success of the mission drove Press Secretary Sean Spicer further into the morass of lies, and as Saturday Night Live relentlessly lampooned him, the hapless Spicer was emerging as one of the most laughable liars ever.[179]

One of Trump's first and most notorious acts as president was to sign a travel ban Executive Order, which temporarily barred travelers from Iraq, Iran, Sudan, Somalia, Syria, Libya and Yemen from entering the U.S. Although Administration officials claimed that the order was not a "Muslim ban," in fact none of the countries proscribed is the birth site of terrorists who committed recent attacks in the United States connected to extremist Islamist ideology, unlike Saudi Arabia, Egypt, Pakistan and other Arab countries where Trump has business interests, yet individuals from countries that did business with Trump were not banned from entry.

Trump's Muslim travel ban unleashed intense protests all over the world as activists, lawyers, and representatives of human rights groups flocked to the nation's airports to help people who suddenly were banned from entering the US, or afraid to take scheduled flights to other countries as they feared that they would not be able to return. The media showed distraught families whose loved ones were prevented from joining them, or people expressing their fear that they or family members would be deported, or not allowed to enter the country. Protestors surrounded airports welcoming Muslims and immigrants, and good Samarians were shown inside the airports helping people and giving them support.

When Sally Yates, acting US attorney general, reviewed the travel ban, she wrote a letter instructing Justice Department officials not to enforce the president's travel ban. The Trumpsters immediately fired her on January 30, 2017, recalling the "Saturday Night Massacre" during the Nixon administration, when an Attorney General was fired for refusing to carry out what he saw as an illegal Richard Nixon Watergate era order, which soon led Nixon to resign in disgrace to avoid impeachment.

After some days of intense chaos at the nation's airports, U.S. District Judge James L. Robart entered a temporary but nationwide stop to the order, saying he concluded the court "must intervene to fulfill its constitutional role in our tripart government." This was a tremendous defeat for the Trump administration which had rushed out an utterly inept travel ban with no exceptions for immigrants with green cards, or those fully vetted for visas, with relatives in the country, or established positions with businesses or universities. Not surprisingly, the TwitterTwat-in-Chief tweeted: "The opinion of this so-called judge, which essentially takes law-enforcement away from our country, is ridiculous and will be overturned!"

Judge Robart had been on the bench since 2004, was nominated by President George W. Bush, and so was not a Democratic Party partisan, and his ruling was upheld by a three-judge panel from the U.S. Court of Appeals for the 9th Circuit which supported Judge Robart's ruling and thus in effect ruled against the Trump administration travel ban. Suspense had been mounting for days, and in a dramatic political spectacle, the appeals court decision was read aloud on the cable news networks and internet sites, probably the first time that many had ever listened to complex legal briefs and argumentation in real time. The result, however, was dramatic and produced a resounding defeat for the Trump administration whose sloppily and hastily-produced immigration ban order was rejected by the courts. In a unanimous, 29-page opinion, three judges with the U.S. Court of Appeals for the 9th Circuit upheld the freeze on Trump's controversial immigration order, meaning previously barred refugees and citizens from seven Muslim-majority countries could continue entering the United States – until the Trump administration appealed the court decision, or issued another travel ban which they announced they would do later in February.

Following Trump's attack on the judiciary, many serious people were angry that he had referred to a "so-called judge" and tweeted: "many very bad and dangerous people may be pouring into our country" because of the judicial decision." It appeared that Trump wanted to create a fall-guy in case of a terror attack, with an insinuation that if terrorists got into the country and carried out an attack because of the blocked Muslim travel ban, the courts would responsible.

While chaos from the travel ban created havoc for the airline and transportation system, and for students, professors, workers, and businesses who found their travel disrupted, the Trumpsters continued to push the worst from the billionaire class and his closest supporters through cabinet hearings. There was intense media scrutiny of his appointments, many of whom came from the depths of the swamps of Wall Street, extreme right politics, or filthy wealth that had been invested in Trump's campaign, but the Democrats just did not have the numbers to defeat Trump's Swamp Creatures, and supine Republicans voted to support even the most unqualified and weak candidates.

For instance, Betsy DeVos, Trump's nominee for education secretary, appeared before the Senate Health, Education, Labor and Pensions Committee for her confirmation hearing January 17, 2017, and demonstrated that she did not know anything about current debates about evaluating student performance, did not know about disability provisions in public education, and generally proved herself to be utterly unqualified to run the Education Department. DeVos, a rightwing billionaire champion of vouchers and charter schools, revealed that she didn't really know anything about public education at all. When asked about her positions on guns in schools, she referred to previous testimony of how guns in a certain school district were needed to protect students and teachers from grizzly bear attacks, yet when reporters questioned officials involved in the school in question, they claimed they had no grizzly bear problems and no guns in their schools.

DeVos' written statement was revealed to be heavily plagiarized, and testimony indicated that the charter schools DeVos had championed in Michigan were failures, yet she squeaked through the Senate committee questioning her, and barely made it through a full Senate vote that required Vice President Mike Pence to cast the tie-breaking vote. This was the first time in history in which the Veep had to break a tie to confirm a cabinet member, linking Pence to DeVos forever.

In her first foray into the public after her confirmation, protesters blocked DeVos from entering a Washington D.C. Middle School with protesters shouting: "You do not represent anything that they stand for," referring to DeVos' attacks on public schools.[180] Demonstrators held signs which noted her position on private education and support for vouchers and charter schools, expressing fears that DeVos would undermine public education which philosopher John Dewey argued was essential to produce democratic citizens and the opportunity for equal advancement for all citizens.[181]

Meanwhile, the Democrats were fiercely questioning the qualifications of Swamp Creature Senator Jeff Sessions, who had a life of opposing civil rights and other progressive legislation, while having a legacy of decisions that blocked African Americans from voting and civil rights. The debate was heated and Senate Majority Leader Mitch McConnell (R-Ky.) silenced Senator Elizabeth Warren's (D-Mass.) attempt to read a letter criticizing Sessions from Coretta Scott King on the floor of the Senate during the debate on Sessions, driving Warren out of the Senate chambers for allegedly impugning the reputation of a colleague in an action interpreted as McConnell flipping out and loosing it. Warren read the letter from Martin Luther King's widow, indicating why Sessions was not fit to serve, outside the doors of the Senate and streamed it live over the Internet, providing days of media coverage and commentary attacking McConnell and making Warren a champion of free speech.

During his first 30 days, Trump continued tweet attacks on anyone who displeased him ranging from federal judges who questioned his Muslim ban to Nordstrom which discontinued Ivanka Trump's fashion line after poor sales in part because of a boycott of her products organized by millennial women. There was an uproar over Trump's tweet attacking Nordstrom for dropping his daughter's clothing line, when he emoted: "My daughter Ivanka has been treated so unfairly by @Nordstrom. She is a great person – always pushing me to do the right thing! Terrible!" Experts in government ethics immediately argued that Trump's promotion of his daughter's products should be referred to the federal ethics office, and that this presented evidence how Trump was incapable of separating his family's businesses from his presidential office.

Nordstrom replied that they had stopped carrying Ivanka's label due to poor sales, stating: "We've said all along we make buying decisions based on performance. We've got thousands of brands – more than

2,000 offered on the site alone. Reviewing their merit and making edits is part of the regular rhythm of our business." Nordstrom's decision followed a mushrooming boycott campaign organized by an anti-Trump activist group called Grab Your Wallet, which demanded Nordstrom sever its business ties with the Trump family. After Trump's tweet, Nordstrom's share prices dropped, but later bounced back. Trump's tweets have in the past also been correlated with changing share prices in US automakers, Boeing and Carrier, but so far stocks that have declined after Trump's Twitter attacks have risen to previous levels or higher.

During the first 30 Days, many of Trump's closest confidents were caught in scandals and there were reports that his administration was in total chaos, as the amateurs made blunder after blunder and the orange-haired Swamp King created utter chaos with his outrageous tweets, intemperate comments, and illegal and chaotic Executive Orders. Kellyanne Conway, the Trump adviser who coined the phrase "alternative facts," produced a media uproar when in an interview with MSNBC's Chris Matthews on February 2, Conway defended Trump's travel ban with claims of a "Bowling Green massacre," by Iraqi terrorists which she (falsely) claimed led to an Iraqi refugee ban under former president Barack Obama. Media fact checkers quickly pointed that there was no "Bowling Green massacre," nor did Obama "ban" Iraqi refugees. Lying Lips Conway's promotion of "alternative facts" as truth provoked CNN to temporarily ban her because of her constant lies, and Conway constant spouting of "alternative facts" revealed how the Trump administration thought it could define reality and tell lie after lie to the American public.

Conway's remark was made in the wake of one of Donald Trump's biggest whoppers of his nascent presidency when he complained that the media didn't cover terrorism and put the U.S. public at risk. In fact, the media have been obsessed with terrorism since the 911 attacks, and the Trump administration had no evidence that there was ever a serious threat of terrorism that the media did not report on. To support Trump's ludicrous claim, the increasingly ridiculous Conway made up a fake terrorist incident that the media in her view did not cover and made herself a figure of ridicule.[182]

Soon after, Conway also made herself a poster-person for exposing Trump family conflict of interests when she promoted Ivanka's Trump's fashion line and urged viewers to go out and buy products, claiming that she was about to do so herself, and then bragging how she was providing an advertisement for Ivanka's stuff.[183] There was an immediate uproar as federal law prohibits government officials from promoting products that would benefit the family of the president, and Conway, already excoriated as the champion of "alternative facts," was outed as a Trump family huckster, adding to her expanding portfolio.[184]

As I was concluding this study I read Matt Taibbi's *Insane Clown President: Dispatches from the 2016 Circus* (2017).[185] Indeed, the Republican presidential primaries were a media circus, as Taibbi well documents, although I would argue that Trump's election is an American Tragedy and Horror Show. Yet there are also comic dimensions to Trump's presidency as he blunders, lies, and creates chaos as has no administration before. Indeed, he has finished his first 30 days without filling many key government posts and many in his administration are already quitting or getting thrown out for maleficence.

Indeed, the biggest scandal of the Trump presidency erupted when President Trump's national security adviser Michael Flynn resigned February 13 after revelations that he had discussed sanctions on Russia with the Russian ambassador to the U.S. during the 2016 presidential campaign and prior to Trump taking office. The *Washington Post* reported that: "The acting attorney general informed the Trump White House late last month that she believed Michael Flynn had misled senior administration officials about the nature of his communications with the Russian ambassador to the United States, and warned that the national security adviser was potentially vulnerable to Russian blackmail, current and former U.S. officials said. The message, delivered by Sally Q. Yates and a senior career national security official to the White House counsel, was prompted by concerns that Flynn, when asked about his calls and texts with the Russian diplomat, had told Vice President-elect Mike Pence and others that he had not discussed the Obama administration sanctions on Russia for its interference in the 2016 election, the officials said."[186]

This shocking report revealed that Trump had appointed Flynn as National Security Advisor despite the fact that U.S. intelligence agencies had made clear that Flynn had broken the law and was compromised by his contacts with the Russians who might have blackmail material on him. It raised once again the curious and perhaps explosive questions concerning relations between the Trump campaign and administration and the Russians, the U.S.'s Cold War antagonist and bete noir of the Republican Party and conservatives, who suddenly had a Republican president in bed with the Russians and rumors of unsavory and perhaps criminal connections.

Questions of impeachment and affinities between Trump and Richard Nixon who had been impeached were widely discussed and a stunning 46% percent of voters in one poll supported impeachment after a mere 30 Days of Trump, a horror show that could go on for years. Like Nixon, Trump was secretive and paranoid, compiling enemy's lists and plotting to destroy rivals. Both were obsessed by Enemies and in one discussion presidential historian Michael Beschloss tweeted: "On December 1972 tape, Nixon told Kissinger, 'The press is the enemy, the establishment is the enemy, the professors are the enemy.'"[187]

The people were also Trump's enemy as protests continued to erupt on a daily basis and a fierce anti-Trump movement was in the making. The Women's Day March had mobilized many who continued protesting and new groups like Indivisible emerged, confronting Congressman in Town Halls or their offices,[188] and strongly arguing for programs like the Affordable Care Act that the Trumpsters threatened to destroy. On February 20, 2017 President's Day, these anti-Trump groups coalesced to wage a nationwide Not My President! Day of Protest all around the country. While Trump had aroused a vast slumbering movement of the forgotten and the deplorable, an active, informed, and militant countermovement emerged with the slogan RESIST!

After a terrible first month, Trump attempted to reset his presidency in an impromptu press conference on February 16, 2017. Dismissing reports of chaos and conspiracy in his administration, Trump claimed that his administration is running like "a fine-tuned machine" and attacked leaks and the press for reports of a dysfunctional administration. "I turn on the TV, open the newspapers and I see stories of chaos, chaos," Trump ranted. "Yet it is the exact opposite. This administration is running like a fine-tuned machine, despite the fact that I can't get my cabinet approved."

The 77 minute psychodrama unfolded a pugnacious defense of his first four weeks as president and a bitter denunciation of the press. Following the firing of his national security advisor Michael Flynn for inappropriately talking to the Russians before the election, Trump denied that he had any connections to Russia whatsoever, or any knowledge of his election campaign team having contacts with Moscow, dismissing these stories as a "ruse." Repeating campaign trail lines, Trump insisted that he "inherited a mess", both domestically and abroad, but claimed that he had achieved more in his first four weeks in office than any previous US president, bragging: "We're just getting started."

Trump attacked "fake news" throughout his press conference, as he was doing daily in a major rhetorical trick of his presidency, deflecting criticism onto the source of the critique which he denounced as "fake news." Henceforth, anyone who attacked him, or any stories critical of his administration, could be dismissed as "fake news." In a contorted twist of Orwellian logic during his 77 minute press conference, Trump proclaimed in response to a question concerning all the news leaks coming out of his administration: "The leaks are absolutely real. The news is fake because so much of the news is fake."

Yet Trump couldn't help producing fake news himself bragging once again that he had achieved the biggest Electoral College win since Ronald Reagan, whereas in real fact Obama, Clinton, and George H.W. Bush had all achieved bigger Electoral College victories. When a reporter confronted Trump with these embarrassing facts, he replied: "I was given that information," raising the question of who was feeding the Informer-in-Chief with so much bad information. Indeed, Trump and his administration were the vanguard of a "post-truth" era in which the president could lie at will and cite alternative facts or information. Checking his discourse against verifiable and falsiable claims, a *Washington Post* "Fact Checker" project indicated that in "the 39 days Trump has been in office, we've counted *140* false or misleading claims."[189] As en example of Trump's constant making up stories, over the weekend of February 18, 2017 Trump told a crowd in Florida of a recent terrorist attack in Sweden because they let so many immigrants in, and, soon after, it was reported around the globe that there was no such attack in Sweden, leading Trump to concede that he had misinterpreted a report from *Fox News*, suggesting that the Chief should take some time out for a media literacy course.

U.S. media commentators were initially dumbfounded by Trump's rambling 77-minute rant, and compared him with the mentally disturbed Captain Queeg of *The Caine Mutiny* and even Dr Strangelove, while a CNN anchor called him "unhinged." Trump continued his tirade against the media later in the day, apparently thinking this excited his base, or maybe he was just outraged by the snide and critical comments on his bizarre press conference: "The FAKE NEWS media (failing @ nytimes, @NBCNews, @ABC, @CBS, @CNN) is not my enemy, it is the enemy of the American people!"

Many commentators noted that Trump's presenting the media as "the enemy of the people" cited Comrade Stalin's and Chairman Mao's attack on the bourgeois press while: "Bill Bishop, the Washington DC-based publisher of the Sinocism newsletter on Chinese politics, said Trump's bid to cow the media into becoming an 'obedient, unquestioning' force came straight out of the Communist party playbook. 'It feels like China ... It's deeply depressing and deeply disturbing and yet every day it gets worse. [with] a stark raving mad president holding Monty Pythonesque press conferences'".[190] Further, "Carl Bernstein, the investigative journalist who helped unearth the Watergate scandal in the early 1970s, was among those appalled by Trump's latest attempt to undermine the media. 'Oh boy,' he told the *New York Times*. 'Donald Trump is demonstrating an authoritarian attitude and inclination that shows no understanding of the role of the free press.'"[191]

Trump's war against media and the judiciary clearly revealed that he was an authoritarian and enemy of democracy who saw any restraints on his power as an illicit limitation on his power to define reality, advising his followers to look to him alone for truth, as he had told them at the Republican National Convention in 2016 that "he alone" could solve the problems facing the country. Never before had such an assault on the basic institutions of democracy been under attack by a president who seemed to have no understanding whatsoever of constitutional democracy and the conception of division of powers. In his rambling press conference, Trump had referenced Jefferson and Andrew Jackson as presidents who also had wars against the press, and while many presidents complain about media coverage, most presidents, including Jefferson and Jackson, attacked specific media, in a period where the press was highly partisan.

And so 30 days into his presidency, Donald John Trump had signed a Muslim travel ban that generated perhaps the most large-scale and widely extended protests in U.S. history against the Trump ban in the U.S. and major cities throughout the world; it had in so doing created chaos in the travel industry, in sectors of business and University life, and had generated a constitutional crisis and started a war with the courts calculated to go on for years, as he prepared to release another, purportedly, more carefully worded and nuanced travel ban (or so we would see). Trump had engaged in chaotic telephone diplomacy, alienating close allies liked Australia and Mexico, creating tension between Pakistan and India, and China and Taiwan, while discussing Trump organization business deals with other world leaders. When North Korea launched a provocative missile test, Trump discussed the U.S. response in a public dinner at his Florida country club Mar-a-Lago with the Japanese Prime Minister and aides from both countries as visitors to the club shot the conversations and documents they were inspecting, thus dealing with national security in an insecure public site.

The forced resignation of Trump's National Security advisor Michael Flynn had set the security and intelligence corps into panic and revealed chaos at the heart of Trump's presidency as successors to Flynn turned down the job, not wanting to get into a "shit storm," as one candidate described the situation. Reince Priebus, Trump's chief of staff, reportedly asked the FBI to deny media reports that Trump campaign advisers were frequently in touch with Russian intelligence agents during the election, and the spectre of Trump Gang/Russian connections cast a dark shadow over his presidency that could shove it into the abyss any moment, a fate that always threatens a scandal-ridden presidency, as Richard Nixon discovered during the Watergate era.

Trump's popularity fell steadily as he careened from one blunder and outrageous comments to another, and top polls indicated that his support had fallen into the high 30s, an all-time-low for a new president, while those in favor of impeachment were in one poll an astonishing 46 percent![192] Resistance to Trump was growing from below as groups who had coalesced at the Woman's March right after Trump inauguration planned more resistance, and a new movement Indivisible gained members and planned actions.

Yet even if Trump were to resign or be forced out, a hardright cabinet and administration is in place, and Mike Pence is fully prepared to push through a rightwing Republican agenda. As Jane Mayer notes in her new Preface to *Dark Money*, not only is Pence, Trump's Vice President, a favorite of the billionaire Koch Brothers who shares their enthusiasm for privatizing social security, deregulating energy industries, and cutting back on environmental regulation and the EPA, but: "Pence's senior advisor in the sensitive task of managing Trump's transition to power was Mark Short, who just a few months earlier had actually run the Kochs' secretive donor club, Freedom Partners." Mayer lists several other top advisors and appointees in the Trump administration who are Koch Brothers cronies, and notes that Mike Pompeo, Trump's choice to run the CIA "was the single largest recipient of Koch campaign funds in Congress." A frightening implication of Mayer's analysis is that even if the polity is lucky enough to drive Donald Trump out of office, we are stuck with Mike Pence and the Rule of the Koch Brothers.[193]

While it is impossible in Winter 2017 to predict the future trajectory of the Trump administration, it is highly likely that this will be an epoch of American Carnage, in which the institutions of liberal democracy and the legislative gains and social progress of the last decades are under threat. Yet powerful forces oppose the authoritarian populist Trump-Pence regime, including the courts which have ruled against Trump's most egregious undermining of the institutions of U.S. democracy, the media that, while under fierce attack from Trump and his anti-democratic supporters, continue to document and critique Trump's daily lies and fake news, and, most saliently, the people, who have demonstrated daily against the Trump administration, and which over the Presidential Day weekend in late February confronted individual members of Congress visiting their home districts in unprecedented displays of outrage and anger against Trump and his policies.

While the power of the people can sometimes be defeated, the diverse resistance movements indicate that the Trump regime will be strongly contested, and already it has shown itself vulnerable to critique and contestation. The Trump team connections with the Russians are particularly explosive in that several Congressional committees and the indefatigable mainstream progressive and alternative media are investigating connections between the Trump election team before the election to see if there was coordination between the Russians who were leaking documents harmful to Hillary Clinton and the Trump campaign team which had many key members with connections to Russia. There was also the question of Donald Trump's economic, political, and personal connections to Russia that involved years of shady business connections and perhaps some explosive scandals. Indeed, Trump's past contained myriad shady deals, connections, and perhaps worse, and never before had the value of a free and independent investigative media been more clear.

The election of Donald J. Trump was an American Nightmare and stunning shock to the political system and body politic unparalleled in recent history. The Trump administration promised to be an American Horror Show and an era of American Carnage that would be difficult to overcome. Yet Trump's war on the media, judiciary system, and other institutions of democracy have been resisted and countered in the early weeks of his administration and although U.S. democracy is in a severe crisis with a highly authoritarian president and administration, the forces of democracy are alive and well and a period of protracted struggle and resistance is likely.

NOTES

1   Maria La Ganga and Ben Jacobs, "More women have come forward saying they have been demeaned or touched inappropriately by Donald Trump," *The Guardian,* October 13, 2016 at https://www.theguardian.com/us-news/2016/oct/12/donald-trump-women-new-sexual-harassment-stories (accessed October 21, 2016).

2   Alexander Burns, Maggie Haberman and Jonathan Martin, "Tape Reveals Trump Boast About Groping Women," *New York Times*, October 8, 2016, on page A1 of the New York   http://www.nytimes.com/2016/10/08/us/politics/donald-trump-women.html?_r=0 (accessed October 21, 2016).

3   The term "meme" became popular in campaign circles in Election 2016; it refers to a "unit of cultural transmission" that circulates by "leaping from brain to brain." Coined by Richard Dawkins in 1976, it appeared in the election as images or phrases used in large part to negatively portray the competing candidates, as with the *Access Hollywood* tape defining Trump as a sexual predator, or the image of Clinton stumbling into a waiting car at the 9/11 memorial, which was used by Trump to portray her as a weak woman without the "stamina" to be President.

4   Gary Legum, "'Such a nasty woman': Donald Trump and the last gasp of an angry id. Donald Trump's rants and insults directed at Hillary Clinton were tantamount to a last impotent, petulant scream," *Salon*, October 20, 2016 at http://www.salon.com/2016/10/20/such-a-nasty-woman-donald-trump-and-the-last-gasp-of-an-angry-id/ (accessed October 21, 2016).

5   David Pierson, "Has Facebook grown too influential?" *Los Angeles Times*, November 13, 2016: C1,6. *The National Enquirer* also circulated outrageously false stories about Clinton throughout the election season, as Rachel Maddow demonstrated in her *TRMS* on January 5, 2017.

6   Jenna Johnson and Karen Tumulty, "Republican women increasingly fear party is alienating female voters," *The Washington Post*, October 26, 2016 at https://www.washingtonpost.com/politics/a-new-war-on-women-breaks-out--this-time-inside-the-republican-party/2016/10/26/9c8f8fa4-9b94-11e6-b3c9-f662adaa0048_story.html (accessed October 21, 2016).

7   Maggie Haberman and Nick Corraniti, "Brand Promotions Suggest Donald Trump Is Looking Past Election Day," *New York Times*, October 26, 2016, at http://www.nytimes.com/2016/10/27/us/politics/donald-trump-brand-promotions.html?_r=0 (accessed October 27, 2016).

8   Jane Mayer, "James Comey Broke with Loretta Lynch and Justice Department Tradition," *The New Yorker*, October 29, 2016 at http://www.newyorker.com/news/news-desk/james-comey-broke-with-loretta-lynch-and-justice-department-tradition?mbid=social_facebook (accessed October 29, 2016). See also Sari Horwitz, "Officials warned FBI that Comey's decision to update Congress was not consistent with department policy," *The Washington Post*, October 29, 2016 at https://www.washingtonpost.com/world/national-security/justice-officials-warned-fbi-that-comeys-decision-to-update-congress-was-not-consistent-with-department-policy/2016/10/29/cb179254-9de7-11e6-b3c9-f662adaa0048_story.html (accessed October 28, 2016).

9   Mayer, op. cit.

[10] The story of Anthony Weiner and Huma Abedin, and Weiner's "sexting" addiction that forced him to resign from Congress and then become disgraced again in a run for Mayor of New York, is told in a documentary film *Weiner*, which became a must-see film of the day for political junkies. Abedin had separated from the Weiner in August, 2016, when it emerged that Weiner continued to exchange lewd messages with women on social media despite having his on-line misbehavers destroying his congressional career and his 2013 mayoral campaign.

[11] Eric Lichtblau, Michael S. Schmidt and Matt Apuzzo, "F.B.I. Chief James Comey Is in Political Crossfire Again Over Emails," *The New York Times*, October 28, 2016 at http://www.nytimes.com/2016/10/29/us/politics/fbi-clinton-emails-james-comey.html (accessed October 30, 2016).

[12] Matthew Miller, "James Comey fails to follow Justice Department rules yet again," *The Washington Post*, October 29, 2016 at https://www.washingtonpost.com/opinions/james-comey-fails-to-follow-justice-department-rules-yet-again/2016/10/29/3a2fad58-9ddd-11e6-b3c9-f662adaa0048_story.html?utm_term=.8562d8ef5567 (accessed October 29, 2016); Greg Sargent, "James Comey needs to clean up his mess. Here's what we need to know." *The Washington Post*, October 29, 2016 at https://www.washingtonpost.com/blogs/plum-line/wp/2016/10/29/james-comey-needs-to-clean-up-his-mess-heres-what-we-need-to-know/?utm_term=.a0bbaa520387 (accessed October 29, 2016); Editorial Board, "The damage Comey's bad timing could do," *The Washington Post*, October 28, 2016, at https://www.washingtonpost.com/opinions/an-october-email-surprise/2016/10/28/df1f98f6-9d46-11e6-a0ed-ab0774c1eaa5_story.html?utm_term=.7518d080d76c (accessed October 30, 2016).

[13] Matthew Miller, "James Comey fails to follow Justice Department rules yet again," *op. cit.*

[14] Ashley Parker and Nick Corasaniti, "Some Trump Voters Call for Revolution if Clinton Wins," *The New York Times*, October 29, 2016 http://www.nytimes.com/2016/10/28/us/politics/donald-trump-voters.html (accessed October 29, 2016).

[15] Comment posted at dailykos.com/ October 30, 2016 http://www.dailykos.com/story/2016/10/30/1588609/-Former-Bush-Ethics-Head-Files-Complaint-Against-Comey-Alleging-Potential-Violations-Of-Hatch-Act (accessed October 30, 2016).

[16] Holder also published an Op Ed in *The Washington* Post: Eric Holder, "James Comey is a good man, but he made a serious mistake," October 30, 2016, at https://www.washingtonpost.com/opinions/eric-holder-james-comey-is-a-good-man-but-he-made-a-serious-mistake/2016/10/30/08e7208e-9f07-11e6-8832-23a007c77bb4_story.html?utm_term=.5fdcda76d1e2 (accessed October 30, 2016).

[17] On, so far, the greatest political crime in U.S. election history, see Douglas Kellner, *Grand Theft 2000. Media Spectacle and a Stolen Election.* Lanham, Md.: Rowman and Littlefield, 2001.

[18] Painter's complaint led to speculation whether Comey himself might soon come under federal investigation; see Spencer Ackerman, "FBI director James Comey may be under investigation for Hatch Act violation," *The Guardian*, October 31, 2016, at https://www.theguardian.com/us-news/2016/oct/31/james-comey-fbi-hillary-clinton-hatch-act-election (accessed November 1, 2016).

[19] Ackerman, Op. Cit.

[20] See Tim Weiner, "The Long Shadow of J. Edgar Hoover," *The New York Times*, November. 1, 2016 at http://www.nytimes.com/2016/11/01/opinion/the-long-shadow-of-j-edgar-hoover.html?action=click&pgtype=Homepage&clickSource=story-

heading&module=opinion-c-col-left-region&region=opinion-c-col-left-region&WT. nav=opinion-c-col-left-region (accessed November 1, 2016), and Scott Shane and Sharon LaFraniere, "James Comey Role Recalls Hoover's F.B.I., Fairly or Not," *The New York Times*, October 31, 2016 at http://www.nytimes.com/2016/11/01/us/politics/james-comey-fbi-emails.html 2016 (accessed November 1, 2016).

21 David A. Fahrenthold "Trump boasts about his philanthropy. But his giving falls short of his words." *The Washington Post*, October 29, 2016, at https://www.washingtonpost.com/politics/trump-boasts-of-his-philanthropy-but-his-giving-falls-short-of-his-words/2016/10/29/b3c03106-9ac7-11e6-a0ed-ab0774c1eaa5_story.html (accessed October 30, 2016).

22 David Barstow, Mike Mcintire, Patricia Cohen, Susanne Craig and Russ Buettner, "Donald Trump Used Legally Dubious Method to Avoid Paying Taxes," *The New York Times*, October, 31, 2016 at http://www.nytimes.com/2016/11/01/us/politics/donald-trump-tax.html?_r=0 (accessed October 31, 2016).

23 Ibid.

24 Lesley Alderman, "An Election sends America to the Couch," *The New York Times*, October 23, 2016: ST1, 13.

25 Rosalind S. Helderman, Tom Hamburger and Sari Horwitz, "After another release of documents, FBI finds itself caught in a partisan fray." November 1, 2016 at *The Washington Post*, November 1, 2016 at https://www.washingtonpost.com/politics/after-release-of-documents-fbi-finds-itself-caught-in-a-partisan-fray/2016/11/01/9d466908-a068-11e6-8832-23a007c77bb4_story.html (accessed November 3, 2016).

26 Op. Cit.

27 Op. Cit.

28 David Smith, "Barack Obama delivers stinging critique of FBI: 'We don't operate on leaks.' President censures James Comey's decision to announce review related to Hillary Clinton days before election as campaigning reaches fever pitch," *The Guardian*, November 2, 2016, at https://www.theguardian.com/us-news/2016/nov/02/barack-obama-fbi-hillary-clinton-emails-election-polls (accessed November 2, 2016).

29 "Here's An Open Letter To Comey From The Teen Who Allegedly Got Sexts From Weiner. 'I thought your job as FBI Director was to protect me.'" *Buzzfeed*, November 3, 2016 at https://www.buzzfeed.com/davidmack/heres-an-open-letter-to-james-comey?utm_term=.xc5zL3elE#.tyrogEl2A (accessed November 3, 2016).

30 Ben Schreckinger and Gabriel Debenedetti, "Gaps in Melania Trump's immigration story raise questions. A racy photo shoot is prompting fresh scrutiny of the would-be first lady's early visits to the United States, *Politico*, August 4, 2016. http://www.politico.com/story/2016/08/melania-trump-immigration-donald-226648 (accessed November 3, 2016). Although there were promises by the Trump camp that Melania would hold a press conference to address the claims that she had worked illegally in the U.S. before getting a visa and working papers, as of early 2017, she has still not had a press conference or addressed the media on this issue.

31 Peter Holley, "KKK's official newspaper supports Donald Trump for president, *The Washington Post*, November 2, 2016 at https://www.washingtonpost.com/news/post-politics/wp/2016/11/01/the-kkks-official-newspaper-has-endorsed-donald-trump-for-president/ (accessed November 3, 2016).

32 Spencer Ackerman, "'The FBI is Trumpland': anti-Clinton atmosphere spurred leaking, sources say," *The Guardian*, November 4, 2016 at https://www.theguardian.com/us-news/

2016/nov/03/fbi-leaks-hillary-clinton-james-comey-donald-trump (accessed November 4, 2016).

[33] Margaret Hartmann, *"National Enquirer* Paid to Suppress Story of Donald Trump Cheating on Melania: Report," *New York,* November 5, 2016 at http://nymag.com/daily/intelligencer/2016/11/national-enquirer-paid-to-kill-trump-affair-story-report.html (accessed November 5, 2016). The *New York* article noted that the *National Enquirer* had run reports attacking Trump's rivals throughout the primary season and had villainized the Clintons for years. The *Enquirer* is run by American Media Chairman and CEO David J. Pecker who has been friends with Trump for many years, endorsed Trump, published columns by Trump, Roger Stone and other Trump supporters, and in the past weeks had published story after story attacking the Clintons, many rehashed from previous years.

[34] See the collection of articles that indicated that the Trump camp was in disarray before the Comey letter gave it a new lease on life at https://www.google.com/?gws_rd=ssl#q=Trump+camp+in+disarray%2C+divided%2C+and+losing (accessed November 3, 2016).

[35] Charles M. Blow, "Trump Is an Existential Threat," *New York Times*, November 3, 2016 at http://www.nytimes.com/2016/11/03/opinion/campaign-stops/trump-is-an-existential-threat.html (accessed November 3, 2016). Blow continued to write fierce denunciations of Trump promising in his last anti-Trump jerimand of 2016 to continue to do so into his presidency; see Charles Blow, *New York Times*, December 19, 2016 at http://www.nytimes.com/2016/11/03/opinion/campaign-stops/trump-is-an-existential-threat.html (accessed December 19, 2016).

[36] On Trump's Brexit obsession, see https://www.google.com/?gws_rd=ssl#q=Brexit+Plus and https://www.google.com/?gws_rd=ssl#q=Brexit+Times+5 (both accessed November 10, 2016).

[37] Interestingly, shortly after the inauguration, the *New York Times* reported that Arron Banks, one of the financiers of the British Brexit campaign, had exchanged ideas with the Trump campaign and accompanied Brexit politician Nigel Farage to Trump rallies. Banks reportedly advised Trump: "facts are white noise" and "emotions rule." Steven Erlanger and Kimiko de Freytas-Tamura, "Godfather of Britain's Exit From E.U. Takes Aim at the Establishment," *New York Times*, January 22, 2017: A15.

[38] On the Trump campaign data collection and strategy, see Kate Brannelly, "Trump Campaign Pays Millions to Overseas Big Data Firm," *NBC News,* November 4, 2016 at http://www.nbcnews.com/storyline/2016-election-day/trump-campaign-pays-millions-overseas-big-data-firm-n677321 (accessed November 5, 2016).

[39] I discuss fake news, which only emerged as a theme after the election, below.

[40] Ferdinand Tönnies, *Community and Society*. New York: Dover, 2011.

[41] On the debates over globalization, see Douglas Kellner, "Dialectics of Globalization: From Theory to Practice," in *Postmodernism in a Global Perspective,"* edited by Samir Dasgupta and Peter Kivisto. London and Delhi: Sage Books, 2014, pp. 3–29, and *Articulating the Global and the Local. Globalization and Cultural Studies*, edited by Ann Cvetkovich and Douglas Kellner. Boulder, Col.: Westview, 1997.

[42] For a collection of articles referring to the stunning of the electorate as the 2016 election stunner played out, see https://www.google.com/?gws_rd=ssl#q=Trump+stun (accessed November 10, 2016).

[43] Key anti-Clinton books include Peter Schweizer, *Clinton Cash. The Untold Story of How and Why Foreign Governments and Businesses Hlped Make Bill and Hillary Rich.* New York: Harper, 2016. For a critique of the anti-Clinton industry, see David Brock, *The Seduction of Hillary Rodha*m (New York: Free Press, 1996), and *Killing the Messenger:*

The Right-Wing Plot to Derail Hillary and Hijack Your Government (New York: Twelve, 2015). Brock started off as a key attack dog on the Clintons and then became one of their major defenders up until this day.

[44] On Limbaugh and Talk Radio, see Al Franken, *Lies: And the Lying Liars Who Tell Them: A Fair and Balanced Look at the Right*. New York: Plume, 2004.

[45] Eliza Collins, "Les Moonves: Trump's run is 'damn good for CBS'" *Politico*, February 29, 2016, at http://www.politico.com/blogs/on-media/2016/02/les-moonves-trump-cbs-220001 (accessed November 10, 2016). Collins wrote: "Donald Trump's candidacy might not be making America great, CBS Chairman Les Moonves said Monday, but it's great for his company. 'It may not be good for America, but it's damn good for CBS,' Moonves said at the Morgan Stanley Technology, Media & Telecom Conference in San Francisco, according to *The Hollywood Reporter* – perfectly distilling what media critics have long suspected was motivating the round-the-clock coverage of Trump's presidential bid."

[46] As a conciliatory victory speech by Trump, a gracious concession by Clinton, and a meeting between Trump and Obama in the White House after the election, the stock market in the U.S. began climbing to all-time highs, as investors contemplated massive profits from a deregulated market and economy and economic policies by the Republican controlled government; other saw Trump as a potential Herbert Hoover whose deregulation and business-oriented government in the late 1920s brought on the Great Depression. See Dana Milbank, "will Donald Trump be Herbert Hoover all over Again?," *Washington Post*, November 11, 2016 at https://www.washingtonpost.com/opinions/will-donald-trump-be-herbert-hoover-all-over-again/2016/11/11/8e533600-a820-11e6-8042-f4d111c862d1_story.html (accessed November 11, 2016). In mid-December, the stock market then plunged as worries about a Trump presidency multiplied, suggesting that the stock market would be a dangerous roller-coaster ride in the immediate future.

[47] One of the bombshells in Megyn Kelly's forthcoming book *Settle for More*, was that an apoplectic Trump called her the night of the first Clinton-Trump debate, incensed that she was going to ask him a tough question about his attitudes and behavior toward women, suggesting that someone at *Fox News*, which was sponsoring the debate, fed the Trump team a question! See the review by Jennifer Senior, "The Hen in the Fox House. Megyn Kelly's Memoir on Life at Fox News and Her Struggles with Trump," *New York Times*, November 12, 2016: C1,4.

[48] See my trilogy of books on the Bush-Cheney Gang, *Grand Theft 2000, op. cit.*; *From September 11 to Terror War: The Dangers of the Bush Legacy*. Lanham, MD: Rowman and Littlefield, 2003; and *Media Spectacle and the Crisis of Democracy*. Boulder, CO: Paradigm Press, 2005.

[49] Christopher Mele and Annie Correalnov, "'Not Our President': Protests Spread After Donald Trump's Election." New York Times, November 10, 2016: P12.

[50] It's true that the next day Trump did a turn-around Tweet in praise of protest, no doubt under orders from his handlers:

Donald J. Trump (@realDonaldTrump)

Love the fact that the small groups of protesters last night have passion for our great country. We will all come together and be proud!

November 11, 2016.

[51] Eugene Scott, "Omarosa: Trump campaign keeping 'list' of enemies," *CNN News*, November 9, 2016 at http://www.cnn.com/2016/11/09/politics/omarosa-list-donald-trump/ (accessed December 8, 2016).

52 Greg Sargent, "The GOP civil war is coming, and Trump will continue to destroy the party," *The Washington Post,* October 26, 2016 at https://www.washingtonpost.com/blogs/plum-line/wp/2016/10/26/the-gop-civil-war-is-coming-and-trump-will-continue-to-destroy-the-party/ (accessed October 31, 2016).

53 Franklin Foer, "Was a Trump Server Communicating With Russia? This spring, a group of computer scientists set out to determine whether hackers were interfering with the Trump campaign. They found something they weren't expecting." *Slate,* October 31, 2016, at http://www.slate.com/articles/news_and_politics/cover_story/2016/10/was_a_server_registered_to_the_trump_organization_communicating_with_russia.html (accessed October 31, 2016).

54 Saikrishna Prakash, "Keep him out of court. Congress should pass a law putting Trump's civil lawsuits on hold," *Los Angeles Times,* November 14, 2016: A13. Trump settled the Trump University lawsuits paying out $25 million in three lawsuits; see Katie Lobosco and Drew Griffin, "Donald Trump settles Trump University lawsuits," *@CNNMoney,* November 19, 2016 at http://money.cnn.com/2016/11/18/news/trump-university-settlement/ (accessed December 8, 2016).

55 Paul Krugman, "Trump Slump Coming?" *The New York Times,* November 14, 2016 at http://www.nytimes.com/2016/11/14/opinion/trump-slump-coming.html (accessed November 15, 2016).

56 Eric Lipton, "Trump Campaigned Against Lobbyists, but Now They're on His Transition Team." *The New York Times,* November 11, 2016 at http://www.nytimes.com/2016/11/12/us/politics/trump-campaigned-against-lobbyists-now-theyre-on-his-transition-team.html?_r=0 (accessed November 12, 2016).

57 Katherine D. Kinzler, "How Kids Learn Prejudice," *Los Angeles Times,* October 26, 2016: SR9.

58 The Southern Poverty Law Center, "Update: Incidents of Hateful Harassment Since Election Day Now Number 701," November 29, 2016, at https://www.splcenter.org/hatewatch/2016/11/18/update-incidents-hateful-harassment-election-day-now-number-701 (accessed November 29, 2016).

59 Jessica McBride, "Trump Election Hate Crime & Violence List: State by State Round Up," *Heavy.com/news,* November 12, 2016 at http://heavy.com/news/2016/11/trump-hate-crimes-violence-election-hoax-fake-donald-muslims-supporters-attacks-protests-riots-islam-racist-graffiti-nazi-california-new-york-louisiana-philadelphia-chicago-video-photos/ (accessed November 15, 2016).

60 Harold Myerson describes how California policies oppose Trump and Republican policies on many key issues leading to potential political wars between state and federal government during the Trump era. See "California Versus Donald Trump," *Los Angeles Times,* November 13, 2016 at http://www.latimes.com/opinion/op-ed/la-oe-meyerson-california-versus-trumpism-20161113-story.html (accessed November 12, 2016).

61 For my earlier critique of the Electoral College, see Kellner, *Grand Theft 2000, op. cit.* See also Christopher F. Petrella, "Slavery, Democracy and the Racialized Roots of the Electoral College," *Truthout,* November 15, 2016, at http://www.truth-out.org/news/item/38373-slavery-democracy-and-the-racialized-roots-of-the-electoral-college (accessed November 15, 2016).

62 NAACP statement, November, 18, 2016, cited in Michelle Ye Hee Lee, "Jeff Sessions's comments on race: For the record," *The Washington Post,* December 2, 2016 at https://www.washingtonpost.com/news/fact-checker/wp/2016/12/02/jeff-sessionss-comments-on-race-for-the-record/?utm_term=.8a6ba28617c4 (accessed December 15,

2016). This article contains a large selection of the Senate testimony on the hearing for a federal judgeship for which Sessions was refused because of his racist actions and comments; as Attorney General, he can now go after his critics and long-time enemies.

63 Matthew Rosenberg and Maggie Haberman, "Trump Is Said to Offer National Security Post to Michael Flynn, Retired General". *The New York Times*. November 11, 2017 at http://www.nytimes.com/2016/11/18/us/politics/michael-flynn-national-security-adviser-donald-trump.html?_r=0 (accessed December 8, 2016).

64 Bryan Bender and Andrew Hanna, "Flynn under fire for fake news. A shooting at a D.C. pizza restaurant is stoking criticism of the conspiracy theories being spread by Donald Trump's pick for national security adviser." *Politico*, December 5, 2016 at http://www.politico.com/story/2016/12/michael-flynn-conspiracy-pizzeria-trump-232227 (accessed December 8, 2016).

65 Ibid. Flynn also pushed conspiracy theories that Islamic terrorists had made deals with Mexican drug cartels to help them cross the border and enter the U.S. illegally and that he had seen photos of signs in the Mexico government in Arabic, claims for which there is no evidence. These sorts of wild conspiracy theories led Paul Waldman to describe Flynn as "Donald Trump's most terrifying appointment," *The Washington Post*, December 6, 2016 at https://www.washingtonpost.com/blogs/plum-line/wp/2016/12/06/donald-trumps-most-terrifying-appointment/?utm_term=.a507a06c6da9 (accessed December 8, 2016).

66 Craig Whitlock and Greg Miller, "Trump's national security adviser shared secrets without permission, files show." *The Washington Post*, December 13, 2016, at https://www.washingtonpost.com/world/national-security/trumps-national-security-adviser-shared-secrets-without-permission-files-show/2016/12/13/72669740-c146-11e6-9578-0054287507db_story.html?utm_term=.68139c1897f4&wpisrc=nl_most-draw7&wpmm=1 (accessed December 13, 2016).

67 Shawn Boburg, "For Trump son-in-law and confidant Jared Kushner, a long history of fierce loyalty," *The Washington Post*, November 27 at https://www.washingtonpost.com/politics/in-fathers-scandal-the-genesis-of-jared-kushners-unflinching-loyalty/2016/11/27/1e9497ba-b378-11e6-840f-e3ebab6bcdd3_story.html?utm_term=.ae88d07b026b (accessed December 5, 2016). Kushner went to Harvard, allegedly after his father, a developer, donated $2.5 million to the university. In his mid-20s, he began buying choice real estate in Manhattan and bought *The New York Observer* which became a mouth-piece for Trump's campaign. Kushner and his wife Ivanka moved in 2017 to Washington to play important roles in the Trump administration.

68 Ken Dilanian and Alexandra Jaffe, "Trump Transition Shake-Up Part of 'Stalinesque Purge' of Christie Loyalists," *NBC News*, November 15, 2016 at http://www.nbcnews.com/politics/2016-election/trump-transition-shake-part-stalinesque-purge-christie-loyalists-n684081 (accessed December 5, 2016). Christie was in political and legal trouble due to the "Bridgegate" trial which claimed that officials in the Christie Administration had ordered the closing of a bridge in rush hour creating a giant traffic jam to punish the major of an adjacent town; Christie denied foreknowledge but in the trial of his underlings charged with the crime, they claimed that Christie was involved in the bridge shutdown and might face prosecution himself, providing another reason for Trump to purge him from his transition team in the Trumpian Saga of Swamp Politics.

69 Kate Zernike, "Betsy DeVos Trump's Education Pick, Has Steered Money From Public Schools," *The New York Times*, November 23, 2016 at http://www.nytimes.com/2016/11/23/us/politics/betsy-devos-trumps-education-pick-has-steered-money-from-public-schools.html?_r=0 (accessed December 5, 2016).

[70]   Greg Windle, Dale Mezzacappa and Darryl Murphy, "Trump taps billionaire Betsy DeVos as education secretary," *The Notebook*, November 23, 2016 at http://thenotebook.org/articles/2016/11/23/trump-taps-billionaire-betsy-devos-as-education-secretary (accessed December 5, 2016).

[71]   Ibid.

[72]   Ibid.

[73]   Indeed, Ross helped Trump keep control of his failing Taj Mahal casino in the 1990s by persuading investors not to push him out, although it eventually failed like all his other Atlantic City ventures.

[74]   Ylan Q. Mui and Robert Costa, "Trump expected to tap billionaire investor Wilbur Ross for commerce secretary." *The Washington Post*, November 24, 2016 at https://www.washingtonpost.com/news/powerpost/wp/2016/11/24/trump-expected-to-tap-billionaire-investor-wilbur-ross-for-commerce-secretary/?utm_term=.d0bf71a8a569 (accessed December 5, 2016).

[75]   Julie Hirschfeld Davis, Binyamin Appelbaum, and Maggie Haberman, "Trump Taps Hollywood's Mnuchin for Treasury and Dines With Romney," *The New York Times*, November 29, 2016 at http://www.nytimes.com/2016/11/29/us/politics/steven-terner-mnuchin-trump-treasury-secretary.html (accessed December 5, 2016).

[76]   Ibid.

[77]   Center for American Progress, "STATEMENT: Elaine Chao is Yet Another Anti-Worker Nominee for the Trump Administration." November 29, 2016 at https://www.americanprogress.org/press/statement/2016/11/29/293876/statement-elaine-chao-is-yet-another-anti-worker-nominee-for-the-trump-administration/ (accessed December 8, 2016).

[78]   Adam Entous, Ellen Nakashima, and Greg Miller, "Secret CIA assessment says Russian was trying to help Trump win White House," *Washington Post*, December 9, 2016 at https://www.washingtonpost.com/world/national-security/obama-orders-review-of-russian-hacking-during-presidential-campaign/2016/12/09/31d6b300-be2a-11e6-94ac-3d324840106c_story.html?utm_term=.5336d30434ce (accessed December 8, 2016).

[79]   David Smith, "Trump's billionaire cabinet could be the wealthiest administration ever. Opponents warn the administration is set to be packed with tycoons who will do nothing to fulfil his promise of helping working-class Americans." *The Guardian*, December 2, 2016 at https://www.theguardian.com/us-news/2016/dec/02/trumps-rich-pickings-president-elects-team-could-be-wealthiest-ever (accessed December 8, 2016).

[80]   Robert Pear, "Tom Price, Obamacare Critic, Is Trump's Choice for Health Secretary," *The New York Times*, November 28, 2016 at http://www.nytimes.com/2016/11/28/us/politics/tom-price-secretary-health-and-human-services.html (accessed December 8, 2016).

[81]   Philip Rucker and Mike DeBonis, "Trump hires a third general, raising concerns about heavy military influence." *The Washington Post*, December 7, 2016 at https://www.washingtonpost.com/politics/trump-hires-a-third-general-raising-concerns-about-heavy-military-influence/2016/12/07/a6273fbc-bca0-11e6-94ac-3d324840106c_story.html?utm_term=.f2ae434e40cd (accessed December 8, 2016).

[82]   Lisa Lerer, "Trump repeating some behaviors he criticized in Clinton," *Associated Press*, December 26 at http://bigstory.ap.org/article/fa4d63080800456291a70f294c49923f/trump-repeating-some-behaviors-he-criticized-clinton (accessed December 28, 2016).

[83]   The Editorial Board, "An Enemy of the E.P.A. to Head It." *The New York Times*, December 8, 2016, at http://www.nytimes.com/2016/12/07/opinion/an-enemy-of-the-epa-to-head-it.html (accessed December 8, 2016).

84   Chris Mooney, Brady Dennis and Steven Mufson, "Trump names Scott Pruitt, Oklahoma attorney general suing EPA on climate change, to head the EPA." *The Washington Post,* December 8, 2016 at https://www.washingtonpost.com/news/energy-environment/wp/2016/12/07/trump-names-scott-pruitt-oklahoma-attorney-general-suing-epa-on-climate-change-to-head-the-epa/?utm_term=.07cac24f974e (accessed December 8, 2016).

85   Michael Hiltzik, "Does Andy Puzder really want to replace his Carl's Jr. workers with robots? No, but..." *Los Angeles Times,* March 30, 2016 at http://www.latimes.com/business/hiltzik/la-fi-hiltzik-puzder-20160322-snap-htmlstory.html (accessed December 8, 2016).

86   The Editorial Board, "Andrew Puzder Is the Wrong Choice for Labor Secretary," of *The New York Times,* December 8, 2016 at http://www.nytimes.com/2016/12/08/opinion/andrew-puzder-is-the-wrong-choice-for-labor-secretary.html (accessed December 8, 2016).

87   Tom Philpott, "Trump's Labor Secretary Pick Hates the Minimum Wage, Loves "Beautiful Women Eating Burgers in Bikinis. Meet Andy Puzder, the miserly, raunchy fast-food magnate who just joined Team Trump." *Mother Jones,* December 9, 2016 at http://www.motherjones.com/environment/2016/12/puzder-labor-secretary-trump-hardees (accessed December 9, 2016).

88   Author Steve Coll, whose book *Private Empire: ExxonMobil and American Power* (Baltimore: Penquin Books, 2013), is considered a major text on ExxonMobil, claimed "reporting on Exxon was not only harder than reporting on the Bin Ladens, it was harder than reporting on the CIA by an order of magnitude," adding: "They have a culture of intimidation that they bring to bear in their external relations, and it is plenty understood inside the corporation too. They make people nervous, they make people afraid." See Mimi Schwartz, "An Extended Interview with Steve Coll," *Texas Monthly.* May 2012 at http://www.texasmonthly.com/articles/an-extended-interview-with-steve-coll/ (accessed December 9, 2016).

89   Nina Agrawal, "U.S. disrupts elections too. Like Russia, America has a long history of meddling in foreign votes." *Los Angeles Times,* December 22, 2016: A2.

90   On the Nicaraguan Sandinistas, the Contra war, and the Reagan administration, see Philip W. Travis, *Reagan's War on Terrorism in Nicaragua: The Outlaw State.* Lexington, Ky.: Lexington Books, 2016.

91   An émigré from Stalin's Russia, Rand was a fanatic anti-communist ideologue and author of the novels *The Fountainhead* and *Atlas Shrugged,* which celebrated extreme entrepreneurial individualism and scorned benevolence and kindness, a philosophy articulated in *The Virtue of Selfishness,* a text that has become a bible for selfish capitalists who fancy themselves superior individuals.

92   James Hohmann, "The Daily 202: Ayn Rand-acolyte Donald Trump stacks his cabinet with fellow objectivists," December 13, 2016 athttps://www.washingtonpost.com/news/powerpost/paloma/daily-202/2016/12/13/daily-202-ayn-rand-acolyte-donald-trump-stacks-his-cabinet-with-fellow-objectivists/584f5cdfe9b69b36fcfeaf3b/?utm_term=.fb25ab966122 (accessed December 28, 2016).

93   Whereas for years I'd seen on TV and read reports that Paul Ryan was a fervent Randist, recently he's said that reports that he was a disciple of Ayn Rand was an "urban legend." See James Rainey, "Paul Ryan loved Ayn Rand, before he said he didn't," *Los Angeles Times,* August 12, 2012 at http://articles.latimes.com/2012/aug/12/news/la-pn-vp-paul-ryan-ayn-rand-20120811 (accessed December 28, 2016).

94   Ayn Rand, *The Virtue of Selfishness*. New York: Signet Classic, 1964. Amazon touts this book as #19 on the "classics" best sellers list of the moment (January 24, 2017), suggesting that Randism is on the move tandem with Trumpism.

95   Adam Smith, *Wealth of Nations*, Book 3, Chapter 04 at https://www.marxists.org/reference/archive/smith-adam/...of.../ch04.htm (accessed December 28, 2016).

96   William Yardley, "Ryan Zinke, Trump's pick as Interior secretary, is all over the map on some key issues," *Los Angeles Times*, December 18, 2016 at http://www.latimes.com/nation/la-na-pol-interior-zinke-2016-story.html (accessed December 24, 2016).

97   Juliet Eilperin and Carol Morello, "Trump team asks State Dept. what it spends on international environmental efforts," *The Washington Post*, December 20, 2016 at https://www.washingtonpost.com/news/energy-environment/wp/2016/12/20/trump-team-wants-state-dept-to-disclose-how-much-it-sends-to-international-environmental-groups/?utm_term=.3e8782e99b1f (accessed December 24, 2016).

98   Brady Dennis "Scientists are frantically copying U.S. climate data, fearing it might vanish under Trump." *The Washington Post*, December 13, 2016 at https://www.washingtonpost.com/news/energy-environment/wp/2016/12/13/scientists-are-frantically-copying-u-s-climate-data-fearing-it-might-vanish-under-trump/?utm_term=.3a5010e8f721 (accessed December 14, 2016).

99   Abby Phillip, "Trump names Rep. Mick Mulvaney, a fiscal hawk, to head budget office," *The Washington Post*, December 17, 2016, at https://www.washingtonpost.com/news/powerpost/wp/2016/12/17/trump-names-rep-mick-mulvaney-a-fiscal-hawk-to-head-budget-office/ (accessed December 5, 2016).

100   Ellen L. Weintraub, "I served five years alongside Donald F. McGahn, President-elect Donald Trump's choice for the post. My experience may be instructive – and disquieting." *The Washington Post*, December 9, 2016 at https://www.washingtonpost.com/opinions/i-worked-with-trumps-pick-for-white-house-counsel-he-doesnt-care-about-corruption/2016/12/09/76f0793c-bcac-11e6-94ac-3d324840106c_story.html?utm_term=.a3441334f464 (accessed December 25, 2016).

101   Julian Borger, "'A recipe for scandal': Trump conflicts of interest point to constitutional crisis. Experts say president-elect does not understand the law and must sell businesses to avoid electoral college disaster. He seems loath to do so." *The Guardian*, November 27, 2016, at https://www.theguardian.com/us-news/2016/nov/27/donald-trump-conflicts-interest-constitutional-crisis (accessed December 5, 2016).

102   *The Washington Post* Editorial Board, "Trump must build a wall – against conflicts of interest," *The Washington Post*, November 24, 2016 at https://www.washingtonpost.com/opinions/trump-must-build-a-wall--against-conflicts-of-interest/2016/11/24/8525c530-b02b-11e6-8616-52b15787add0_story.html?utm_term=.6c864ec1046b (accessed December 5, 2016).

103   Sherisse Pham, "Is Ivanka Trump mixing Japanese business with politics?" *CNN Money*, December 5, 2016 at http://money.cnn.com/2016/12/05/news/donald-trump-japan-ivanka-clothing-deal/ (accessed December 8, 2016).

104   Rosalind S. Helderman and Tom Hamburger, "Trump's presidency, overseas business deals and relations with foreign governments could all become intertwined." *The Washington Post*, November 25, 2016 at https://www.washingtonpost.com/politics/trumps-presidency-overseas-business-deals-and-relations-with-foreign-governments-could-all-become-intertwined/2016/11/25/d2bc83f8-b0e2-11e6-8616-52b15787add0_story.html?utm_term=.cb6879accc40 (accessed December 5, 2016).

[105] Drew Harwell and Anu Narayanswamy, "A scramble to assess the dangers of President-elect Donald Trump's global business empire." *The Washington Post*, November 20, 2016, at https://www.washingtonpost.com/business/economy/a-scramble-to-assess-the-dangers-of-president-elects-global-business-empire/2016/11/20/1bbdc2a2-ad18-11e6-a31b-4b6397e625d0_story.html?utm_term=.6f87640713dd (accessed December 5, 2016).

[106] E.J. Dionne Jr, "A year to protect democracy," *The Washington Post*, January 1, 2017 at https://www.washingtonpost.com/opinions/a-year-to-protect-democracy/2017/01/01/ec384014-ce98-11e6-a87f-b917067331bb_story.html?utm_term=.25cd443f2b12 (accessed March 1, 2017).

[107] Anne Gearan, "What is the story behind Trump's phone call with Taiwan?" *The Washington Post*, December 3, 2016 at https://www.washingtonpost.com/world/national-security/trump-spoke-with-taiwanese-president-a-major-break-with-decades-of-us-policy-on-china/2016/12/02/b98d3a22-b8ca-11e6-959c-172c82123976_story.html?utm_term=.5432b4d0bd54 (accessed December 5, 2016).

[108] Nicola Smith, "Woman who talked to mayor about airport expansion plans said she was associated with Trump Organization, official says," *The Guardian*, December 3, 2016 07.14 EST at https://www.theguardian.com/world/2016/dec/03/trumps-taiwan-phone-call-preceded-by-hotel-development-inquiry (accessed December 5, 2016).

[109] Dana Milbank satirized Trump's telephone diplomacy with the Prime Minister Nawaz Sharif. See his "Trump, the pleaser president," *The Washington Post*, December 2, 2016 at https://www.washingtonpost.com/opinions/trump-the-pleaser-president/2016/12/02/b8014256-b88f-11e6-b994-f45a208f7a73_story.html?utm_term=.6c3f4243c738 (accessed December 5, 2016). Summarizing the Pakistani government's Ministry of Information *Press Release No. 298*, Pakistan's official "readout" of the phone call reads:

> Prime Minister Muhammad Nawaz Sharif called President-elect USA Donald Trump and felicitated him on his victory. President Trump said Prime Minister Nawaz Sharif you have a very good reputation. You are a terrific guy. You are doing amazing work which is visible in every way. I am looking forward to see you soon. As I am talking to you Prime Minister, I feel I am talking to a person I have known for long. Your country is amazing with tremendous opportunities. Pakistanis are one of the most intelligent people. I am ready and willing to play any role that you want me to play to address and find solutions to the outstanding problems. It will be an honor and I will personally do it. Feel free to call me any time even before 20th January that is before I assume my office.

> On being invited to visit Pakistan by the Prime Minister, Mr. Trump said that he would love to come to a fantastic country, fantastic place of fantastic people. Please convey to the Pakistani people that they are amazing and all Pakistanis I have known are exceptional people, said Mr. Donald Trump.

Milbank noted that "what made Trump's conversation with Sharif all the more terrific, amazing, tremendous, fantastic and exceptional was that only days earlier, a member of Trump's transition team had told journalists in India that Trump is in favor of legislation declaring Pakistan a '*terror state*.' The promise, consistent with Trump's previous complaints about Pakistan's '*betrayal and disrespect*,' was huge news on the subcontinent."

[110] Eric Lipton and Maggie Haberman, "'Going Once': Bids for Coffee with Ivanka Trump," *The New York Times*, December 16, 2016: A1, A17.

[111] In his movie *Trumpland*, Michael Moore was referring to parts of mid-America small town and rural areas where Trump had electoral support, but I am referring to Trumpland as the economic, political, and family empire that encompasses to ever-expanding world of Donald J. Trump and his family and associate and the scandals, cons, and outrages involved in the expansion of Trumpland as empire ruled by King Donald J.

[112] *Kali Holloway,* "14 Fake News Stories Created or Publicized by Donald Trump. Fake news is the one thing Trump hasn't claimed to have invented that he actually deserves some credit for inventing." *AlterNet,* January 12, 2017 at http://www.alternet.org/media/14-fake-news-stories-created-or-publicized-donald-trump (accessed January 13, 2017).

[113] Neal E. Boudette, "Ford Move, Cited as Victory by Trump, Has No Effect on U.S. Jobs," *The New York Times,* November 18, 2016 at http://www.nytimes.com/2016/11/19/business/ford-move-cited-as-victory-by-trump-has-no-effect-on-us-jobs.html?_r=0 (accessed December 5, 2016).

[114] Drew Harwell and Rosalind S. Helderman, "Trump's unpredictable style unnerves corporate America," *The Washington Post,* December 6, 2016, at https://www.washingtonpost.com/business/economy/trumps-unpredictable-style-unnerves-corporate-america/2016/12/06/6e3f3976-bbea-11e6-94ac-3d324840106c_story.html?utm_term=.085eb1523b3f (accessed December 5, 2016).

[115] David Smith and Julian Borger, "Clinton accuses Putin of acting on 'personal beef' in directing email hack." *The Guardian,* December 16, 2016 at https://www.theguardian.com/us-news/2016/dec/16/clinton-putin-email-hack-revenge (accessed December 16, 2016).

[116] John Podesta, "Something is deeply broken at the FBI," *The Washington Post,* December 26, 2016 at https://www.washingtonpost.com/opinions/john-podesta-something-is-deeply-broken-at-the-fbi/2016/12/15/51668ab4-c303-11e6-9a51-cd56ea1c2bb7_story.html?utm_term=.70174bfce24d (accessed December 26, 2016).

[117] For a full account of the Carrier deal, its role in Trump's campaign, the issues involved, how Trump negotiated the deal, its initial celebration, and criticism of its limitations, see David Smith, "Everything you need to know about Trump and the Indiana Carrier factory. He made the company a punchbag during his anti-globalisation election crusade, and now takes credit for saving jobs. But how did it happen, and who really won?" *The Guardian,* December 3, 2016 at https://www.theguardian.com/us-news/2016/dec/03/donald-trump-carrier-factory-indiana-jobs-tax-breaks (accessed December 12, 2016).

[118] Ibid.

[119] Adam Entous, Ellen Nakashima and Greg Miller, "Secret CIA assessment says Russia was trying to help Trump win White House," *The Washington Post* December 9, 2016 at https://www.washingtonpost.com/world/national-security/obama-orders-review-of-russian-hacking-during-presidential-campaign/2016/12/09/31d6b300-be2a-11e6-94ac-3d324840106c_story.html?utm_term=.c6d9ad649bef (accessed December 12, 2016).

[120] "The Podesta E-Mails," http://www.politico.com/live-blog-updates/2016/10/john-podesta-hillary-clinton-emails-wikileaks-000011 (accessed December 12, 2016).

[121] Liz Wahl, "Trump Is Using Our Old Putin TV Propaganda Playbook. Former Russia Today presenter sees the hallmarks of Putin's propaganda style in the way Trump is treating reality." *The Daily Beast,* December 12, 2016, at http://www.thedailybeast.com/articles/2016/12/13/donald-trump-is-mirroring-vladimir-putin-s-disinformation-machine.html (accessed December 12, 2016).

[122] Jugal K. Patel and Wilson Andrews, "Trump's Electoral College Victory Ranks 46th in 58 Elections," *New York Times,* December 18, 2016 at https://www.nytimes.com/

interactive/2016/12/18/us/elections/donald-trump-electoral-college-popular-vote.html?_r=0 (accessed December 19, 2016).

[123] Jennifer Rubin, "Moscow rules? *The Washington Post*, December 10, 2016, at https://www.washingtonpost.com/blogs/right-turn/wp/2016/12/10/moscow-rules/?utm_term=.7caf761c333d (accessed December 12, 2016).

[124] Jugal K. Patel and Wilson Andrews, "Trump's Electoral College Victory Ranks 46th in 58 Elections." *The Washington Post*, December 18, 2016 at http://www.nytimes.com/interactive/2016/12/18/us/elections/donald-trump-electoral-college-popular-vote.html (accessed December 22, 2016).

[125] The Editorial Board, "Time to End the Electoral College." *The New York* Times, December 19, 2016 at http://www.nytimes.com/2016/12/19/opinion/time-to-end-the-electoral-college.html?action=click&pgtype=Homepage&clickSource=story-heading&module=opinion-c-col-left-region&region=opinion-c-col-left-region&WT.nav=opinion-c-col-left-region (accessed December 20, 2016).

[126] Ibid.

[127] The Editorial Board, "Time to End the Electoral College," *The New York Times*, December 19, 2016 at https://mobile.nytimes.com/2016/12/19/opinion/time-to-end-the-electoral-college.html (accessed December 26, 2016).

[128] Greg Sargent, "Could Trump help unleash nuclear catastrophe with a single tweet?" *The Washington Post*, December 26, 2016 at https://www.washingtonpost.com/blogs/plum-line/wp/2016/12/26/could-trump-help-unleash-nuclear-catastrophe-with-a-single-tweet/?utm_term=.909d059fa3b7 (accessed December 26, 2016).

[129] In early January. Bill and Hillary Clinton and George W. and Laura Bush also announced they were going to Trump's inauguration.

[130] Dave Barry, "Dave Barry's Year in Review: Trump and the 'hideous monstrosity' that was 2016" in *The Washington Post*, January 1, 2017 at https://www.washingtonpost.com/lifestyle/magazine/dave-barrys-year-in-review-trump-and-the-hideous-monstrosity-that-was-2016/2016/12/29/17c84a14-b7d6-11e6-b8df-600bd9d38a02_story.html?utm_term=.8c619c5fb4ea (accessed January 1, 2017).

[131] David Horsey, "A Fake News History of 2016" *Los Angeles Times*, January 1, 2017: A17.

[132] Editorial Board, "Take a Bad Year. And Make it Better." *New York Times*, December 30, 2017: A20.

[133] *Ibid.*

[134] On the Occupy movements, see Douglas Kellner, *Media Spectacle and Insurrection, 2011: From the Arab Uprisings to Occupy Everywhere*. London and New York: Continuum/Bloomsbury, 2012.

[135] Tom Cahill, "New Years' video reveals Trump partying with mob associate Joey 'No Socks' Cinque. Where is the media?" *U.S. Uncut,* January 3, 2017 at http://usuncut.com/politics/media-silent-trump-seen-partying-mob-associate/ (accessed January 7, 2017).

[136] Randy Parker, "Bob Goodlatte – the swamp thing," *WN.com News*, January 10, 2017 at https://article.wn.com/view/2017/01/10/Parker_Bob_Goodlatte_the_swamp_thing/ (accessed January 10, 2017). On the 1982 movie *Swamp Thing*, see http://www.imdb.com/title/tt0084745/?ref_=fn_al_tt_1 (accessed January 7, 2017). There were also 1990 and 1991 *Swamp Thing* TV-series.

[137] Actually, there were arguments that it was not Trump's tweet, but a massive response by the public which pressured the Republicans to drop their abolition of the Ethics Commission; see Jon Queally, "Public Outrage, Not Trump's Tepid Rebuke, Upends GOP Attack on Ethics Panel," *Common Dreams,* January 03, 2017 at http://www.commondreams.org/

news/2017/01/03/public-outrage-not-trumps-tepid-rebuke-upends-gop-attack-ethics-panel (accessed January 7, 2017). This article also points out that Michael Moore tweeted that Trump wasn't against gutting the independent congressional watchdog, but just questioned the "timing" of the move.

138   Renae Merle, "Trump to tap Wall Street lawyer Jay Clayton to head SEC," *Washington Post,* January 2, 2017 at https://www.washingtonpost.com/pb/news/wonk/wp/2017/01/04/trump-to-tap-wall-street-lawyer-jay-clayton-to-head-sec/?outputType=accessibility&nid=menu_nav_accessibilityforscreenreader (accessed January 7, 2017).

139   See Tom Phillips, "'Brutal, amoral, ruthless, cheating': how Trump's new trade tsar sees China. Peter Navarro has been picked to lead US trade and industrial policy – a move that may upset Beijing," *The Guardian*, December 22, 2016, at https://www.theguardian.com/world/2016/dec/22/brutal-amoral-ruthless-cheating-trumps-trade-industrial-peter-navarro-views-on-china (accessed January 1, 2017).

140   Ibid.

141   Michael D. Shear and David E. Sanger, "Putin Led a Complex Cyberattack Scheme to Aid Trump, Report Finds," *New York Times*, January 6, 2017 at https://www.nytimes.com/2017/01/06/us/politics/donald-trump-wall-hack-russia.html (accessed January 1, 2017).

142   It should be noted for posterity, if there is any after the Reign of the Swamp King, both Donald J. Trump and Arnold Schwarzenegger were accused of multiple sexual assaults by multiple women. Further, Arnold's royal wife Maria Schriver eventually left Der Gropenfuhrer when it was revealed that Arnold had been having a decades long affair with a house-maid and sired a son with her, driving the royal member of the Kennedy family, Princess Maria, to dump the Arnold who, nonetheless, was chosen as an appropriate host for his TV-show *The Apprentice* by the Swamp King. Such were affairs of state during the reign of the country's first reality-TV show president.

143   Philip Rucker and Danielle Paquette, "How a week of Trump tweets stoked anxiety, moved markets and altered plans," *Washington Post,* January 7, 2017 at https://www.washingtonpost.com/graphics/politics/week-of-trump-tweets/?hpid=hp_hp-top-table-main_trumptweets-animated%3Ahomepage%2Fstory (accessed January 7, 2017).

144   David Ferguson, "Keith Olbermann pleads with Trump supporters: 'His illness is putting your family at risk'" *Rawstory*, January 6, 2017 at https://www.rawstory.com/2017/01/keith-olbermann-pleads-with-trump-supporters-his-illness-is-putting-your-family-at-risk/ (accessed January 7, 2017).

145   Michael S. Rosenwald, "Gun silencers are hard to buy. Donald Trump Jr. and silencer makers want to change that. Trump Jr. visits company that makes gun silencers to show his support." *Washington Post,* January 7, 2017 at https://www.washingtonpost.com/local/gun-silencers-are-hard-to-buy-donald-trump-jr-and-silencer-makers-want-to-change-that/2017/01/07/0764ab4c-d2d2-11e6-9cb0-54ab630851e8_story.html?utm_term=.821013f12dcb (accessed January 7, 2017).

146   Here's Meryl Streep's speech on YouTube at https://www.youtube.com/watch?v=NxyGmyEby40 (accessed January 10, 2017).

147   Scott Shane, Nicholas Confessore, and Matthew Rosenberg, "How a Sensational, Unverified Dossier Became a Crisis for Donald Trump," January 11, 2017 at https://www.nytimes.com/2017/.../11/us/.../donald-trump-russia-intelligence (accessed January 11, 2017).

148   The full dossier was published by *Buzzfeed* at https://www.documentcloud.org/documents/3259984-Trump-Intelligence-Allegations.html (accessed January 10, 2017).

149 Jeff Stein, "Trump, Russian Spies and the Infamous 'Golden Shower Memos': *Newsweek*, January 10, 2017 at http://www.newsweek.com/trump-russian-spies-infamous-golden-shower-memos-541315 (accessed January 10, 2017).

150 Ibid.

151 Doyle McManus, "Trump just compared the U.S. intelligence community to Nazi Germany. Let that sink in," *Los Angeles Times*, January 11, 2017 at http://www.latimes.com/opinion/opinion-la/la-ol-trump-intelligence-nazi-dossier-buzzfeed-20170111-story.html (accessed January 11, 2017).

152 *New York Times* reporters noted: "a new Gallup poll on Friday morning found that only 44 percent of Americans approve of the way Mr. Trump has handled his transition – compared with 83 percent who approved of President Obama's transition and 61 percent who approved of George W. Bush's. That followed a Quinnipiac University poll this week that put Mr. Trump's approval rating at 37 percent." Julie Hirschfeld Davis, Christopher Drew, Nicholas Fandos and Jeremy W. Peters, "Transition Briefing. Trump National Security Adviser Called Russian Envoy Day Before Sanctions Were Imposed." *New York Times*, January 13, 2017 at https://www.nytimes.com/2017/01/13/us/.../donald-trump-transition.html (accessed January 14, 2017).

153 Lisa Rein, Tom Hamburger and Mike DeBonis, "After Trump rebuke, federal ethics chief called to testify before House lawmakers." *The Washington Post*, January 13, 2017 at https://www.washingtonpost.com/news/powerpost/wp/2017/01/12/federal-ethics-chief-called-to-testify-before-house-lawmakers/?utm_term=.f5eb4a013963 (accessed January 14, 2017).

154 On Flynn's close connections with Russia, as well as the close Kremlin connections of many others in the Trump inner circle, see Malcolm Nance, *The Plot to Hack America. How Putin's Cyberspies and WikiLeaks Tried to Steal the 2016 Election*. New York: Skyhorse Publishing, 2016, pp. 54ff.

155 Tony Blair was derisively known as "Bush's Poodle" during the 2003 Iraq War when the UK joined the US in a venture to overthrow Saddam Hussein which had brought chaos into the region; see Douglas Kellner. *Media Spectacle and the Crisis of Democracy.* Boulder, CO: Paradigm Press, 2005.

156 Tillerson and Exxon signed a multibillion dollar deal to explore the Artic region for oil, a bonanza that had been postponed due to the Obama administrations sanctions on Russia after revelations of Russian hacking the 2016 election. No doubt the Trump-Tillerson-Putin Troika would make their joint war on the artic a major priority of their emerging partnership.

157 NAACP statement, November, 18, 2016, cited in Michelle Ye Hee Lee, "Jeff Sessions's comments on race: For the record," *The Washington Post*, December 2, 2016 at https://www.washingtonpost.com/news/fact-checker/wp/2016/12/02/jeff-sessionss-comments-on-race-for-the-record/?utm_term=.8a6ba28617c4 (accessed December 15, 2016). This article contains a large selection of the Senate testimony on the hearing for a federal judgeship for which Sessions was refused because of his racist actions and comments.

158 Barry Meier, "Trump's Role in Son's Failed Deal May Yield First Test for a State Regulator," *New York Times*, December 21, 2016 at https://www.nytimes.com/2016/12/21/business/north-charleston-donald-trump.html?_r=0 (accessed January 14, 2017).

159 David Smith, "Donald Trump starts MLK weekend by attacking civil rights hero John Lewis," *The Guardian,* January 14, 2017 at https://www.theguardian.com/us-news/2017/jan/14/donald-trump-john-lewis-mlk-day-civil-rights (accessed January 14, 2017).

[160] Charles M. Blow, "John's Gospel of Trump's Illegitimacy," *New York Times*, January 16, 2017 at https://www.nytimes.com/2017/01/16/opinion/johns-gospel-of-trumps-illegitimacy.html (accessed January 16, 2017).

[161] David Lauter, "Trump's transition hits a rough patch," *Los Angeles Times,* January 16, 2017: A7.

[162] Dan Balz and Scott Clement, "Poll: Trump draws low marks for transition, response to Russian hacking," *Washington Post*, January 17 at https://www.washingtonpost.com/politics/poll-trump-draws-low-marks-for-transition-response-to-russian-hacking/2017/01/17/0926302a-dc25-11e6-ad42-f3375f271c9c_story.html?hpid=hp_hp-top-table-main_poll-710a%3Ahomepage%2Fstory&utm_term=.27e220a28968 (accessed January 17, 2017).

[163] See the *Washington Post* website at https://www.washingtonpost.com/ (accessed January 17, 2017).

[164] One of George W. Bush's sole contributions to global culture was his invention of the nickname "Pootie Poot" for Putin, whose soul W reportedly looked into, yet never became a real soul brother to Vladimir as Donald was aspiring to be; W's other contribution to global culture was coming up with the designation "Turd Blossom" for his enabler Karl Rove. On Bush and Pootie Poot, in case you think I'm making this stuff up, see Wikipedia's "List of nicknames used by George W. Bush" at https://en.wikipedia.org/wiki/List_of_nicknames_used_by_George_W._Bush (accessed January 17, 2017).

[165] David A. Fahrenthold, Philip Rucker and John Wagner, "Trump to be sworn in, marking a transformative shift in the country's leadership," *Washington* Post, January 20, 2017 at https://www.washingtonpost.com/politics/trumps-arrival-on-eve-of-inauguration-ushers-in-real-change-to-washington/2017/01/19/f2134a40-de62-11e6-918c-99ede3c8cafa_story.html?utm_term=.09162fab5ad0 (accessed January 20, 2017).

[166] The term "America First" is associated with Charles Lindberg's movement in the early 1940s to keep the U.S. out of the war against Hitler's fascism, and has isolationist, pro-fascist, and anti-Semite overtones. When confronted with the history of the term, Trump rebutted that he was using a "new" and "more modern" concept.

[167] Although Trump had been bragging how he was writing the speech himself, it was allegedly written by Bannon and Steve Miller; on the latter, see Lisa Mascaro, "How a liberal Santa Monica high school produced a top Trump advisor and speechwriter." *Los Angeles Times*, January 17, 2017 at http://www.latimes.com/politics/la-na-pol-trump-speechwriter-santamonica-20170117-story.html (accessed January 20, 2017).

[168] William Rivers Pitt, "American Carnage: The Obscenity of Trump's Inauguration," *Truthout*, January 21, 2017 at http://www.truth-out.org/news/item/39176-american-carnage-the-obscenity-of-trump-s-inauguration (accessed January 21, 2017).

[169] This initial crowd estimate and comparison that was broadcast on inauguration day was contested by the Trump administration as I note below. Whatever the actual numbers all evidence indicate that Obama's inaugurations were significantly bigger than Trumps by any measurement.

[170] Emily Eakin, "What Can Artists Accomplish by Saying No to Trump?" *New Yorker*, January 20, 2017 at http://www.newyorker.com/culture/cultural-comment/what-artists-accomplish-by-saying-no-to-trump (accessed January 20, 2017).

[171] Steve Lopez collected his favorite placards in "Massive D.C. march steps all over Trump." *Los Angeles Times*, January 22, 2017: B1, B5: "We Shall Overcomb"
"Make America Think Again"
"Think Outside My Box"

"IKEA Has Better Cabinets"

"Did You Remember To Set Your Clocks Back 60 Years Last Night?"

"Tweet All People Kindly"

[172] *Time* countered that it did begin to rain as Trump began his inauguration speech and included a batch of Tweets that confirm this. See Martin Pengelly, "It Started Raining the Moment Donald Trump Was Inaugurated President," *Time*, January 22, 2017 at http://time.com/4641165/donald-trump-inauguration-rain/ (accessed January 22, 2017).

[173] Julie Hirschfeld Davis and Matthew Rosenberg "Slamming Media, Trump Advances Two Falsehoods. Bitter Attack in Speech. Claims on Crowd Size and C.I.A. Rift Are at Odds with Facts." *New York Times*, January 22, 2017A1, A17. D.C. Metro riders broke the record on the day of the Women's March with over 1 million riders reported, far more than for the Trump inauguration.

[174] In an article on "Bushspeak and the Politics of Lying" written during the Bush/Cheney era, I distinguished between *Big Lies* that were endlessly repeated until they had the ring of truth, like the claim that Saddam Hussein was hiding "weapons of mass destruction" and was in alliance with al Qaeda (a favorite whopper of Dick Cheney and his minions), contrasted to *Bold Lies* that informed people knew were not true (like the Saddam-al Qaeda connection), and *Brazen Lies* where the lying liar as well as those being lied to knew were not true, but that the spin patrol repeated anyway, like Spicer and Conway on the numbers of people attending the Obama vs. Trump inauguration. See Douglas Kellner, "Bushspeak and the Politics of Lying: Presidential Rhetoric in the 'War On Terror,'" *Presidential Studies Quarterly*, 37, no. 4 (December 2007), special issue on "Presidential Rhetoric," pp. 622–645.

[175] The Editorial Board, "Donald Trump and a Sea of Empty Desks," *New York Times* By, January 23, 2017:A22.

[176] For an excellent analysis of how Trump's cabinet and administration choices benefited the capitalist class, see Elizabeth Drew, "Terrifying Trump," *The New York Review of Books*, March 9, 2017: 37–41.

[177] On Orwellian language, see Douglas Kellner "From *1984* to *One-Dimensional Man*: Reflections on Orwell and Marcuse," *Current Perspectives in Social Theory*. JAI Press: Greenwich, Conn.: Vol. 10, 1990, 223–252. For applications of Orwellian critique to Trump, see Jean Seaton, Tim Crook and DJ Taylor, "Welcome to dystopia – George Orwell experts on Donald Trump," *The Guardian*, January 25, 2017 at https://www.theguardian.com/commentisfree/2017/jan/25/george-orwell-donald-trump-kellyanne-conway-1984 (accessed on February 17, 2017).

[178] Eric Schmitt and David E. Sanger, "Raid in Yemen: Risky From the Start and Costly in the End," *The New York Times*, February. 2, 2017: A01.

[179] Sophie Gilbert, "The Genius of Melissa McCarthy as Sean Spicer on *Saturday Night Live*. The actress made a surprise appearance as the White House press secretary." *The Atlantic*, February 5, 2017 at https://www.theatlantic.com/entertainment/archive/2017/02/the-genius-of-melissa-mccarthy-as-sean-spicer-on-saturday-night-live/515715/ (accessed on February 17, 2017). Sarah Jones, "First Melissa McCarthy And Now A Top House Democrat Has Humiliated Sean Spicer," *Politicus USA*, February 12th, 2017 at http://www.politicususa.com/2017/02/12/maxine-waters-humiliates-sean-spicer-takes.html (accessed on February 17, 2017). Jones wrote: "After yet another brutally on point lampooning of Sean Spicer by Melissa McCarthy on Saturday Night Live, Representative Maxine Waters (D-CA) rubbed salt in the wound by telling Joy Reid 'Nobody takes him seriously anyway… Let's have fun with him while he's there.'"

[180] Alexandra Rosenmann, "Protesters Block Education Secretary Betsy DeVos From Entering D.C. Middle School," *AlterNet*, February 10, 2017 at http://www.alternet.org/activism/protesters-block-education-secretary-betsy-devos-entering-dc-middle-school (accessed on February 16, 2017).

[181] See John Dewey, *Democracy and Education*. New York, NY: Simon & Brown, 2012.

[182] Jim Rutenberg notes that many of Trump's most outrageous and quickly refuted claims of massive election fraud, media underreporting of terrorism, and other whoppers repeat wild claims made in Alex Jones radio show and Infowar site;, see "In Trump's Volleys, Echoes of Alex Jones's Conspiracy Theories." *New York* Times, February 19, 2017 at https://www.nytimes.com/2017/02/19/business/media/alex-jones-conspiracy-theories-donald-trump.html?_r=0 (accessed on February 20, 2017).

[183] On Ivanka Trump's life-time of promotion for herself and her family, and attempts to rebrand herself as an icon for young women, see Amy Wilentz, "This Particular Daddy's Girl. What does Ivanka Trump have to say to Women Who Work?" *The Nation*, February 18, 2017: 14–19.

[184] Curiously, Conway had announced that she was not going to play a role inside the Trump White House in order to stay home and care for her young children, yet she seems to have accepted a position as Trump's "Counselor to the President," and was perhaps the most visible media representative of the Trump administration during its early weeks, until her constant spinning and outright lies led some media organizations to distance themselves from her.

[185] Matt Taibbi's *Insane Clown President: Dispatches from the 2016 Circus*, New York, NY: Spiegel & Grau, 2017.

[186] Adam Entous, Ellen Nakashima and Philip Rucker, "Justice Department warned White House that Flynn could be vulnerable to Russian blackmail, officials say," *Washington Post*, February 13, 2017 at https://www.washingtonpost.com/world/national-security/justice-department-warned-white-house-that-flynn-could-be-vulnerable-to-russian-blackmail-officials-say/2017/02/13/fc5dab88-f228-11e6-8d72-263470bf0401_story.html?utm_term=.fc130b7a9480 (accessed on February 20, 2017).

[187] Michael Beschloss, Twitter at https://twitter.com/BeschlossDC/status/832712935956885505 (accessed on February 20, 2017).

[188] The Indivisible Movement was organized by congressional staffers who wrote a booklet on how to protest and organize against the Trump administration; see the handbook at https://www.indivisibleguide.com/ (accessed on February 21, 2017).

[189] Chris Cillizza, "Donald Trump's streak of falsehoods now stands at 33 days," February 21, 2017, with documentation at https://www.washingtonpost.com/graphics/politics/trump-claims/?tid=a_inl (accessed on February 18, 2017).

[190] Tom Phillips. *The Guardian,* Trump's media attacks play into China's hands, says Beijing Press," February 18, 2017 at https://www.theguardian.com/world/2017/feb/18/media-attacks-by-trump-play-into-china-hands-global-times (accessed on February 18, 2017).

[191] Ibid. Echoing his Fuhrer, alt-right maverick become Rasputin/Cromwell to Trump, Steve Bannon launched an all-out attack on the media: "Stephen K. Bannon, Trump's chief strategist, told reporters: that news organizations had been 'humiliated' by the election outcome and repeatedly describing the media as 'the opposition party' of the current administration. 'The media should be embarrassed and humiliated and keep its mouth shut and just listen for a while.' See Michael M. Grynbaum, "Trump Strategist Stephen Bannon Says Media Should 'Keep Its Mouth Shut'" *The New York Times*, January 26,

2017 at https://www.nytimes.com/2017/01/26/business/media/stephen-bannon-trump-news-media.html (accessed on February 18, 2017).

[192] Nick Kristof, "How Can We Get Rid of Trump?" *New York Times,* February 19, 2017: SR 11.

[193] Jane Mayer, *Dark Money. The Hidden History of the Billionaires Behind the Rise of the Radical Right.* New York, NY: Anchor Books, 2017, pp. xiiiff.

Printed in the United States
By Bookmasters